AUSTRALIAN SYMBOLISM
The art of dreams

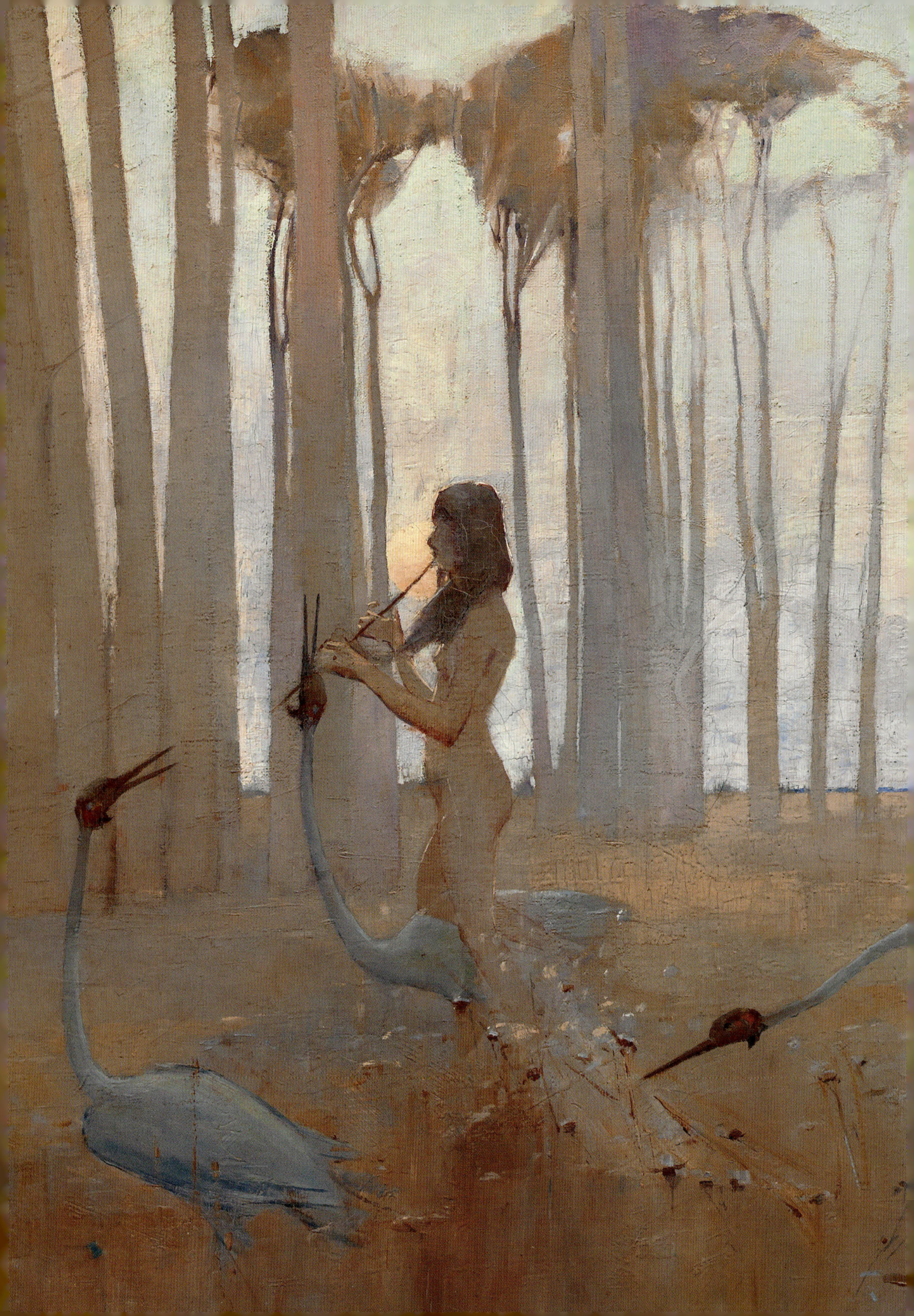

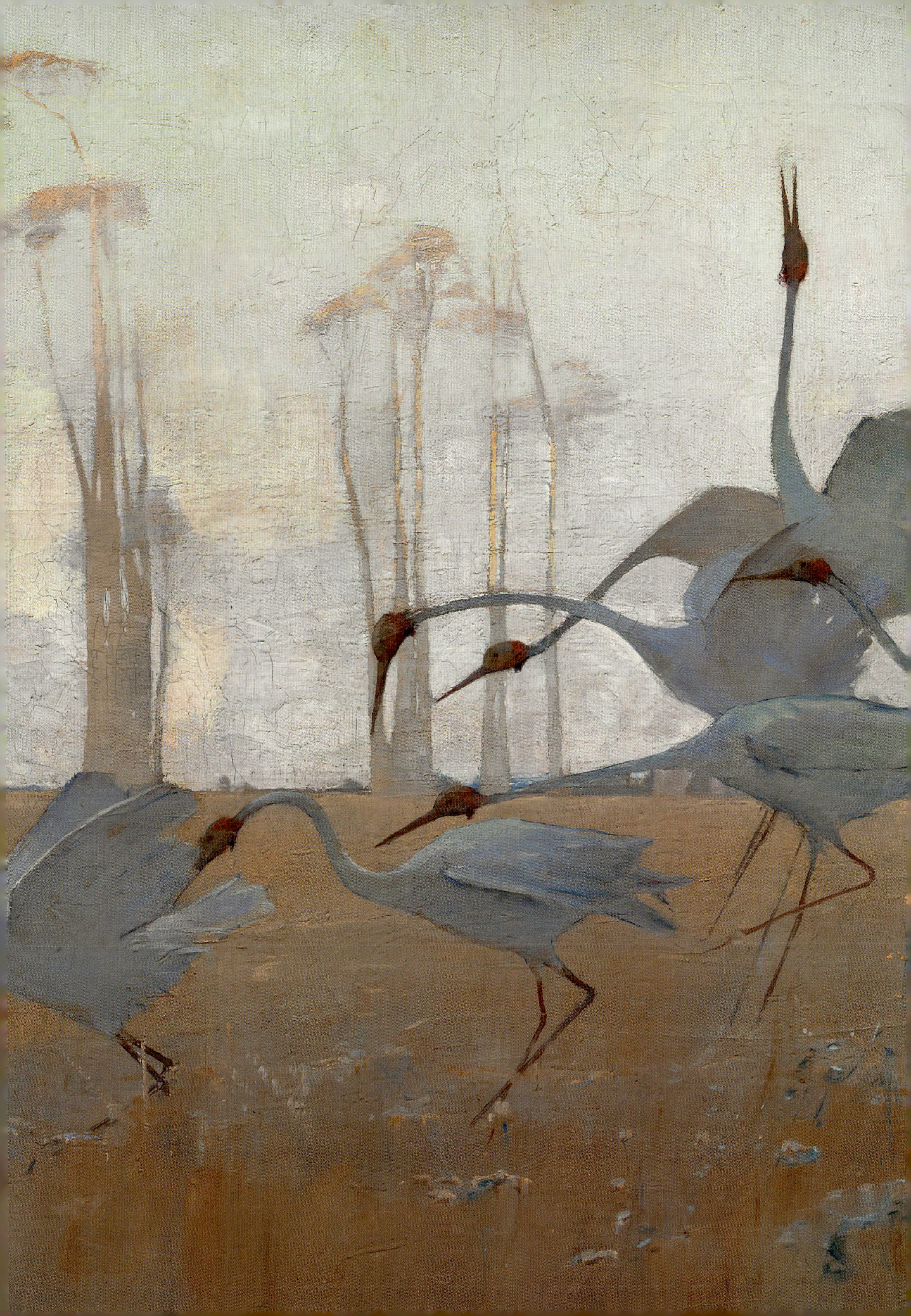

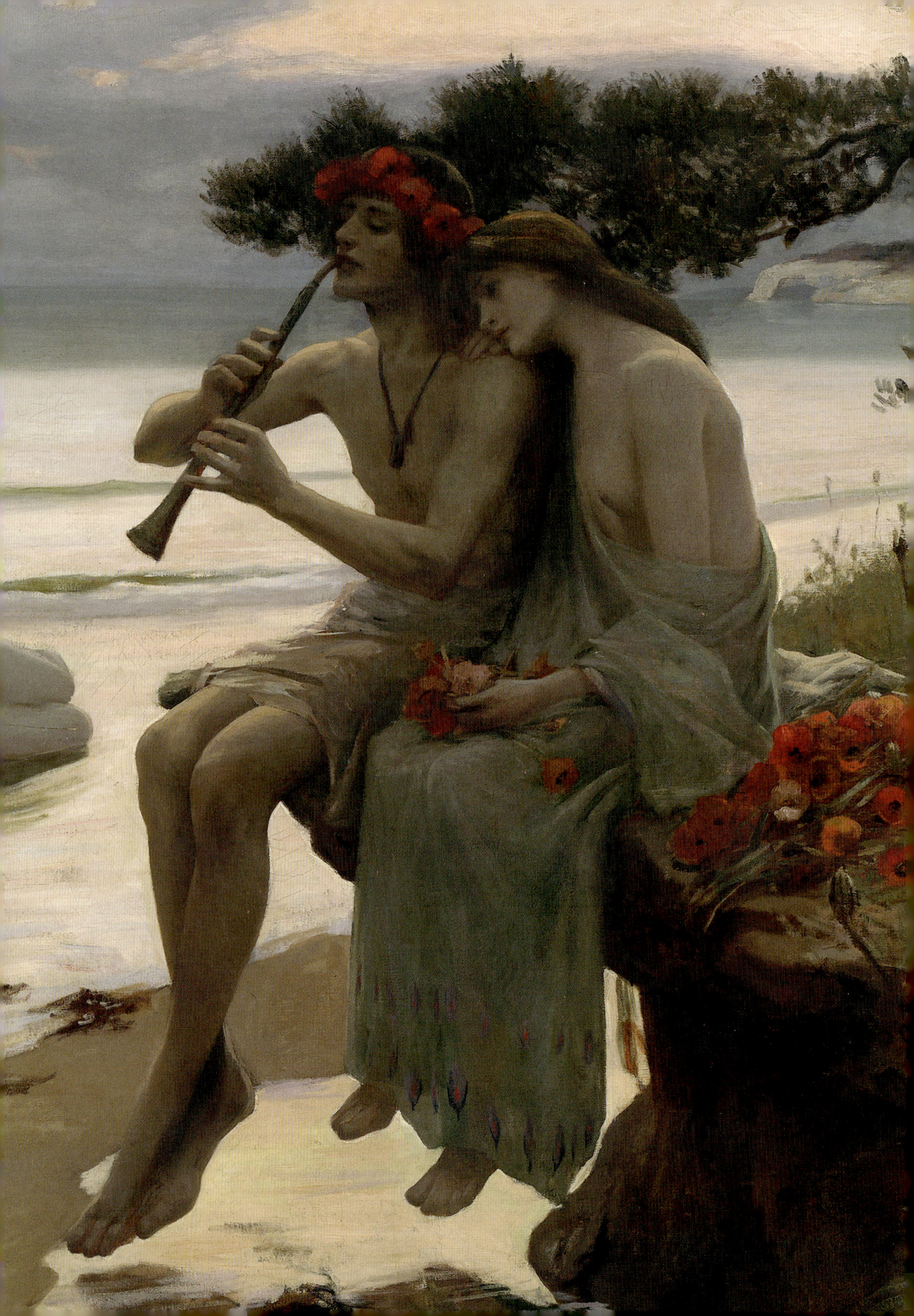

AUSTRALIAN SYMBOLISM
The art of dreams

Denise Mimmocchi

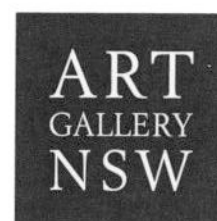

CONTENTS

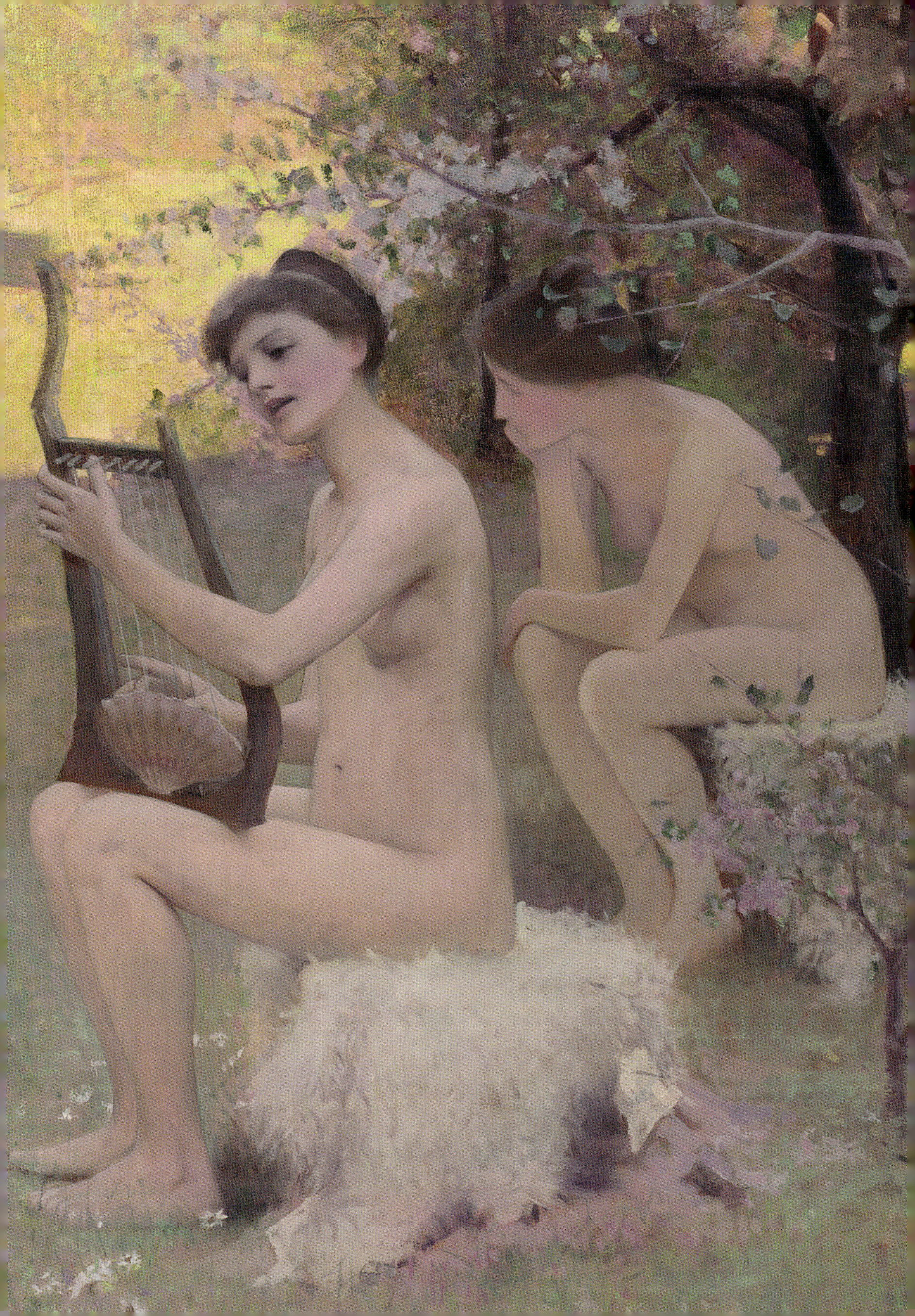

FOREWORD

The Art Gallery of New South Wales is proud to present *Australian Symbolism: the art of dreams*, the first exhibition to explore this fascinating area of Australian art. The Symbolist movement has recently been the subject of renewed international interest yet remains surprisingly neglected in relation to Australian practices. *Australian Symbolism: the art of dreams* is a timely exhibition, establishing the significance of the movement in Australia by showcasing the diversity of artistic responses toward its themes and ideas. Bringing together more than 70 works, including paintings, sculpture, photography and decorative arts, the exhibition surveys the varied terrain of Symbolism in Australia during a period when enigmatic figures of fantasy and mythology and works espousing poetic sensations gained an increasing presence in Australian art. *Australian Symbolism: the art of dreams* builds on the major retrospectives presented by the Art Gallery of New South Wales in recent years on some of the key protagonists of Australian Symbolist art, such as Bertram Mackennal, Rupert Bunny and Charles Conder. We are delighted to revisit and recontextualise the Symbolist-inspired works of these artists, alongside others, to bring fresh insight into late nineteenth-century Australian art history.

While the theme of Symbolism may be unfamiliar to Australian audiences, this publication and exhibition reveals how the movement has shaped some of the period's most significant and admired artworks. To properly showcase the reach and diversity of Symbolism in Australia we have relied on the generosity of a number of public institutions and private collectors, and my gratitude goes to all the lenders to this exhibition. I must make special mention of the gallery directors who have contributed a number of important works from their collections: Ron Radford at the National Gallery of Australia, Gerard Vaughan at the National Gallery of Victoria, and Tony Ellwood at the Queensland Art Gallery. My thanks also to the President's Council for their crucial support of this exhibition. Finally, I thank curator Denise Mimmocchi and acknowledge the many staff members at the Art Gallery of New South Wales who have helped to bring this exhibition and publication to fruition.

Anne Flanagan
Acting director, Art Gallery of New South Wales

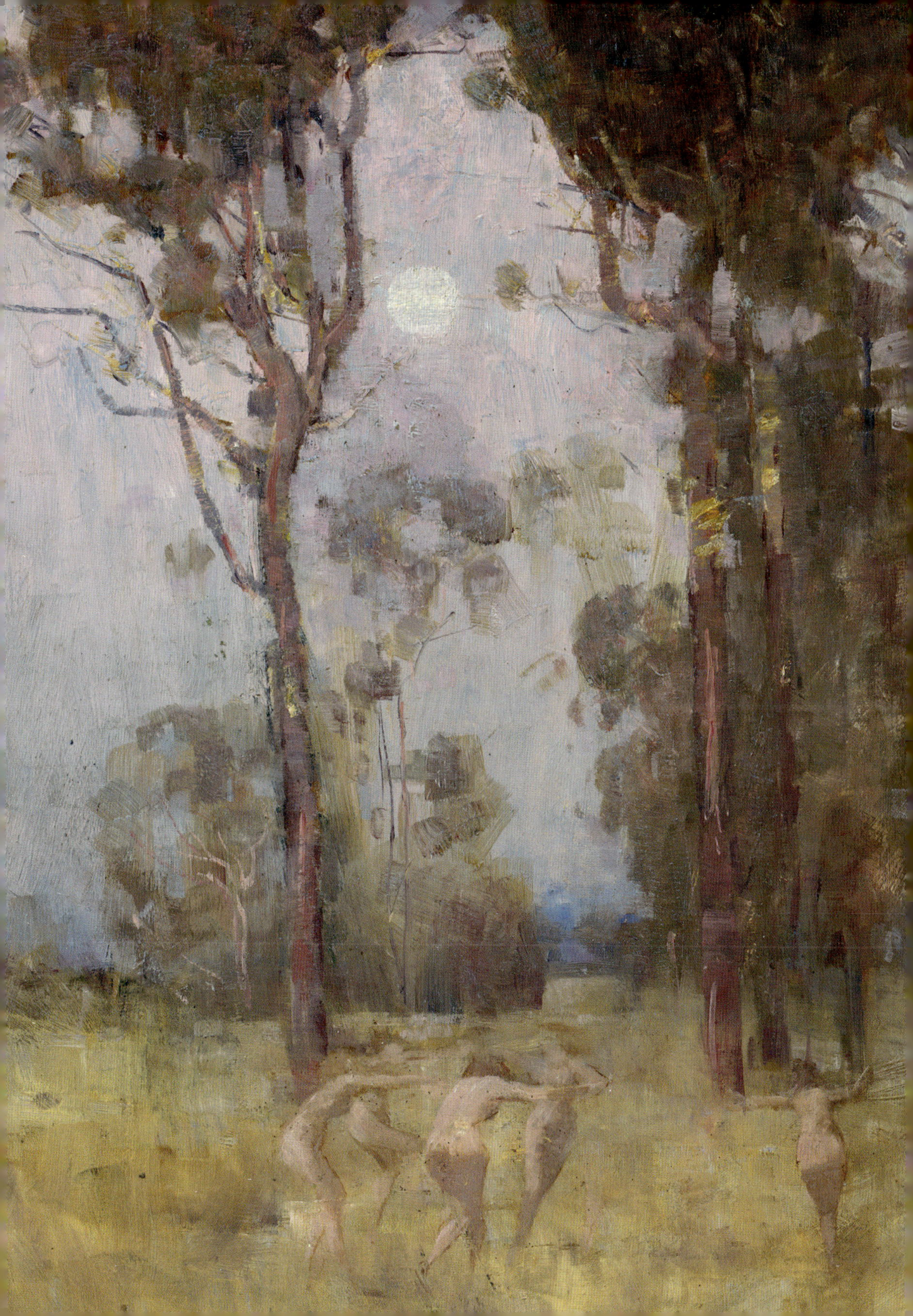

THE ART OF DREAMS

In 1889 there was a notable shift in Charles Conder's painting that highlighted certain new tendencies in Australian art. Conder acknowledged the artistic reorientation in his work in a letter to his friend GF Mann, citing the paintings he submitted to the Victorian Artists' Society that year: 'I have been painting allegorical pictures for this exhibition and one is I think the best work I have done at present.'[1] He was referring to *Hot wind* 1889, a small painting that received much attention at the time and subsequently – despite the fact that until 2006 its whereabouts was unknown.[2]

In *Hot wind* Conder depicts a dangerous westerly wind in the guise of an orientalised temptress. In his smoke-hazed, mirage-like vision she leans towards a brazier, blowing a flame that threatens to wreak havoc over the parched environment. *Hot wind* was first exhibited in the Melbourne winter of 1889, yet its allusion to the environment's annihilation recalled the effects of the stifling drought of the summer past, the worst on record, which had greeted Conder as he travelled through Victoria from Sydney in late 1888. Conder had arrived in Melbourne with an Impressionist's focus on extracting the ambient qualities of place, developed during his formative experiences of painting en plein air on Sydney's coastline and rural outskirts. It therefore made sense for a landscape marked by the extremities of the Victorian drought, and the terrible threat of bushfire, to have captured the painter's attention. Yet, as Conder suggested to Mann, *Hot wind* also reveals an artistic mind that was venturing elsewhere.

Hot wind reveals Conder's oscillation between the Impressionist aim to render general atmospheric conditions and a sharp manoeuvre away from such intentions. This shift is detected in the composition's sweep from naturalistic detail to poetic abstraction: the drought-stricken land on the left is channelled through the figure and transformed into smoke-filled negation on the right. While Conder adopts a creamy gold palette to reference the drought's bleaching effects, he infuses it with opalescent inflections of blues and rose-madder reds. The clearest indication of Conder's artistic transformation is, however, his subject matter. Conder may have referred to *Hot wind* as 'allegorical' in his letter to Mann, but it is not a straightforward metaphor of nature's destructive power. Nature had been traditionally allegorised in art as a woman who could be both maternal and cruel. Yet Conder represents

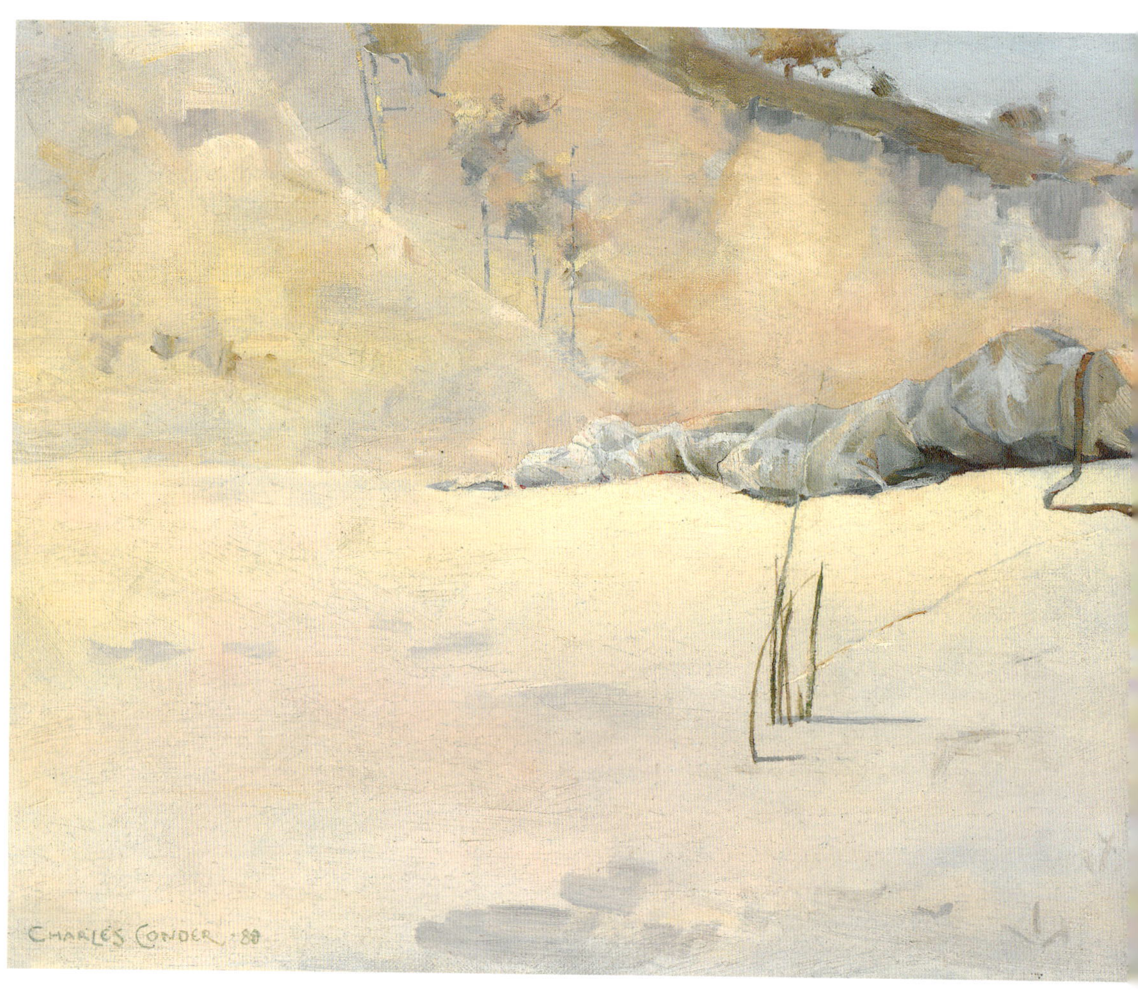

Charles Conder *Hot wind* 1889, oil on board
National Gallery of Australia, Canberra. Acquired with the assistance of the Yulgibar Foundation 2006

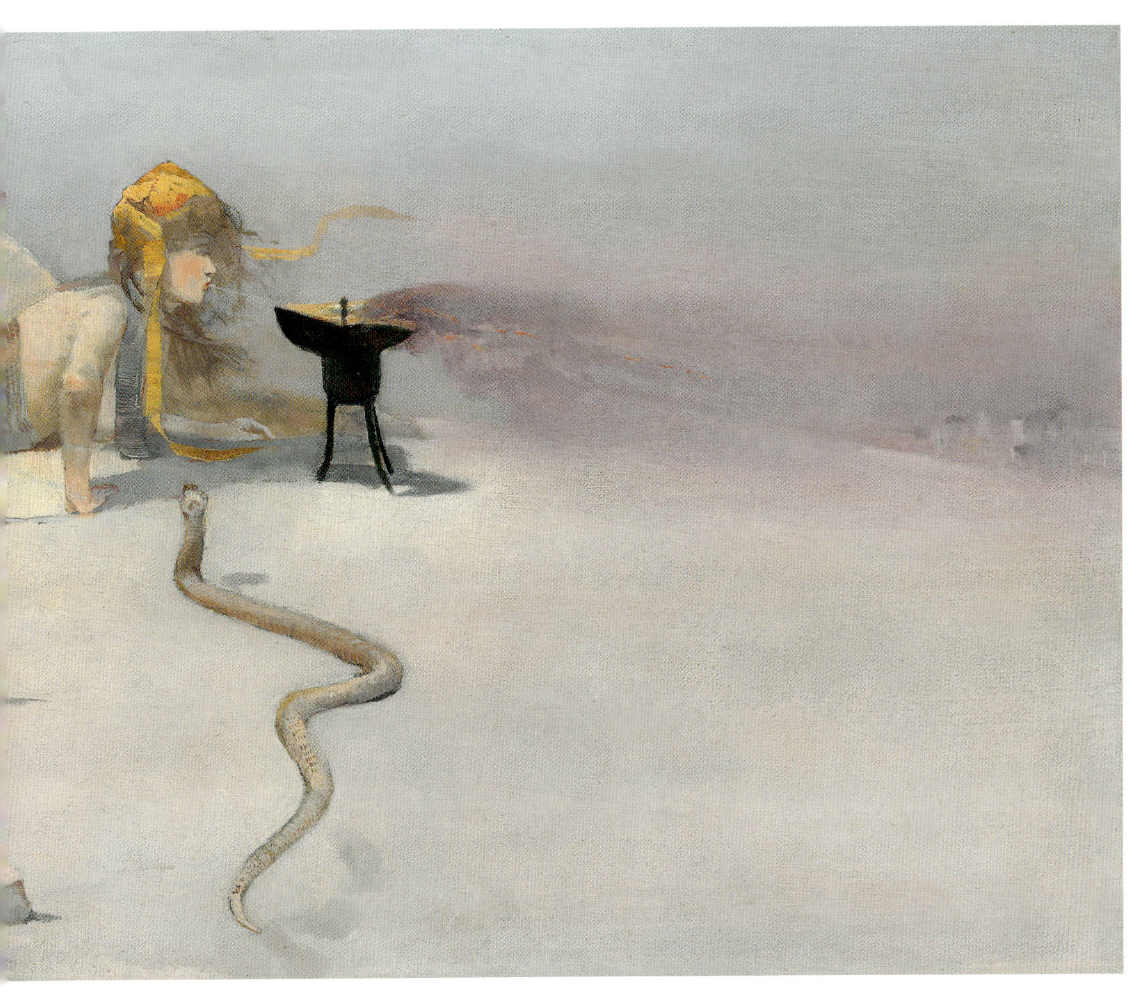

Nature as a treacherous femme fatale – the figure of the tantalising yet maliciously sexual woman that had been popularised by the late nineteenth century in art and literature and as a hallmark figure of Europe's fin-de-siècle culture.

In *Hot wind* Conder lets this malevolent figure loose in the Australian environment. Exotically draped and slithering along the burning desert sand, she is symbolically united with the deadly reptile that approaches her from the foreground in a shared capacity for destruction. Although familiar with brown snakes as a ubiquitous feature of the Australian landscape from his painting excursions in the bush, Conder metaphorically transcribes its form as an extension of his femme fatale in order to symbolically allude to the biblical Eve. As the instigator of original sin and human downfall in Old Testament myth, Eve had long been depicted as the mother of all femme fatales. By intersecting the figure and snake in a lascivious dance of arabesque forms echoed in the woman's drapery and headdress, Conder depicts a sexualised presence that commands the annihilation of the environment. *Hot wind* was painted during a much-mythologised period of Australian art defined in terms of the development of landscape painting as national emblem – and certainly the snake, hot wind and fire are elements of destruction which have a specific meaning and urgency in Australian terms. Conder also fuses the landscape with a larger idea of the elemental and exotic and in so doing reorients his Impressionist agenda. Using the Australian landscape as his platform, he conjures a seductive dream of oblivion.

While the 1880s and 90s have been more commonly associated with Impressionist- and Naturalist-inspired art practices in Australia, *Hot wind* reveals an alternative set of influences operating concurrently in these decades. It demonstrates the impact of tendencies that had been recently labelled 'Symbolist' by the poet Jean Moréas in a manifesto published in Paris in 1886. Moréas eloquently established the Symbolists' aim as being to 'clothe the idea in sensuous form', to give expression to thoughts and feelings through means that sidestep description or narrative and appeal primarily to the senses.[3] While the manifesto was written in relation to a current school of French poetry, the characteristics he described as Symbolist more broadly distinguished a set of practices that could be identified across the arts by the 1880s, ranging from the opera of Richard Wagner to the sculpture of Auguste Rodin. The British Pre-Raphaelite artists, the French painters Pierre Puvis de Chavannes and Gustave Moreau, the Swiss-German painter Arnold Böcklin and the avant-garde offerings of Paul Gauguin all fulfilled Moréas's definition of Symbolism as turning the artistic gaze inwards to register the terrains of the imagination, dreams and desires.

Australian Symbolism: the art of dreams explores how the visual language and themes of the Symbolist movement were established in Australian art in the late nineteenth and early twentieth centuries. Its impact is considered through a series of encounters, engagements and exchanges between Australian artists and Symbolist art forms at the turn of the century to trace the ways in which Australian artists incorporated Symbolist characteristics in their work.

The decades when Symbolism was established as an influential art movement across Europe were those of unprecedented urban and cultural expansion in Australia, when the role of the arts and the status of artists gained greatly in focus and scope. As Australian artists became more cosmopolitan in their ambitions they sought further training in Europe where they encountered a more nuanced set of aesthetic and conceptual principles. At the turn of the century, as Charles Harrison and Paul Wood have claimed, 'to think of modern art was to think of modern French art. This was not because all modern art was French, but rather because France was the acknowledged source ... to which artists of other countries referred when they intended to mark their own work as modern.'[4]

Hence, while the term Symbolism is understood as an internationally dispersed set of tendencies, Australians followed the common pattern of artists who sought the experience of the Paris art world in their search for contemporary forms of expression. Yet as suggested by *Hot wind* – a work produced by a painter whose artistic experiences had to that point evolved only in Australia – encounters with Symbolism in this country are not confined to a study of the work of expatriate artists. *Hot wind* attests to a wider circulation of ideas that may have been sourced from an international model but were developing concurrently in Australia in relation to local conditions.

Unlike the movements of Impressionism or Naturalism, Symbolism was not tied to a particular style but rather to a set of conceptual concerns that gave visual shape to ideas and the imagination. Nonetheless, the stylistic shifts adopted by Symbolists to convey these inner realms corresponded to the late-century development of decorative aesthetics. The term 'decorative' was used at this time to describe an art of abstracted expression, where depictions of the physical world were subordinate to compositions based on relationships between subjective colour and form, and rhythmical emphasis. At this time, Art Nouveau had infiltrated a range of artistic fields, including the visual arts, craft, design, illustration and architecture, to the extent that it became known as the 'modern style'. With its arabesque line driving the internal logic of the painting and the expression of emotions and sensations, Art Nouveau became a key decorative strategy and a style often adopted by Symbolists.

As *Hot wind* demonstrates, Conder's shift in subject matter broadened the parameters of his formal expression. In this context, to study the art of Symbolism in Australia is also to explore the development of decorative practices and how artists turned to principles of abstraction to register subjective states and break from Naturalism. While Symbolism was a short-lived influence on Australian artists, its wider impact is in its transformation of the art of the material world into one of abstract thought.

Chapter 1

AUSTRALIAN ARTISTS AND COSMOPOLITAN CURRENTS

The lessons of imaginative design

Arthur Loureiro's paired oval paintings, *The spirit of the Southern Cross* and
The spirit of the new moon, were first exhibited in November 1888 at the Victorian
Artists' Society in Melbourne. Illustrated in the press in a review of the exhibition
highlights, *The spirit of the new moon* stood out, as its companion would also have
done, as distinct in its format and conception from an otherwise traditional array
of subjects.[1] In these works Loureiro presents the idea of a feminine, classicised
beauty as an essence of the universe presiding over Australia. He equates the female
form with celestial design to symbolically encapsulate the mysteries of the cosmos
and its intangible depths. Critics praised Loureiro's works for being 'thoroughly
poetical in conception', and the paintings were given special notice in reviews not
only for their artistic merit but also because their subject matter eluded the genre
categorisations of the exhibition.[2] Distinct as an art of the imagination, with their
primary aim of evoking mood over narrative and suggestion over description,
The spirit of the Southern Cross and *The spirit of the new moon* are recognised
as the first works produced in Australia which reveal elements of Symbolist art.[3]

The Portuguese-born Loureiro arrived in Australia in September 1884 as part of
what Frederick McCubbin described as the healthy influx of 'young artists from the
old countries [who] served to create a cosmopolitan atmosphere' during the 1880s.[4]
Loureiro came to Australia after more than a decade of art training that had been
dispersed internationally from his native Oporto to Lisbon, Rome, Florence and
Madrid, and a period in Paris from 1880 to 1882. Here he completed his studies in
the atelier of Alexandre Cabanel whose 1863 painting the *Birth of Venus* epitomised
the model of a flawlessly designed, erotically posed, female allegorical subject that
was an academic ideal of mid- to late-century Salon art. Following medical advice,
Loureiro migrated to Australia, the native home of his wife Marie Thérèse Huybers
whom he had married in 1881. He subsequently rose to prominence in Melbourne's

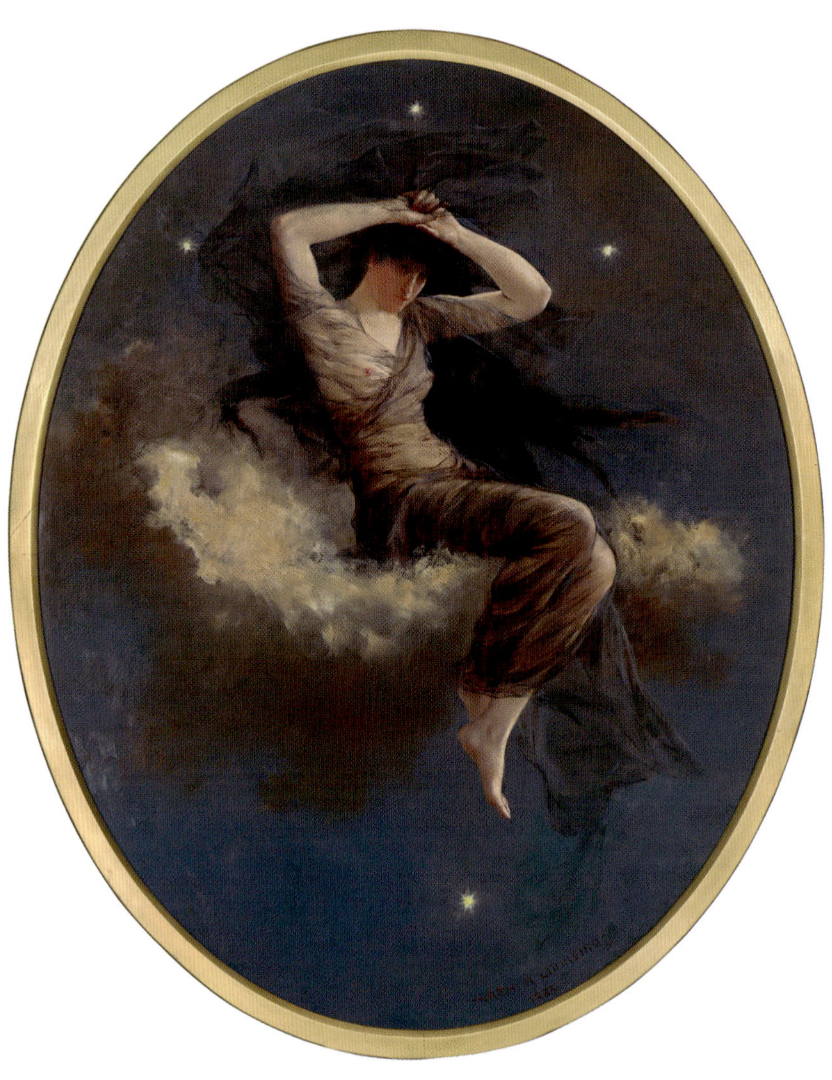

Arthur Loureiro *The spirit of the Southern Cross* 1888 (above) and *The spirit of the new moon* 1888 (opposite),
oil on canvas

 National Gallery of Victoria, Melbourne. Purchased 2003

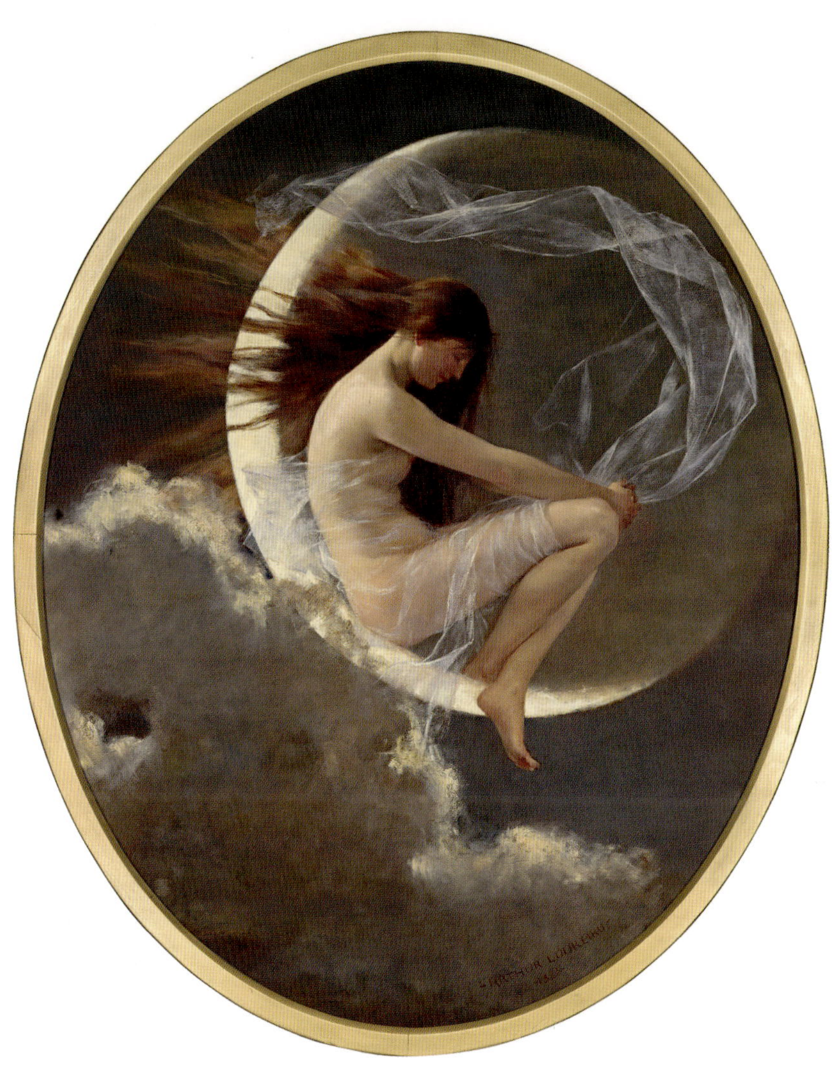

bourgeoning artistic circles as an exhibitor and founding council member of the Australian Artists' Association and subsequent Victorian Artists' Society, and also as an influential teacher.[5] Loureiro built his career during the opportune years of Melbourne's economic boom, which saw an expansive residential building program in its affluent suburbs. Within a year of his arrival Loureiro had secured a commission for a mural design for a Toorak mansion, which he decorated with 'emblematic figures' as allegories of the four seasons.[6]

Loureiro's attention to the decorative qualities of mural design appears to have shifted the parameters of his art. Continuing the tandem practice he established in Europe, he moved between Naturalism and plein-air genres of landscape and rustic scenes, and allegorical works of female subjects. While Loureiro was aware of the female allegories of Salon art, he would have also been alert to the Symbolist reformulation of such subjects from his time in Europe. Loureiro remained connected to the ideas of the Parisian avant-garde in Australia through his sister-in-law, the journalist Edith Huybers.[7] As the Paris arts correspondent for the London *Spectator* and *Universal Review* magazines, Huybers was professionally and socially connected to the city's literary and artistic avant-garde, including the notorious writer Joris-Karl Huysmans with whom she began an affair in 1888. Huysmans was renowned as the author of *A rebours (Against nature)*, the 1884 novel considered central to literary Symbolism. The novel was embraced by the Parisian avant-garde for its branding of an artistic decadence in which the creative individual consciousness, fuelled by art, eroticism, madness and perversion, governed a new hedonistic reality. Although Loureiro's work was removed from Huysmans's type of artistic decadence, Edith Huybers represented a vital link to the ideas of the Parisian avant-garde that informed a Symbolist conception of Loureiro's art. His incorporation of moderated aspects of Symbolism, along with his concerns of a decorative art form, allowed him to stray from the domains of the natural world to expand on the conventional formulation of the allegorical female model in his work and to signal an order beyond the rational and material, central to Symbolist preoccupation.

Produced as a residential commission for a residence in the Melbourne suburb of Kew, *The spirit of the Southern Cross* and *The spirit of the new moon* were adapted from an earlier panel which shows the moon-cradled figure in *The spirit of the new moon* as well as a ferocious old man, prophetic in his guise, whose commanding presence is envisaged from the clouds as a gale-like force.[8] Although the painting is known as *Study for 'The spirit of the new moon'*, it was based on the nationalistic sixteenth-century Portuguese poem *Os Lusíadas* by Luís Vaz de Camões,[9] a fantastical epic of Portuguese voyages and conquests that takes place under the gaze of various charitable and malevolent gods. The imagery in *Study for 'The spirit of the new moon'* relates to the account of the great navigator Vasco da Gama's journey to India, in the course of which a violent tempest was unleashed on him by the Olympic council of gods led by Neptune.[10] A watchful Venus guiding Vasco's journey summons her nymphs to calm the storm gods and restore order to the expedition. Loureiro conjures the raging force of the storm through the figure of the old man, and the celestial guidance of Venus's calm repose. He sheds the specifics of Camões's narrative for a broader vision of opposing spiritual forces, suggesting the chaotic and radiant orders that govern the play of universal fate.

Transferring the original concept into a more generalised mural format, Loureiro transposed the composition from the figuration of a cosmic battleground to a set of decoratively paired female motifs where the ferocious storm figure is adapted into the darkly veiled, tempestuous Southern Cross. The Portuguese inspiration for the work was replaced by the anglicised sentiments of Percy Bysshe Shelley's 1820 poem *The cloud*: 'That orbed maiden with white fire laden whom mortals call the moon.' These lines were displayed alongside *The spirit of the new moon* when it was exhibited at the Victorian Artists' Society and were also published in the catalogue. While maintaining the fundamental quality of poetically driven form, Loureiro's adaptation of his original painting was not only in terms of its decorative format, but also with the pragmatic view of creating imagery more accessible to Melbourne audiences. The Southern Cross was adopted as a potent national symbol – the constellation unique to southern skies and the popular political emblem of the 1854 Eureka Stockade. In *The spirit of the Southern Cross* in particular, we see Loureiro modify the language of French Symbolism for an imaginative art of national inflection.

The Symbolist conception of decorative commissions suggests how Europe's fin-de-siècle cultural fashions were registered by the 1880s in the bourgeoning taste of Melbourne's middle class and employed as part of the artistic embellishment of the city during the decade of its prosperous expansion.[11] The classical allegorical figure had become visually entrenched in Melbourne at this time through sculpted decorations of the city's new landmarks. However, *The spirit of the Southern Cross* and *The spirit of the new moon* are not straightforward ornamental allegories. Loureiro's work was noted in the press for investing 'decorative painting with an imaginative quality which makes his pictures of this order something more than mere dainty designs of form and colour'.[12] This 'imaginative quality' provides the terms of the works' Symbolist distinction. The figures resonate as allusive beings, with their forms the poetic embodiment of the infinite – the abstract 'spirit of' referred to in the title of the works. It was through such terms that Jean Moréas characterised Symbolism in his 1886 manifesto, claiming that 'the essential part of symbolic art is never to reach the idea itself'.[13] As such, Symbolism, from its formal inception, was promoted as a movement encouraging ambiguity, and one where

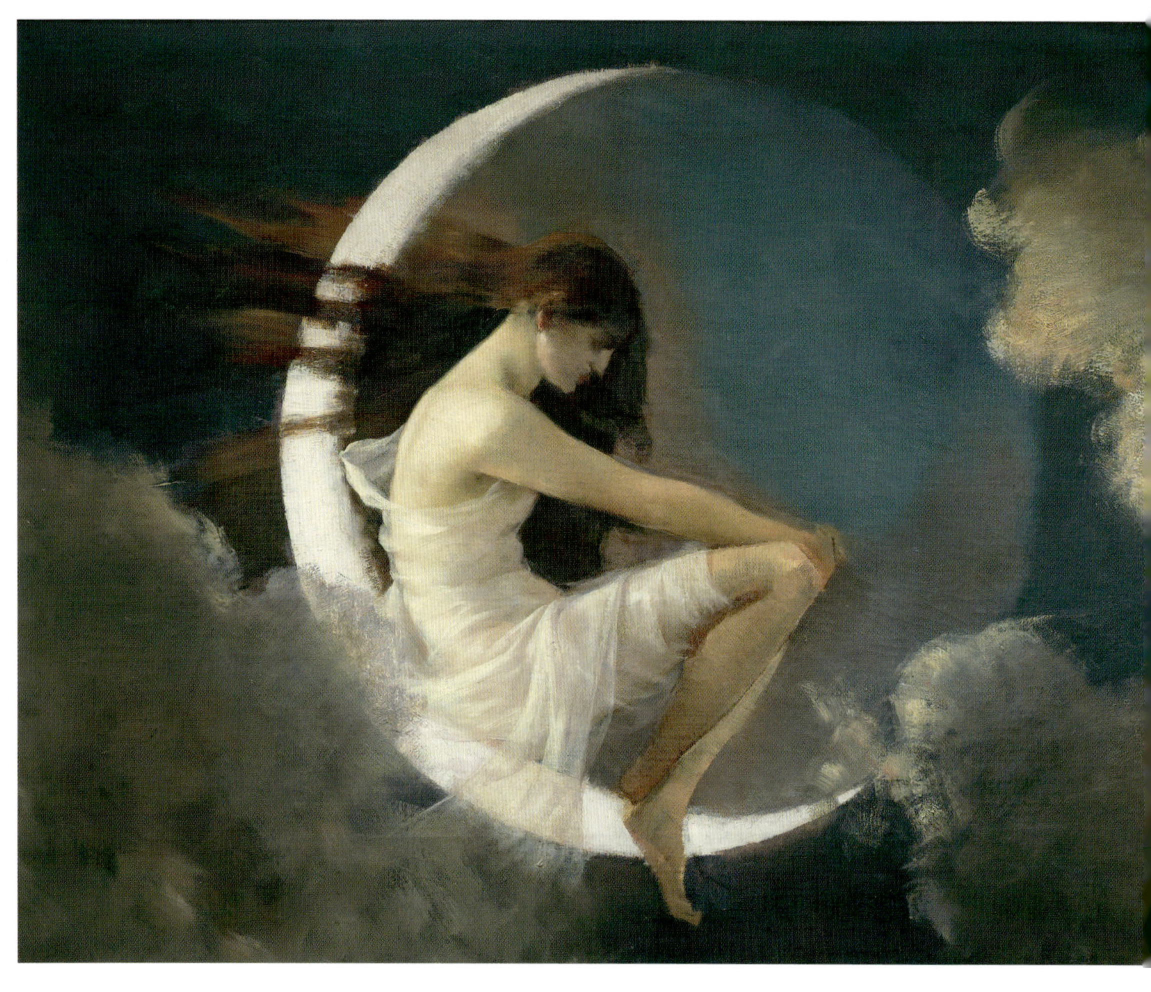

Arthur Loureiro *Study for 'The spirit of the new moon'* **1888,** oil on canvas (see detail page 159)
Queensland Art Gallery, Brisbane. Purchased 1995. Queensland Art Gallery Foundation Grant with the assistance of Philip Bacon
through the Queensland Art Gallery Foundation. Celebrating Queensland Art Gallery's Centenary 1895–1995

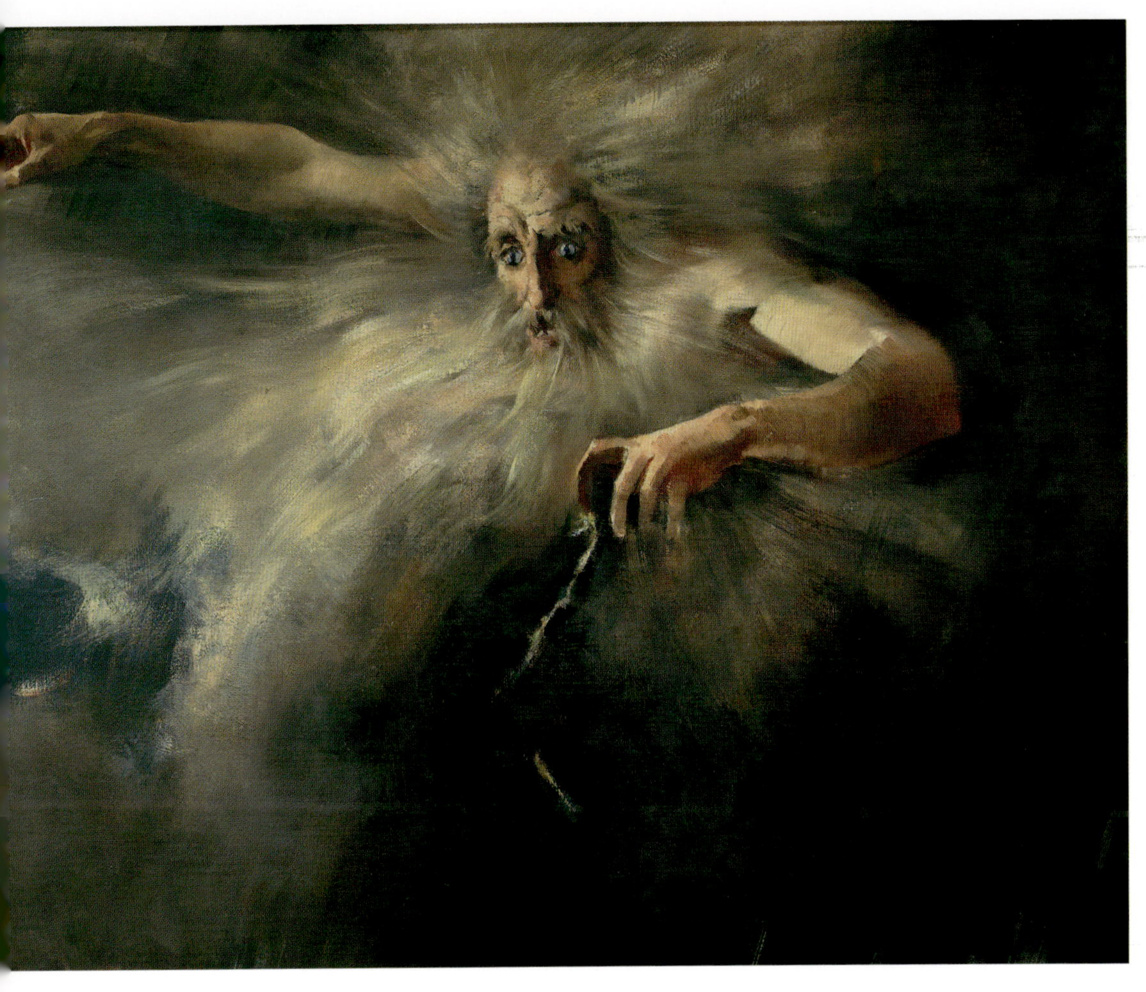

the appearances of the external world were used to imply the deeper, spiritual or psychological arenas existing beyond them. While classically informed, Loureiro's work relies on Symbolism's mode of interpretation, where meaning was not exact or didactic, but rather registered through sensual form.

'Enigmatic goddess and mortal woman': the Symbolist female

If *The spirit of the Southern Cross* and *The spirit of the new moon* can be considered the first Symbolist-inspired paintings created in Australia, then they reveal the source of such inspiration through their representations of women. The engagement with female imagery, overwhelmingly generated by male artists, was central to fin-de-siècle art. The ideal female figure of the late-century Salon was epitomised by the Venus figures of Alexandre Cabanel and William-Adolphe Bouguereau: polished, fleshy, empty vessels that served to allegorise their form of beauty as universal truth. The Symbolists' emphasis on inner life challenged the vacancy of this model, and they instead depicted the female form through a range of guises broadly oscillating between angelic, ethereal beings, and figures of exaggerated sexuality.

This duality broadly approximates the divisions between the French and British modes of Symbolism: while artists of British Aestheticism and late Pre-Raphaelism art adopted female motifs of poetically allusive beauty and subjects of internal resonances, from the French emerged her polemic other – the femme fatale. With its modern roots in the literature of Charles Baudelaire and Gustave Flaubert, the femme fatale was a demonic and sexually engulfing force. By the late nineteenth century the popular translation of this figure into the visual arts was informed by the psychological backlash against the emerging New Woman who was gaining greater political legitimacy and independence through the period's key legislated reforms. The 1880s and 90s witnessed the increased awareness of the ideals of the suffragette movement but also the promotion of the New Woman as a socially corrosive force by conservative commentators. Thus while women enjoyed gradual shifts from the political peripheries of society, images shaped by the apprehensive reactions to women's changing social status became increasingly pronounced in both art and literature.

The Symbolists aligned the social ambivalence about female empowerment with developing psychoanalytical theories of (female) sexual deviancy with representations of the sexually enticing malevolent woman.[14] Seizing on mythological precedents and biblical prototypes of the powerful female sexual force, the figures of Salome, Judith, Eve and Homer's Circe became recurring subjects in their art. In the 1870s Gustave Moreau provided an enduring archetype of the femme fatale with a series of works based on Salome's dance before Herod. With his jewel-like palette encrusting

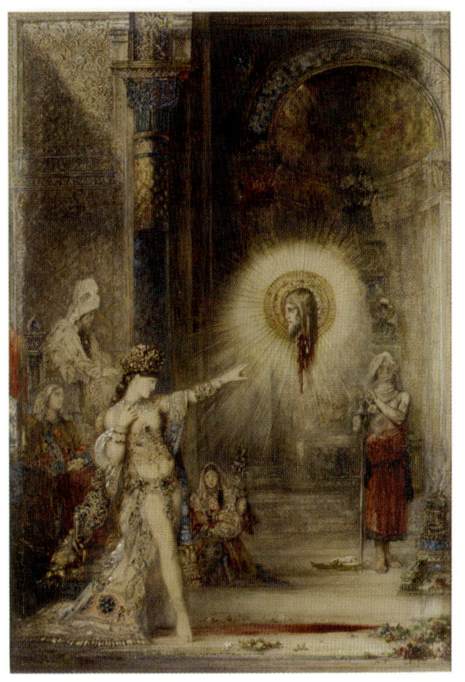

the figure with exotic orientalised ornament, Moreau's Salome performs a captivating dance, combining a seductively posed body with the commanding gesture of outstretched arms. It was with the fertile fusion of literary and visual modes of expression, the correlation between art forms that the Symbolists held as ideal, that Moreau's Salome came to epitomise the Symbolists' femme fatale. The protagonist of *A rebours*, Des Esseintes, famously fantasises before a Moreau watercolour of Salome, and reconstructs the work through the incantations of his mind and senses. He concludes that Moreau's 'enigmatic goddess' is a 'mortal woman, the soiled vessel, ultimate cause of every sin and every crime'.[15] The Symbolist woman represented this same strange disjuncture: the goddess who was subversively mortal, sensually real yet perennially ideal. Armed with her sexuality as a weapon of power over the (rational) male, she was no longer an annex of mythology but a devastatingly present force and, as such, became a key figure in Symbolist art.

Within the ranks of Australian artists responding to such Symbolist modelling of the female, Bertram Mackennal's *Circe* 1892–93, the sorceress of Homer's *Odyssey*, is the most accomplished and potentially malevolent within the terms of French Symbolism. Mackennal was among the first generation of artists born and trained in Australia to travel to Europe in the 1880s to further their studies. He arrived in London in 1882 and studied at the Royal Academy Schools in 1884 but, dissatisfied, left for Paris after a few months. During the decade of his studentship, which was broadly divided between Paris and London, Mackennal's practice was informed by his immersion in both the traditions and contemporary developments of these centres. The 1880s and 90s witnessed an unprecedented level of sculptural activity in both cities. In England this became known as the New Sculpture movement, which incorporated a broad range of tendencies sourced from French developments that revitalised the lifeless neoclassical model that had dominated sculpture practice throughout the century. New Sculpture used a diverse set of strategies to animate sculptural surfaces in terms of the 'values of the flesh' and how such values signalled

Gustave Moreau *The apparition (L'Apparition)* c1876, watercolour
Musée de Louvre on loan to Musée d'Orsay, Paris. Gift of Charles Hayem 1898
Photo ©RMN (Musée d'Orsay)/Jean-Gilles Berizzo

the spirit within. [16] In the work of its most notable practitioners, such as Alfred Gilbert (who had offered Mackennal special tuition), such preoccupations were identified by a heightened idealised naturalism in the figure together with decorative or abstracted ornament. While the lessons learnt by Mackennal from his association with the New Sculptors was varied, it was this Symbolist-inspired tendency to infuse the physical with suggestions of the spiritual that was the ideal that he sought for *Circe*.

In *Circe* Mackennal brought to fruition the experience he gained over a decade of study in Europe. He wrote from Paris in the summer of 1893 to his friends and supporters in Melbourne reporting on his progress on the work: it was his first lifesize sculpture with which he was determined to make his mark at the Paris Salon.[17] While informed by New Sculpture, *Circe*, as a work created in Paris for Salon success, was ultimately shaped with a feel for the present-day concerns of the art of that city. *Circe* was a creature of the Salon: a figure identified with a moral distortion that the Symbolists had aligned with the feminine, albeit with a malignant guise moderated by its idealised natural form. In the course of *Circe*'s production Mackennal emphasised its conception in such terms, stating that the 'mystic feeling of the head and the character of the outstretched hands are my main points of interest'.[18] It was with this combination of taut physicality, irrational sexual powers, hypnotic command and a hieratic pose encapsulating the power and poise of Moreau's *Salome*, that Mackennal created the figure as a psychological fortress.

Circe's heightened corporeality – a body that is both naturally real and figuratively ideal – positions it in the New Sculpture context, but such 'British' qualities are harnessed to forcefully assert the femme fatale. Depicted at the critical moment when the sorceress Circe transforms humans into swine, Mackennal equates her power with a potent and mysterious sexual force. The French press praised *Circe* as a figure of beauty, but one that is 'nervous, dry, tough and domineering', suggesting an anxious allure on the part of the viewer.[19] Mackennal emphasises her forceful physicality through frontality: a confrontational, even intrusive, positioning of the figure in relation to the viewer. Crowned with coiled serpents, physically inviting and yet psychologically repellent, *Circe* encapsulates the Symbolist definition of woman as sorceress.

The impact of Rodin: 'great dreams in marble'[20]

Mackennal claimed that it was from the example of Auguste Rodin, the widely recognised leader of modern sculpture, that he came to understand the Symbolist definition that 'art is not nature, but something grander and superimposed on nature'.[21] Rodin's treatment of sculptural surfaces as the means for suggesting animating forces beneath the flesh, of using (as he said) 'the forms and attitudes

Bertram Mackennal *Circe* 1892–93, original lifesize plaster 1893, lifesize bronze 1901
National Gallery of Victoria, Melbourne. Felton Bequest 1910

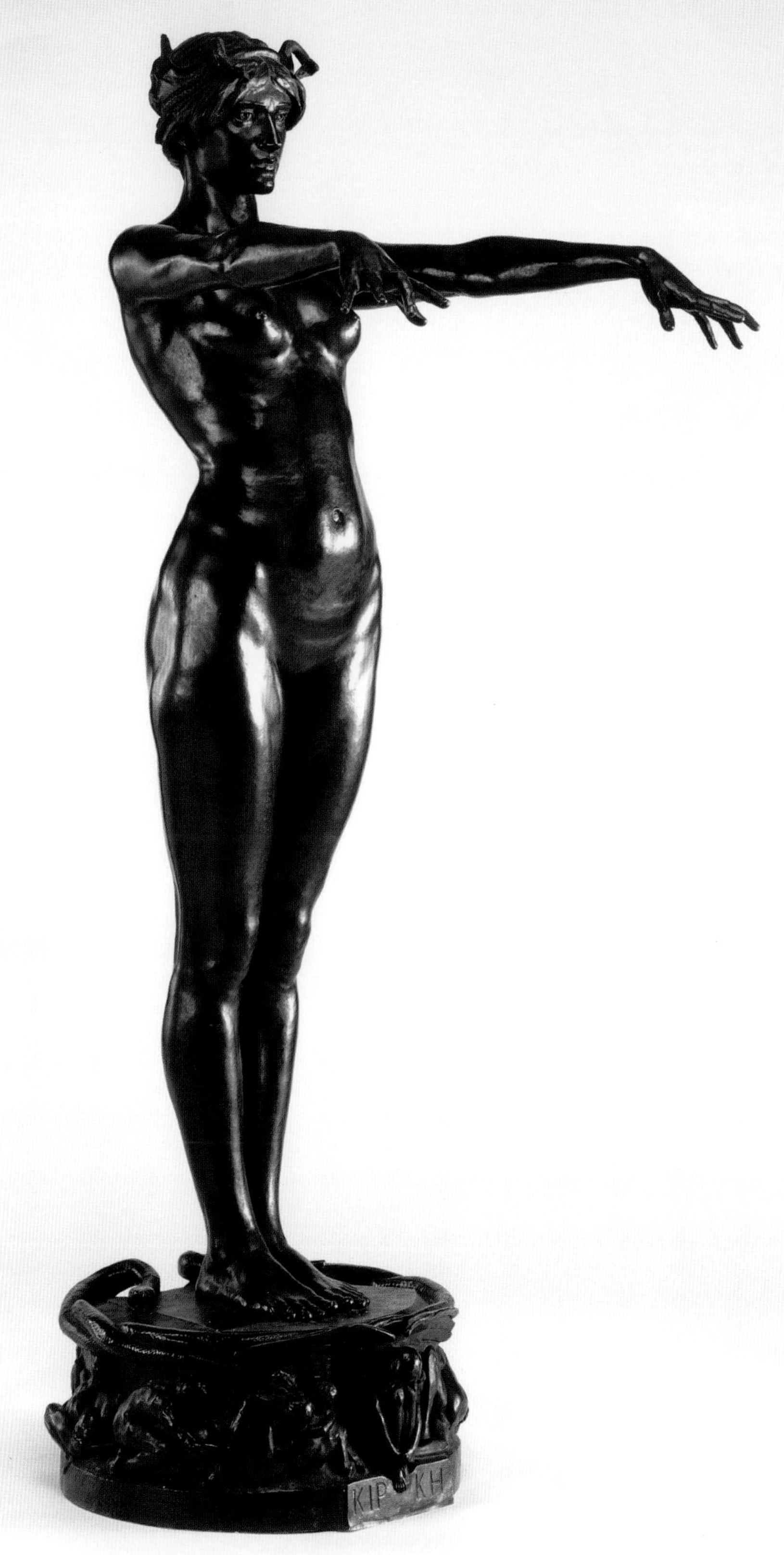

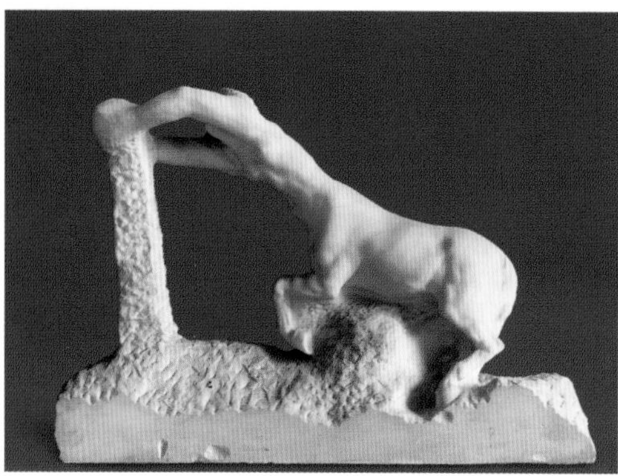

of human beings ... [to] reveal the emotions of his soul', provided a fundamental model not only for Mackennal but for many subsequent Australian sculptors.[22] Through Rodin's directive, inner realities could be made outwardly manifest by expressive modelling, while maintaining a fundamental attachment to figurative form.

The aesthetic imprint of Rodin on Mackennal's work is most clearly inscribed on the base of *Circe*. With its coupling bodies contained within a tightly compressed band, this circular relief recalls the undulating figurative surfaces of Rodin's *The gates of hell* 1880–c1900. Like the fated figures of Rodin's masterwork, Mackennal evokes a chaotic humanity tumbling from grace as the metaphoric outcome of the eroticised power of the femme fatale and of humanity's capacity to transform into an animalistic force. Rodin's enduring influence was evident in 1907 when, 'in a flash of Rodinesque inspiration', Mackennal produced *The Earth and the elements* with a beautifully conceived sense of vaporous movement in stone.[23] The work gives evocative shape to the perennial motion of its personified elements. These ethereal beings are evoked through the rolling rhythm weaving between the textured surface of the marble and the sensual smoothness of their flesh.

Rodin's aesthetic of fragmentation, combining rusticated and modelled surfaces, had by the new century become part of the academic language of sculpture. As *The Earth and the elements* suggests, it became established as a means of invoking the expressive, sensual qualities of the stone medium. Charles Web Gilbert emulates this model in *The Sun and the Earth* 1918. While his success at the Royal Academy the previous year with *The critic* 1917 embraced an Edwardian shift to more factual, pragmatic form, *The Sun and the Earth* holds to the Symbolist ideal of evoking sensuous existence through Rodinesque innovations. And while similar in theme to Mackennal's personification of the elements, Web Gilbert's figures are more erotically earthbound.[24] Responding to the fused lovers of Rodin's *The kiss* 1889, the figures' softened forms are cradled within the coarsened features of the stone, with both surfaces dynamically combined in an Art-Nouveau flow. Web Gilbert referenced Rodin's conceptual shaping – his ability to convey intangible human emotion captured within a grander physical structure.

Auguste Rodin *Female centaur (Centauresse)* 1889, marble
Musée Rodin, Paris. Photo ©RMN François Vizzavona 2010

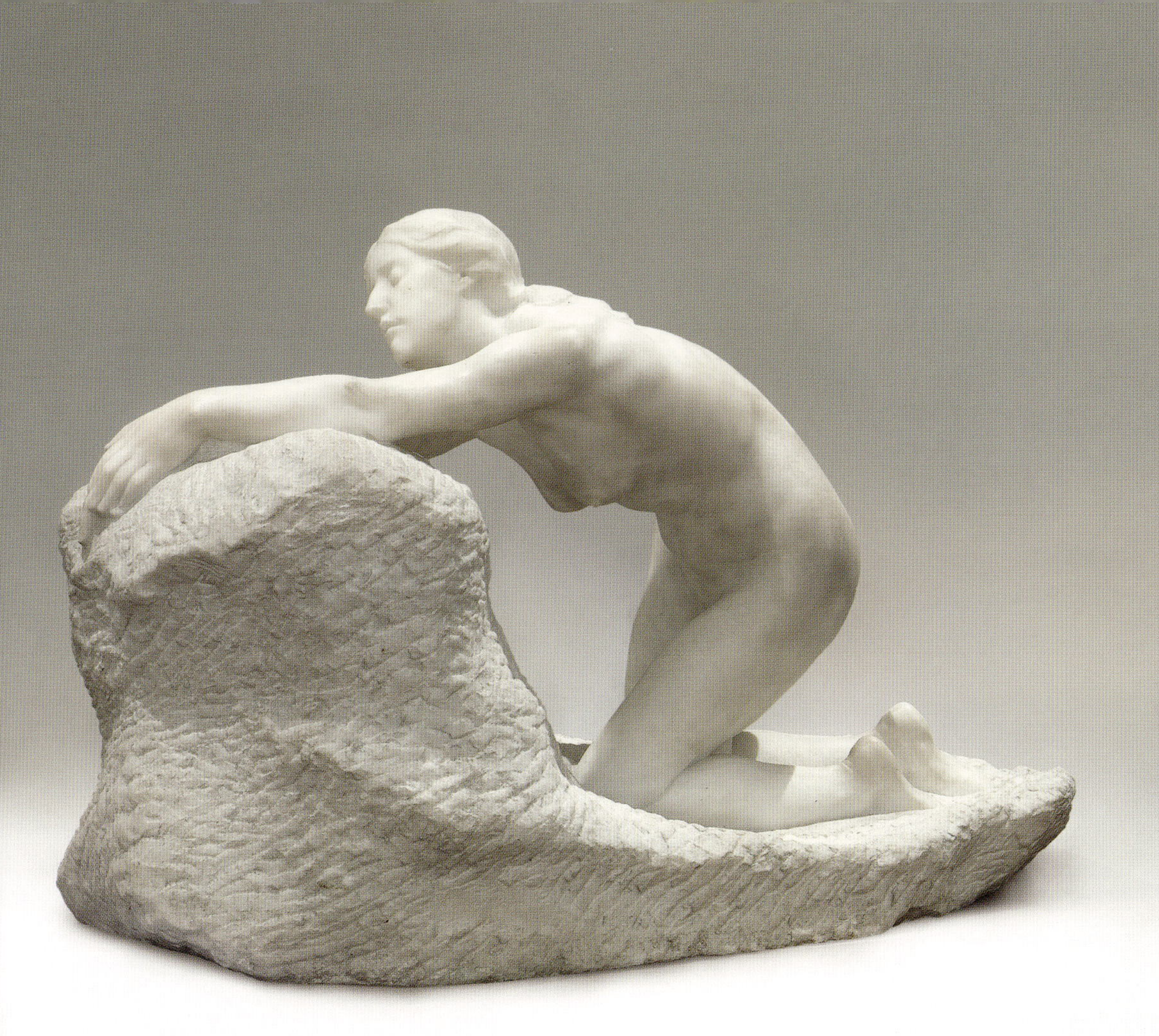

Harold Parker *Ariadne* 1919, marble
National Gallery of Victoria, Melbourne. Felton Bequest 1921

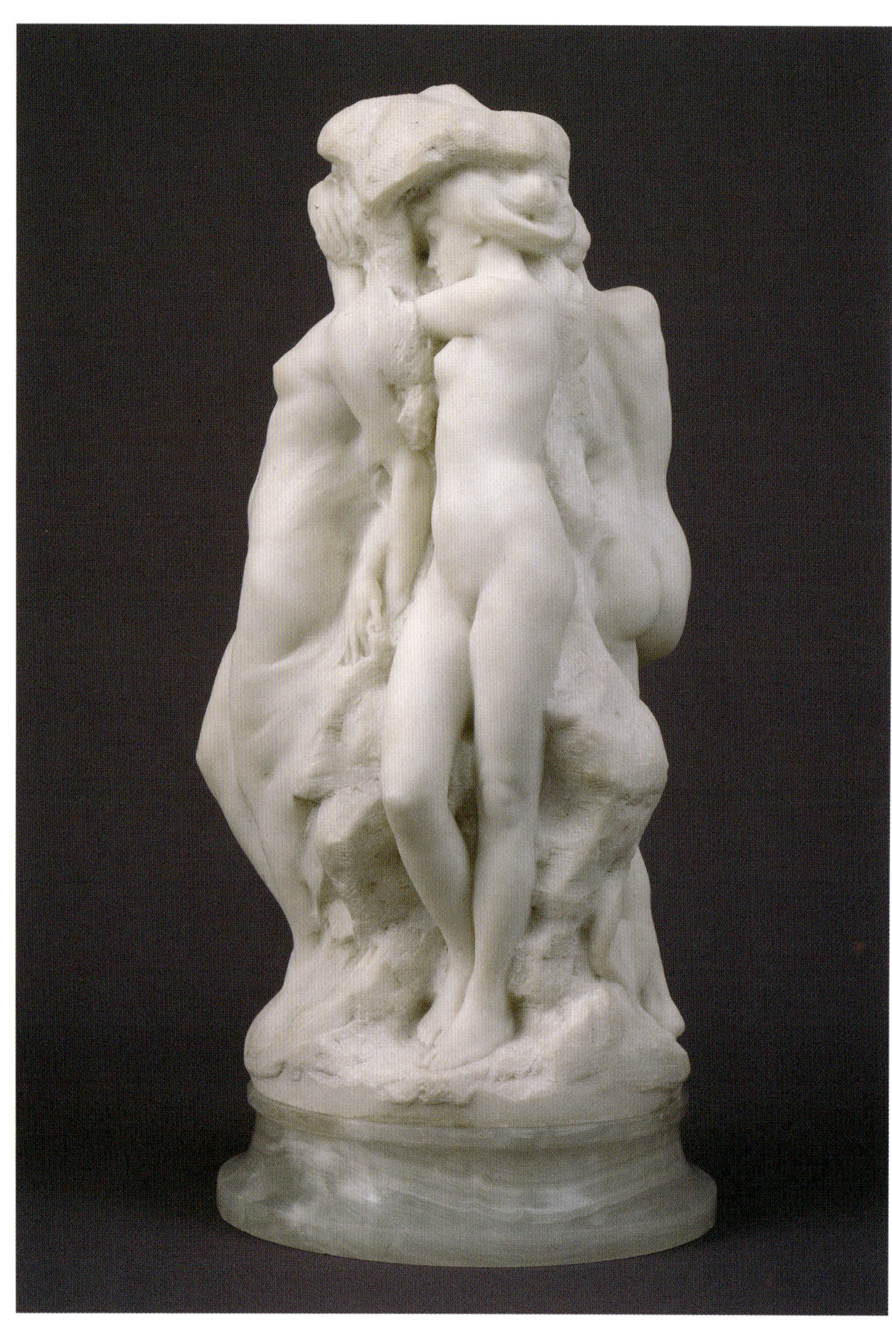

(above) **Bertram Mackennal** *The Earth and the elements* **1907**, marble on onyx base
Art Gallery of New South Wales. On loan from the Tate Gallery, London,
presented by the Trustees of the Chantrey Bequest 1907

(opposite) **Charles Web Gilbert** *The Sun and the Earth* **1918**, marble
National Gallery of Victoria, Melbourne. Gift of Mrs Web Gilbert 1927

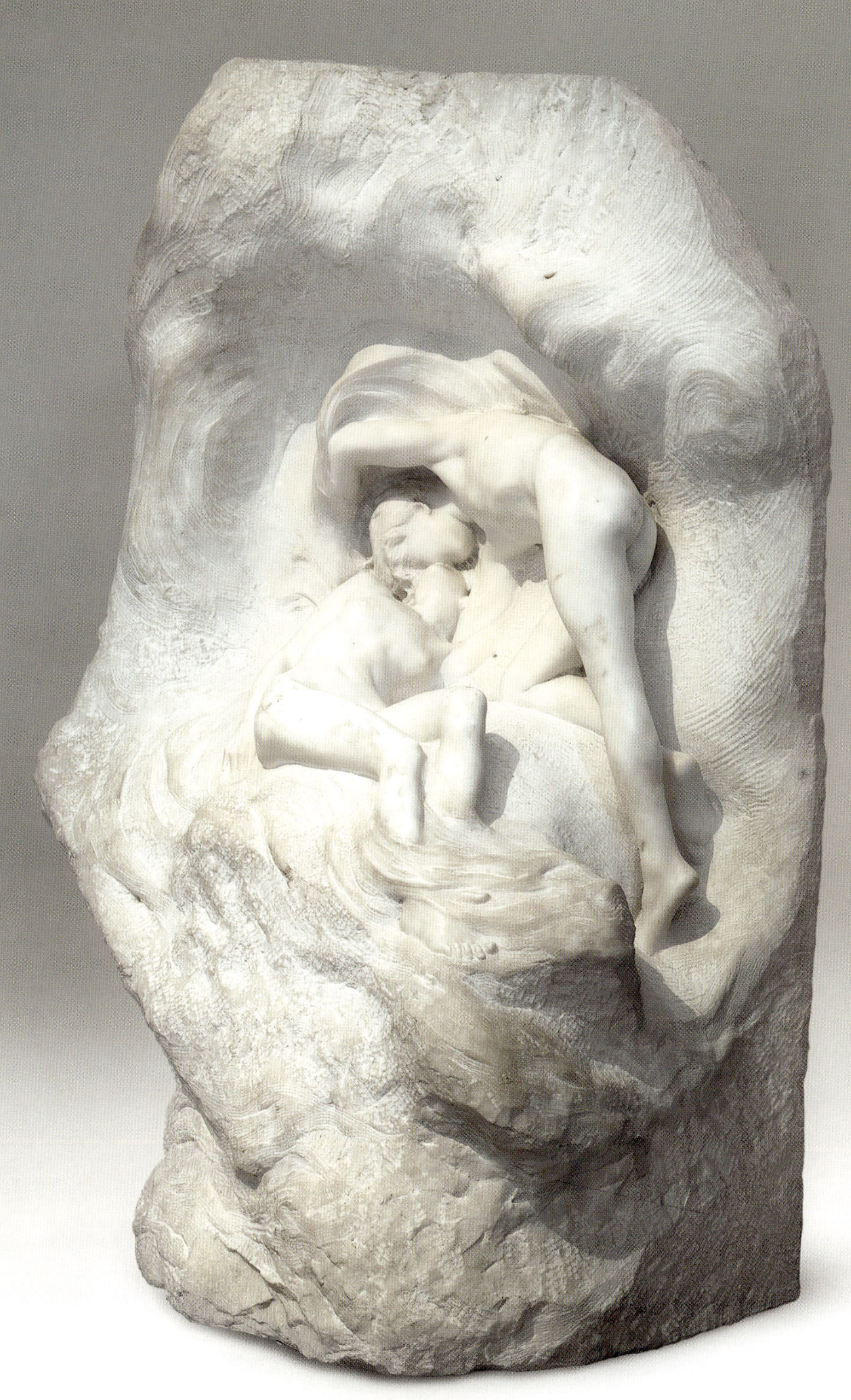

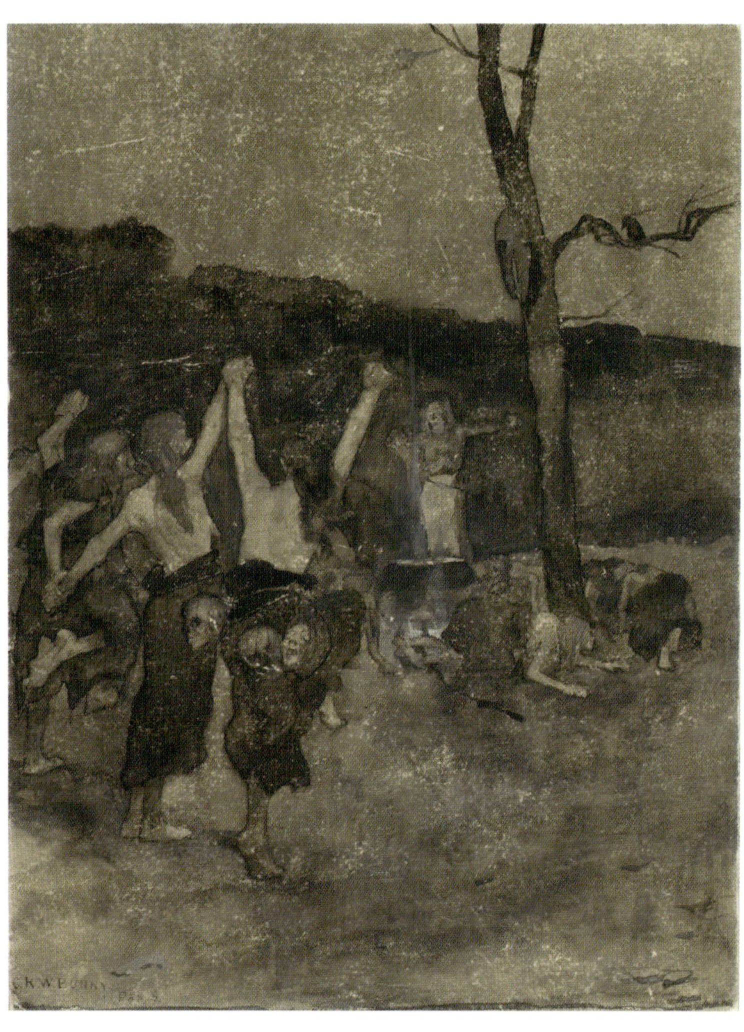

Rupert Bunny *Untitled (Witches' sabbath)* 1887, probably originally exhibited as *Une nuit de Valpurgis*, watercolour on paper

 The University of Melbourne Art Collection. Gift of the Bunny Estate 1948

It was with reference to Rodin's aesthetic that Brisbane-born sculptor Harold Parker achieved his greatest success in London. *Ariadne* 1919 (a version of larger 1904 work) was enthusiastically received when the lifesize marble was exhibited in 1908 and subsequently purchased by the Tate Gallery. Parker composes the body of *Ariadne* into a seductive corporeal expression that essentialises the yearning, grief and desire of this mythical figure. While Parker, like Mackennal, clearly worked from the life model, he also encompassed Rodin's emphasis on figurative gesture as a means of exploring emotional content. Extending outstretched from a textured block base, *Ariadne* echoes the example of Rodin's 1889 marble *Female centaur*, which represents the desperate struggle of the soul trapped within the body. Parker similarly positions the body of *Ariadne* stretching from the stone block, imploring for release. Described by William Moore as 'exquisite in its tense sadness', *Ariadne* was instantly recognised as a crucial Australian sculpture.[25]

Rupert Bunny: myth and the occult

It was through an engagement with Symbolist themes that Melbourne-born artist Rupert Bunny (who had arrived in Paris in 1887) made his notable entrée at the Paris Salon. *Un sabbat*, exhibited in 1888, is known only through its contemporary description as well as a watercolour on paper, *Une nuit de Valpurgis* 1887 (opposite), probably its study. In contrast to the seductive femme fatale, the women in Bunny's work are depicted as deviants of an irrational order, their diabolical charge referencing primordial energy rather than sexual agency.[26] Bunny's friend in Paris, the Hungarian poet Zsigmond Justh, speculated that Bunny's 'tendency toward the mystical' stemmed from the stories told to him by his father, who nurtured his youthful imagination with tales of Greek myth.[27] However, *Une nuit de Valpurgis* suggests that a different set of sources claimed Bunny's attention. The subject of these works is the 'Wulpurgis night' of Germanic myth where witches gathered on the spring night of pagan worship. The work evokes myth through macabre ritual and women of primeval spirit that together provide a sinister shaping of fantastic subject matter.

By igniting realms of the fantastic and displacing the scientific rationalism, materialism and positivist thought exerted over nineteenth-century culture, the figures and landscapes of ancient mythologies were crucial subjects for Symbolist artists. While myth encapsulates a nostalgic yearning for an imagined idyllic past, it features more significantly in Symbolist art as the masking of deeper human drives and as a tool for interpreting the modern sensibility. When Freud famously defined the formation of male sexual identity in terms of the story of Oedipus, he exemplified the way that classical myths were adopted in the psychological sciences to fathom deeper elemental desires. Like Freud, the Symbolists equated the irrational order

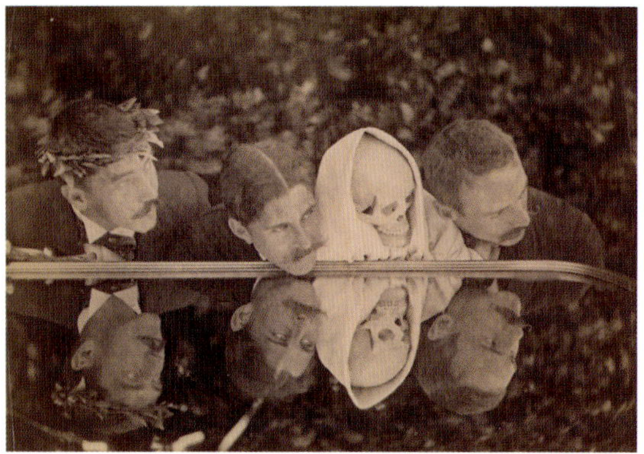

of mythological subjects with the realm of the spirit and the psyche. In claiming such legitimacy for classical myth in contemporary expression, the playwright Alfred Poizat declared that 'they were no longer Greek myths, they were our own; they were no longer part of Greek legend, but the legend of our own souls'.[28]

Related to this interest in myth and legend, occultism also played a part in Symbolist expression, especially in Paris and Belgium. In late-century terms the occult referred to the investigation of spiritual forces and combined aspects of science, mysticism and ancient wisdom to explain the unseen elements of the universe. When Huysmans declared that 'space is peopled by microbes. Is it more surprising that space should not also be crammed with spirits?' he was articulating the Symbolist defense of the intangible in an age of scientific and positivist thinking.[29] The general impact of the occult on artistic culture was well publicised by the end of the century through frequent references in the pages of Symbolist journals in Paris where it was positioned as part of the flow of ideas between the psychological sciences, poetry, literature and music that contributed to the formation of Symbolist aesthetics.[30]

When the fascination for the occult was at its most pronounced in Paris, Bunny explored the subject in his art, although his preoccupations were more aesthetic than mystical.[31] Photographs of Bunny and his friends in the late 1880s posing with shrouds, skulls and daggers declare a farcical attitude toward the fin-de-siècle fashion for the occult. Nonetheless Bunny explored the expressive potential of Symbolist devices and themes as evidenced by a handful of paintings and a substantial archive of sketches that plot his preoccupation with subjects of sorcery and the macabre.[32] Bunny also pursued these themes in a series of experimental monotypes exhibited in 1898.[33] Monotypes enable a more unmediated form of painting, and Bunny matched this quality of the medium with a turbulent and psychologically denser subject matter than found in his paintings. The subjects of his monotypes included ghoulish visions of sea monsters, grim reapers in various guises, demons, and strange gods of the underworld. Through such forms Bunny introduced a sub-genre of horror imagery extracted from the occult.

In his exploration of such themes, Bunny's early monotypes evidence the impact of the Swiss-German artist Arnold Böcklin, whose idiosyncratic paintings are

Rupert Bunny (right) and unidentified friends c1887–88
The University of Melbourne collection

a significant precursor to the Symbolist movement. *Out of the sea* c1898, depicting
a figure's flight from an ocean monster emerging as an engulfing force from the deep,
suggests his emulation of Böcklin's work. It is one of several monotypes by Bunny
depicting futile escape attempts from overwhelming forces – death, rape and other
unknown terrors – and referencing the generated panic states of Böcklin's creation.
Out of the sea encapsulates a sense of primordial fear, externalising into mythical
form the ambience of nightmares through an overarching mood of anxiety and
tension that is accentuated by rushed and animated brushwork. Through such means,
Bunny engaged with the Symbolists' strategies for decoding the psychological realism
of myth to explore reality as altered by human fears and desires.

In his monotype *(Orpheus)* c1898 Bunny reworked mythical imagery through the
Symbolist theme of decadence. The work is based on Ovid's account of Orpheus
when he was decapitated during a Bacchanalian orgy. His head, along with his lyre,
was washed up on the Mediterranean shore and discovered by the locals of a nearby
village. Bunny diminishes the visual links to this narrative, imaging instead a dramatic
moment where a woman lifts the decaying head in prelude to a gruesome kiss. The
gesture is not sourced from Orpheus's tale but reprised from the climactic moment
of Oscar Wilde's play *Salome*. Wilde had Salome kiss the decapitated head of John
the Baptist in what is the play's decadent encounter between seduction, murder
and necrophilia. Bunny composed *(Orpheus)* as a theatrical mise-en-scène, with
the woman draped in flowing robes, centrally positioned in a shallow space against
a painted ocean backdrop and turning the head of Orpheus outwards, implying
revelation to an audience. It is a moment of both repose and climax: the kneeling
figure lovingly holds the rotting head as the fetishised remains of a lover in the
suspended moment of Salome's heretical kiss. Wilde had premiered *Salome*
in Paris in 1896, capitalising on the city's delight in theatricised vice, and the play
was subsequently banned from theatres in London. Yet its censorship, along with
Aubrey Beardsley's darkly seductive accompanying illustrations, aided the play's
notoriety, and ensured that Wilde's *Salome* was one of the enduring embodiments
of the fin-de-siècle femme fatale.

Sarah Bernhardt: the 'serpent of the old Nile'[34]

When Wilde's *Salome* premiered in Paris, the stage sensation Sarah Bernhardt
starred in its title role. Bernhardt was the ultimate Symbolist celebrity: the epitome
of the femme fatale imagined by writers and painters. Closely attuned to the aesthetic
fashioning of her public persona, Bernhardt turned the male-driven imaging of the
dangerous woman into an assertive tool for self-promotion. By the late nineteenth
century, associations with Bernhardt were held as a highly prized mark of cultural
prestige, a pertinent point for young Australian artists as they sought their entrée

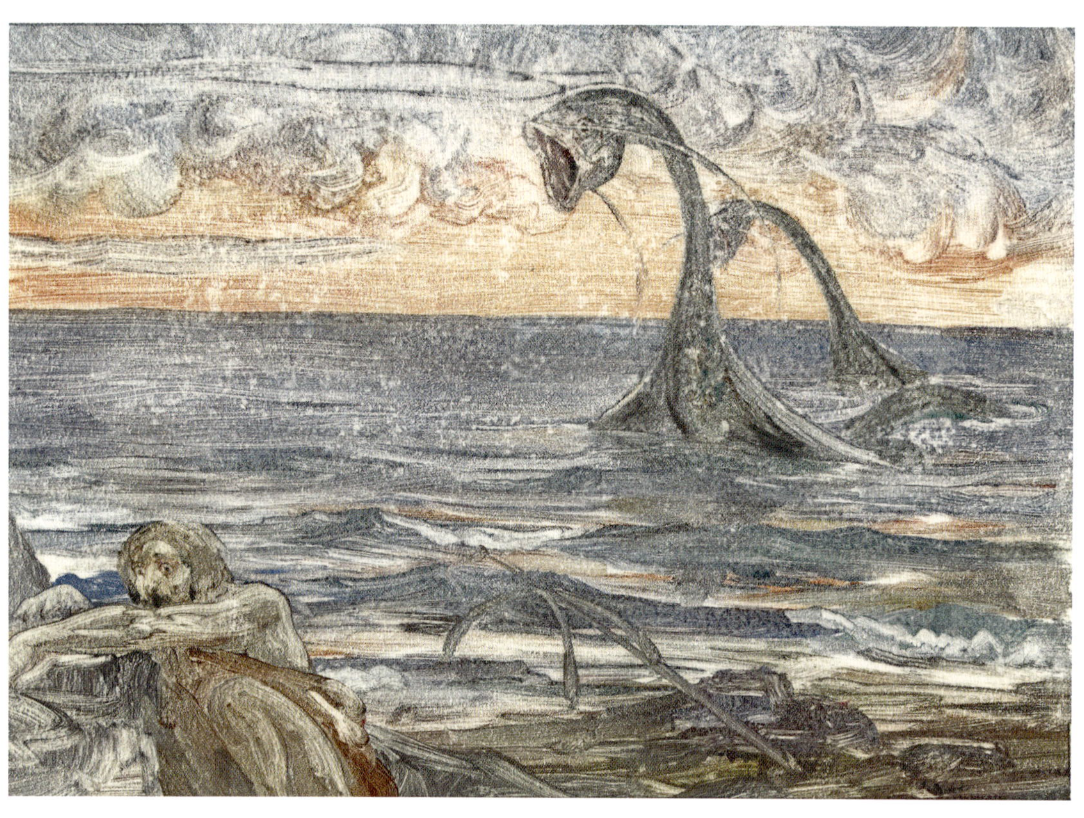

Rupert Bunny *Out of the sea* c1898, monotype
National Gallery of Victoria, Melbourne. Gift of Mr CC Chisholm 1962

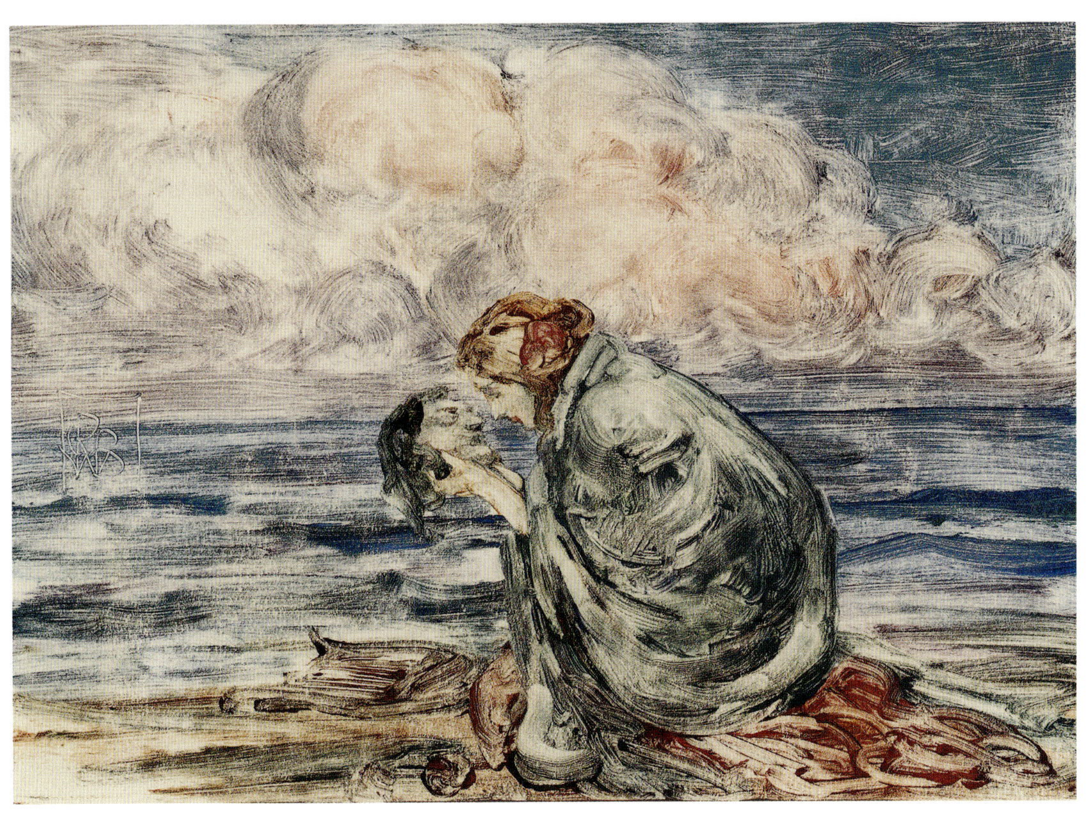

Rupert Bunny *(Orpheus)* c1898, colour monotype
Art Gallery of New South Wales. Purchased 1969

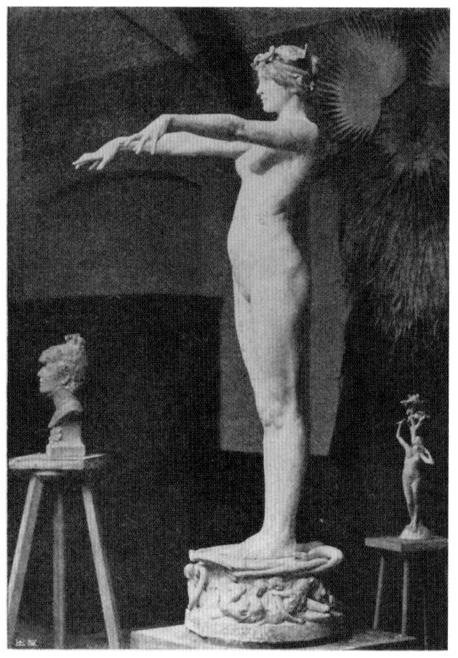

into the Paris art world. Thus Rupert Bunny's social standing in Paris during these decades can be measured in part by Bernhardt's documented visits to his studio, and his own frequenting of her salons.[35] Bernhardt also acquired at least one of Bunny's early paintings, *Illusion – the eternal Maya* c1890 (not located). Its subject, an enigmatic female figure, the 'world's creator and destroyer' who 'floats in a foggy space' with a 'skull's death head', parallels the mystical model of feminine power with which Bernhardt aligned herself.[36]

Bernhardt, herself a practising sculptor, featured in the early promotion of Bertram Mackennal's artistic reputation. The actress, on tour in Melbourne in 1891, became a vocal supporter of the young sculptor when, with a degree of controversy fuelled by her involvement, Mackennal failed to secure the first prize in a competition for a sculpture for Melbourne's public library. In retaliation, Bernhardt dramatically declared that she had commissioned a portrait bust from Mackennal, which she intended to exhibit at the Paris Salon and make his name known to all leading Parisian critics.[37] Mackennal produced three portraits of Bernhardt in various formats, yet it was the bust that he planned to exhibit with *Circe* at the 1893 Salon.[38] The intended grouping of these works implies an association in their conception. Bernhardt's femme fatale is aligned to Mackennal's interpretation of female power in *Circe*, as a figure whose malevolence is ultimately tied to a position of command, and whose nudity and sensuality are assertive guises.

In *Phedre*, his 1879 sonnet dedicated to Bernhardt, Wilde cast her as a hybrid born of a commingling of Ancient Greece and the lascivious fires of hell transcending the common world.[39] He purportedly scoured ancient coin collections in the British Museum searching for her likeness.[40] In Mackennal's extant portrait *Sarah Bernhardt* c1892–93, the actress is figured as this Symbolist visionary. Modelled in the low-relief profile format of coin design, Bernhardt is depicted with her eyes half-closed, appearing somewhere between dream and waking and the inward momentum of a trance. The tangible physicality of sculpture has been

Circe in plaster in Mackennal's studio with a bust of Sarah Bernhardt in the background c1896, featured in *The Sketch* 29 April 1896. Photo courtesy State Library of New South Wales

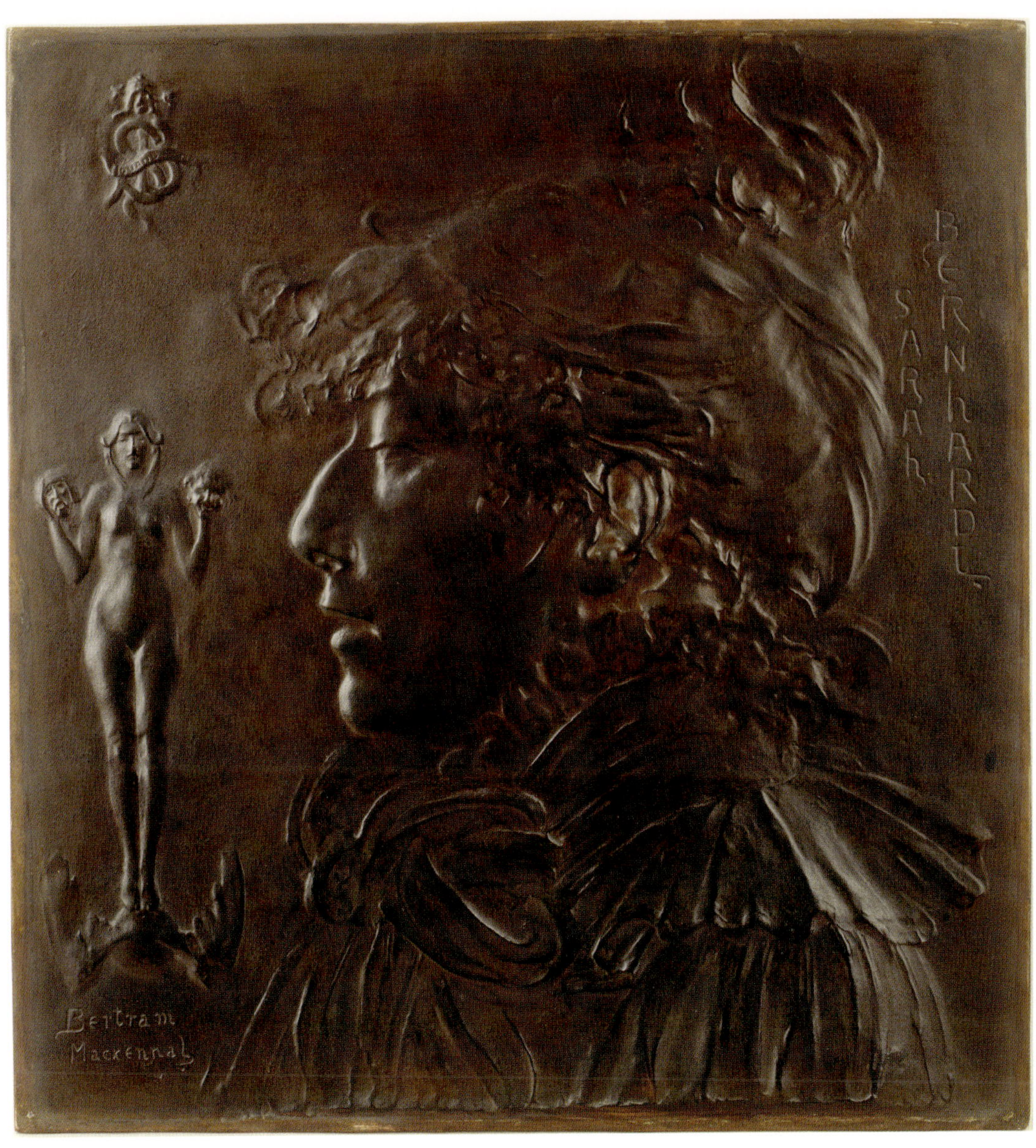

Bertram Mackennal *Sarah Bernhardt* c1892–93, bronze relief
Art Gallery of New South Wales. Bequest of Mrs JR McGregor 1944

described as being at odds with the Symbolist expression of the immaterial.[41] Of
its forms, the relief format is most compliant with the description of allusive states,
paralleling the Symbolists' tendency towards dematerialised imagery as a means
of distancing their subjects from the real.[42] Bernhardt's relief portrait hovers
between this articulation and recession of the image. It was produced as a motif of a
transformed state, implying that the conditions of Bernhardt's theatrical profession,
registered in the masks of comedy and tragedy, are part of her being. Mackennal
capitalises on Bernhardt's celebrity, clearly inscribing her name and monogram on
the work. For him, this was an exercise in evoking a Symbolist personage and aligning
his practice with a fin-de-siècle icon.

'The ideal somnambulist'[43]

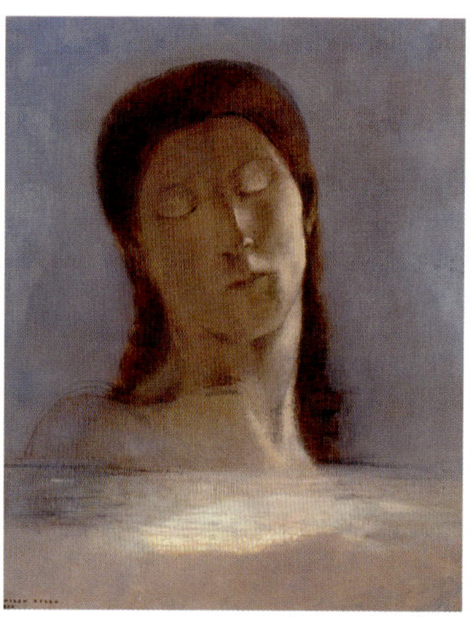

In depicting Bernhardt with her eyes half-
closed, Mackennal portrayed her in terms
of a key motif of Symbolist art and one
epitomised by Odilon Redon in his 1890
painting *Closed eyes*. Redon's androgynous
figure is depicted with eyelids shut,
enigmatically poised between water and
sky, and all material and narrative elements
negated to suggest the transcending force
of the mind. *Closed eyes* became an emblem
of the potency of inner consciousness,[44]
although imagery of closed eyes, sleepers
and dreamers already had wide resonances
in late-century European art. In England,
for example, Edward Burne-Jones's hallmark
depictions of elegant dreamers gave poetic
shape to introspective reasoning. Redon's figure, however, is a more ambiguous force
– not a sleeper or a dreamer perhaps, but one in a trance. The fashioning of such
subjects was broadly informed by the scientific charting of the subconscious in this
period. Freud's influential book *The interpretation of dreams*, published in German in
1899, reinforced earlier understandings of dreams as manifestations of subconscious
activity through symbolic forms. Prior to this, in 1882 in France, hypnotism had
been established as a therapeutic tool for exploring psychoses and had developed as a
popular fascination by the 1890s. With its potential to externalise the inner dynamics
of human consciousness, hypnosis became a potent source for Symbolist art. By the
end of the century, when inner consciousness was recognised as a vital part of waking
life, hypnotically induced sleep increasingly featured as a subject of art.

Odilon Redon *Closed eyes* 1890, oil on canvas
Musée d'Orsay, Paris, acquired from the artist by the state for the Luxembourg Palace, 1904.
Photo © RMN (Musée d'Orsay)/Hervé Lewandowski

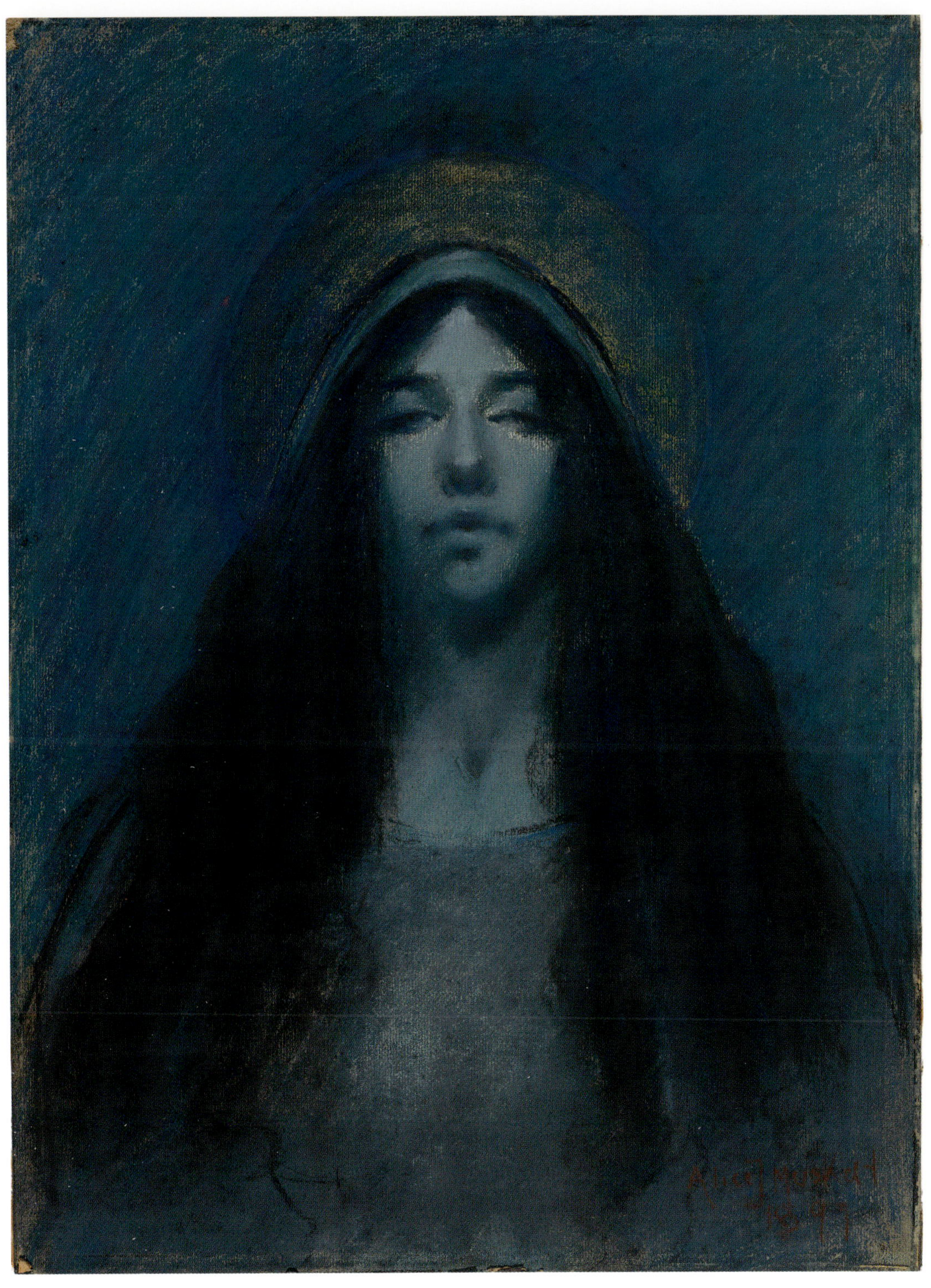

Alice Muskett *A lost halo* 1897, pastel
National Gallery of Australia, Canberra. Purchased 1992

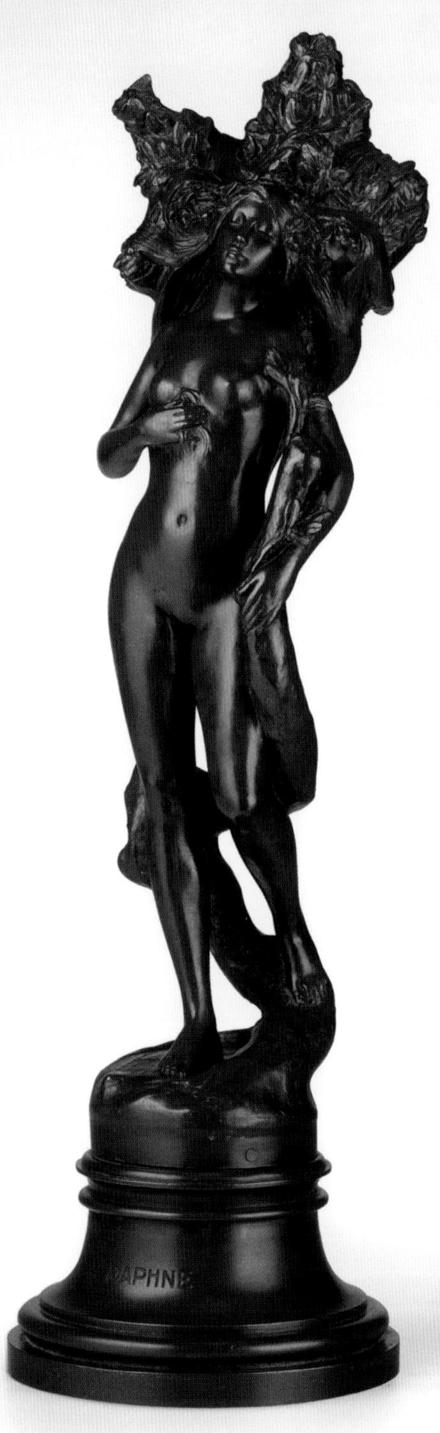

Bertram Mackennal *Daphne* 1897, bronze statuette
Queensland Art Gallery, Brisbane. Purchased 1974

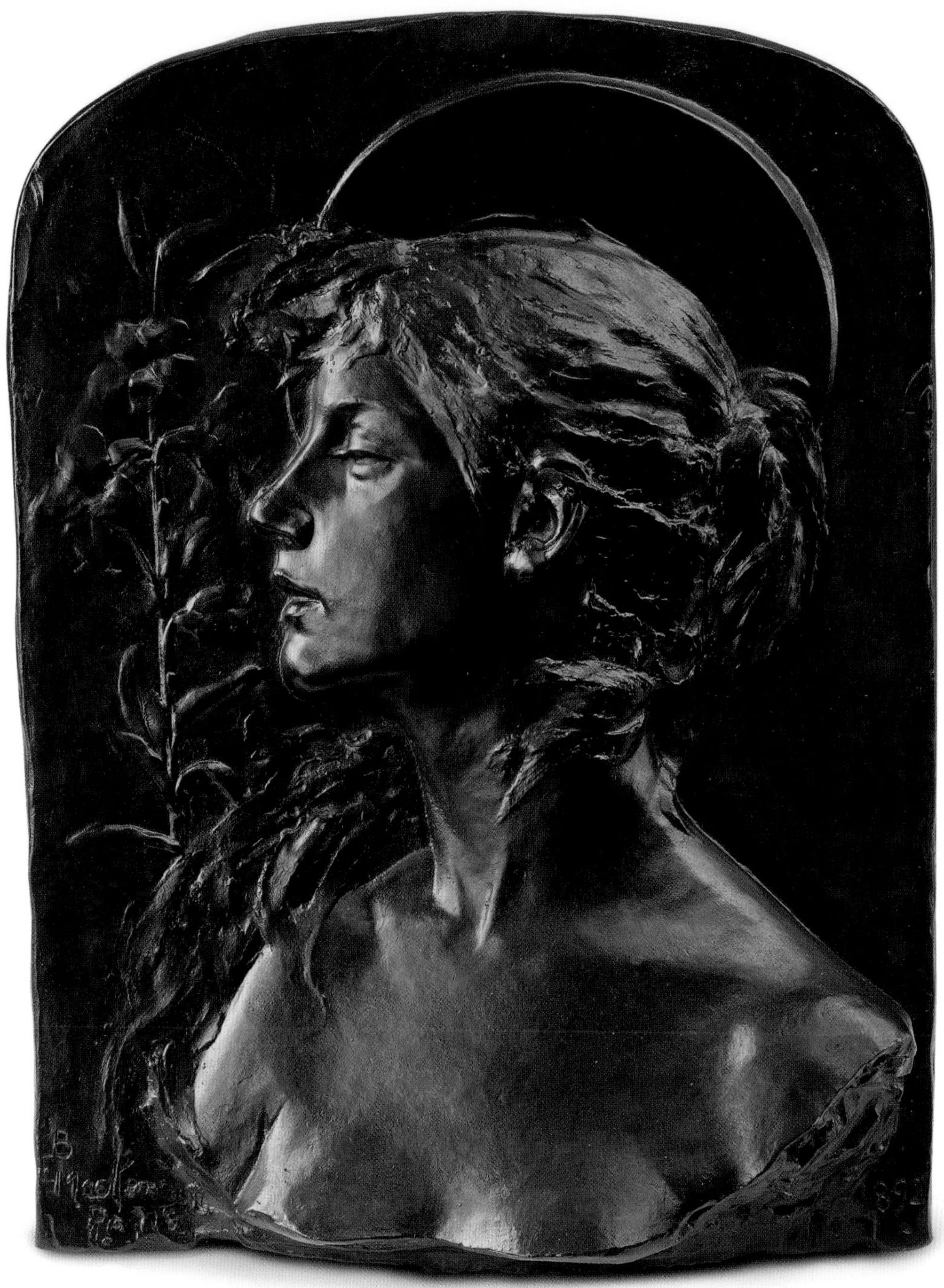

Bertram Mackennal *La tête d'une sainte (Head of a saint)* 1892, bronze relief
Private collection

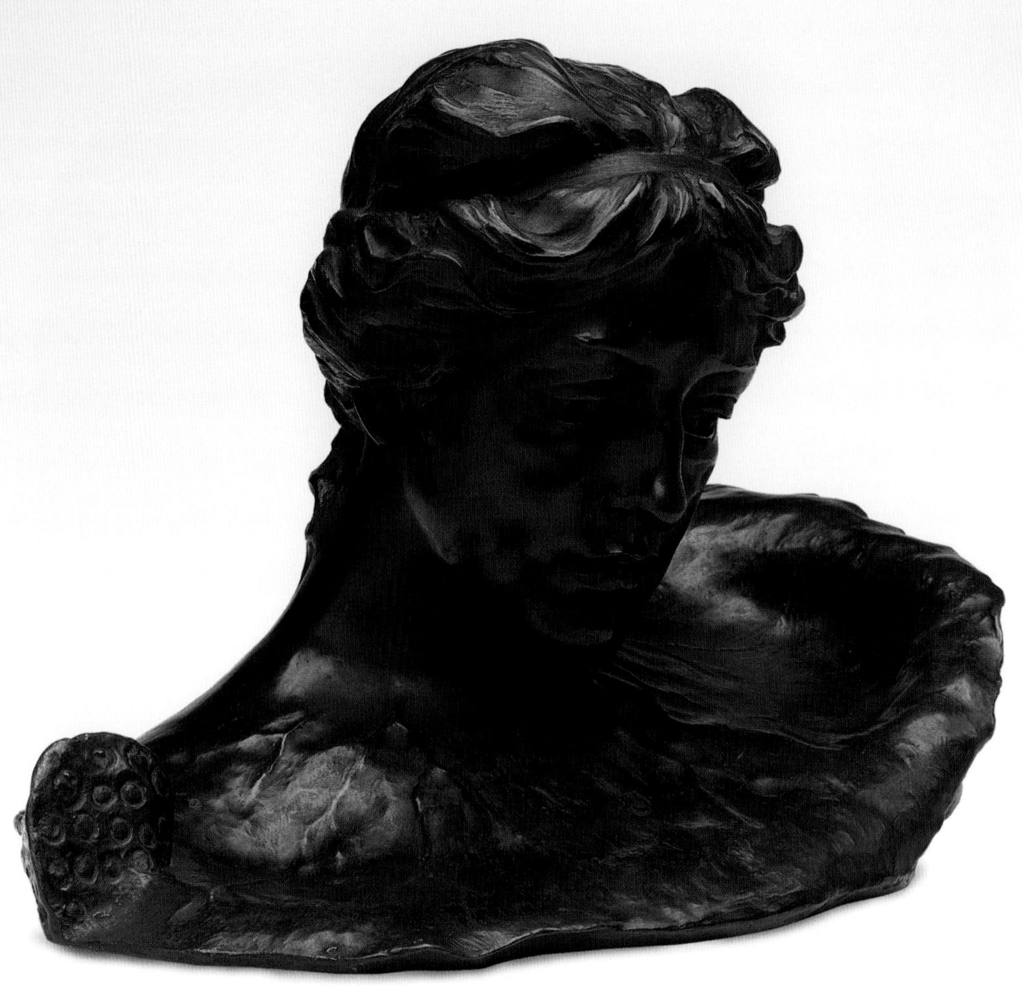

Charles Web Gilbert *The dreamer* 1915, bronze
National Gallery of Victoria, Melbourne. Felton Bequest 1922

Alice Muskett's *A lost halo* 1897 is a striking invocation of the Symbolist trance.
Muskett, who initially studied at the newly formed Julian Ashton Art School in
Sydney in 1886, travelled to Paris between 1895 and 1898 where she studied at the
Académie Colarossi. While establishing a professionally rigorous routine through
her training, it was in the current art of the day that she found inspiration for her
practice. When Muskett returned to Sydney in 1898 she exhibited works that were
readily identified as 'Symbolist' by the local press. Muskett produced the pastel *A lost
halo* in Paris, and in its figure she amalgamates the Symbolists' divided depictions of
woman as sinner and saint. Crowned with a golden halo and coloured by the shades
of a deep numinous blue, *A lost halo* alludes to mystical aspects of Marion saintliness
while simultaneously portraying the figure as a soporific seductress. The overlap of
the sacred and the profane, and the loss of purity indicated by the title, was reinforced
by the serpents and 'innocent flowers' carved into the work's original frame, making
A lost halo an evocative Symbolist ornament.[45]

In the late nineteenth and early twentieth centuries Australian artists responded
readily to subjects of mystical trances and hypnotic states. These subjects became an
indication of their interest in and familiarity with Symbolist themes. Unlike Redon's
asexual personage, which suggested that somnambulistic states transcended even
the specifics of gender, the principal subject of the waking sleep in Australian work
was female. Thus Australian artists seized on the poetic currency of the dreamer as
established by Pre-Raphaelite artists, their references to Symbolism relating more
to British than Continental sources. Mackennal produced a series of early works
that use the motif of the trance to allude to a sense of female mystery. *La tête d'une
sainte (Head of a saint)* 1892, which anticipates the format of his Sarah Bernhardt
portrait, depicts a dreaming, windswept being and describes her passage of mystical
transformation in a poetic synthesis of low and high relief modelling. While the
symbols of lily and halo suggest the motifs of the Annunciation, it is the sensuous
qualities of the figure that are used to imply a sacred ideal. Using the format of
an altarpiece, the work alludes to a more generalised veneration of the sensualist
aesthetic in fin-de-siècle culture.[46] The suggestive imagery of closed eyes was also
used in the beautifully resolved statuette *Daphne* 1897, depicting the moment of
Daphne's transformation into a tree in order to escape Apollo's amorous pursuit. Yet
Mackennal suggests her metamorphosis is from the physical to the psychological realm.
He composes the figure with Art-Nouveau line, using this arabesque form to infer
inner sensations and the fusion of the figure with the metaphysical rhythms of nature.

Charles Web Gilbert's *The dreamer* 1915, the first work he exhibited at the Royal
Academy, demonstrates how the female figure as ideal somnambulist continued
to resonate in the new century. As in Mackennal's *Daphne*, the entities of woman
and nature are fused to create a compelling introspective being. *The dreamer* is
the cumulation of Web Gilbert's largely self-taught practice as a sculptor. While

untutored in the medium, he drew example from his mentor Charles Douglas
Richardson in Melbourne (see pages 56–66) and Mackennal, whose work, well
publicised in Australia, provided a Symbolist model of international success.
The impact of both artists on Web Gilbert is evident in the aesthetic emphasis of
The dreamer. While maintaining a firm attachment to the life model, the figure and
lotus leaf are seamlessly integrated in an Art-Nouveau sweep, their common veins
pulsating as an organic life force fuelling the figure's thoughts. Web Gilbert used
the image of the lotus leaf as an eastern symbol of purity of mind and body in his
bas-relief *The wheel of life* 1910.[47] In *The dreamer* he uses the lotus via a Symbolist
conception, where it features as a sleep-inducing opiate, producing an embodiment
of the dreaming state.

Madness and the Symbolist female subject

The Symbolist interest in hypnotic detachment gained impetus during the decades
when hypnosis was sanctioned as the treatment for hysteria.[48] In the early development
of nineteenth-century psychiatry, hysteria had been diagnosed as a predominantly
female malady and, according to late-century Darwinian views, was attributed to
their feeble mental constitution.[49] Consequently, in the overlap between aesthetic
and psychological discourses in fin-de-siècle culture, women became ready signifiers
and embodiments of irrational states in artistic practices.

Sydney Long drew on these connections in *Isabella* 1904, created at a time when
the artist, known for his Art-Nouveau pastorals (see pages 110–23), had reverted
to a realist style. The painting was based on the 1820 poem of obsessive grief and
love *Isabella; or The pot of basil* by John Keats (which in turn had been sourced
from Boccaccio's *Decameron*). Keats's poem tells of a woman's insane grief, which
led her to keep her murdered lover's head in a pot of basil. Such a tale of unhinged
bereavement lends itself well to Symbolist thematics: the American John White
Alexander painted an evocative rendition of Isabella in 1897, conjuring the subject's
fragile mental state through a muted palette and arabesque forms. Like Alexander,
Long depicts the figure with her eyes closed, in the grip of an internal drama. Long's
model for Isabella was the actress Vivienne Powis-Stuart, whose theatrical air is the
keynote of the composition. Lavishly robed and enthroned, Isabella sits in a trance state
enacting a dramatic solitary séance. Behind her, a round window composed as a halo
provides a concave view of the landscape as a projection of her distorted state of mind.

The mark of madness in George Lambert's *The serpent* 1898 is the figure's imposing
and demonically alert eyes. This work was created in the formative years of Lambert's
career when his output, which consisted mainly of portraits and paintings of rural
themes, was dotted with works indicating a youthful investigation of Symbolist

Sydney Long *Isabella* **1904,** oil on canvas
 Private collection

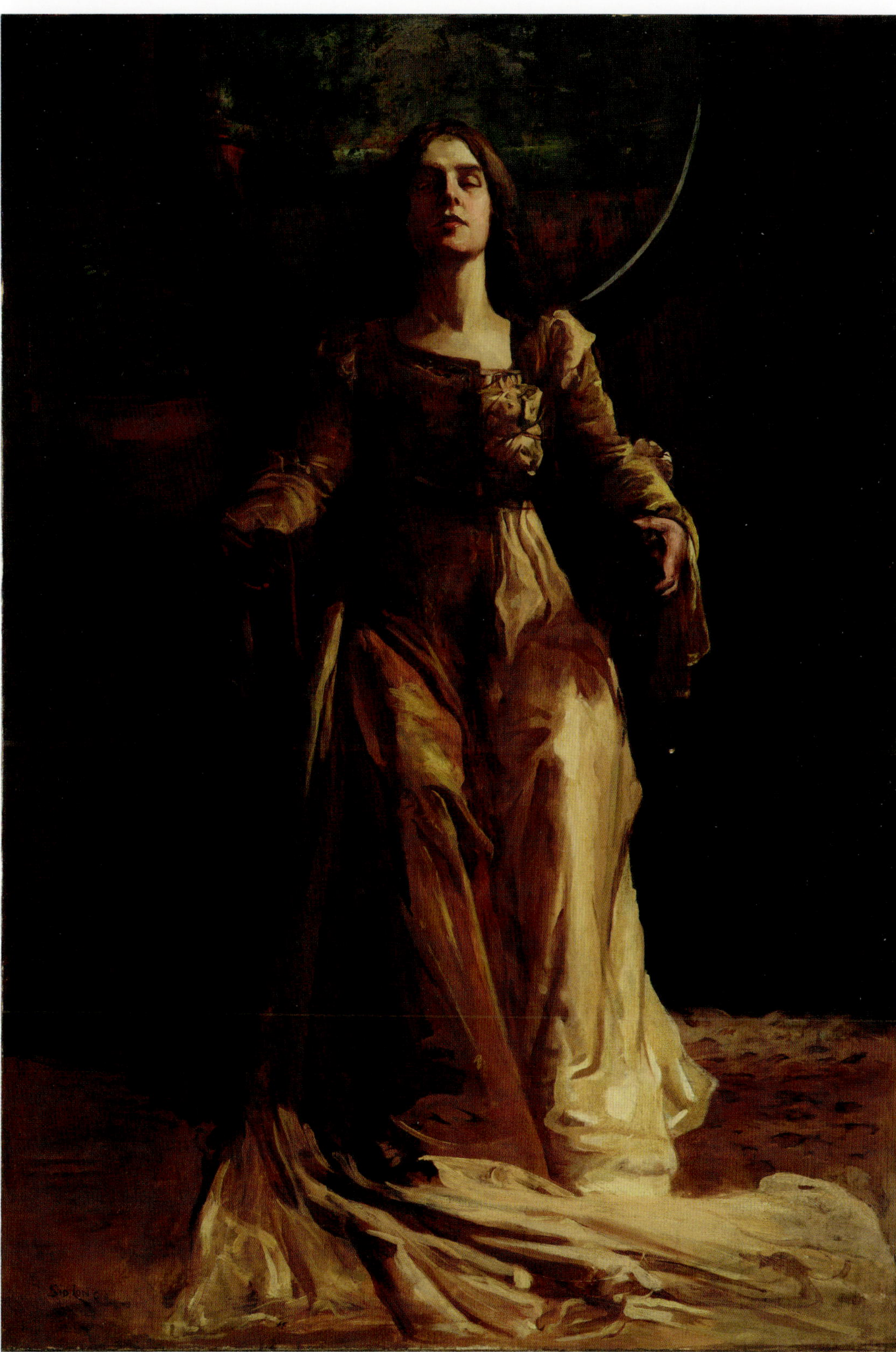

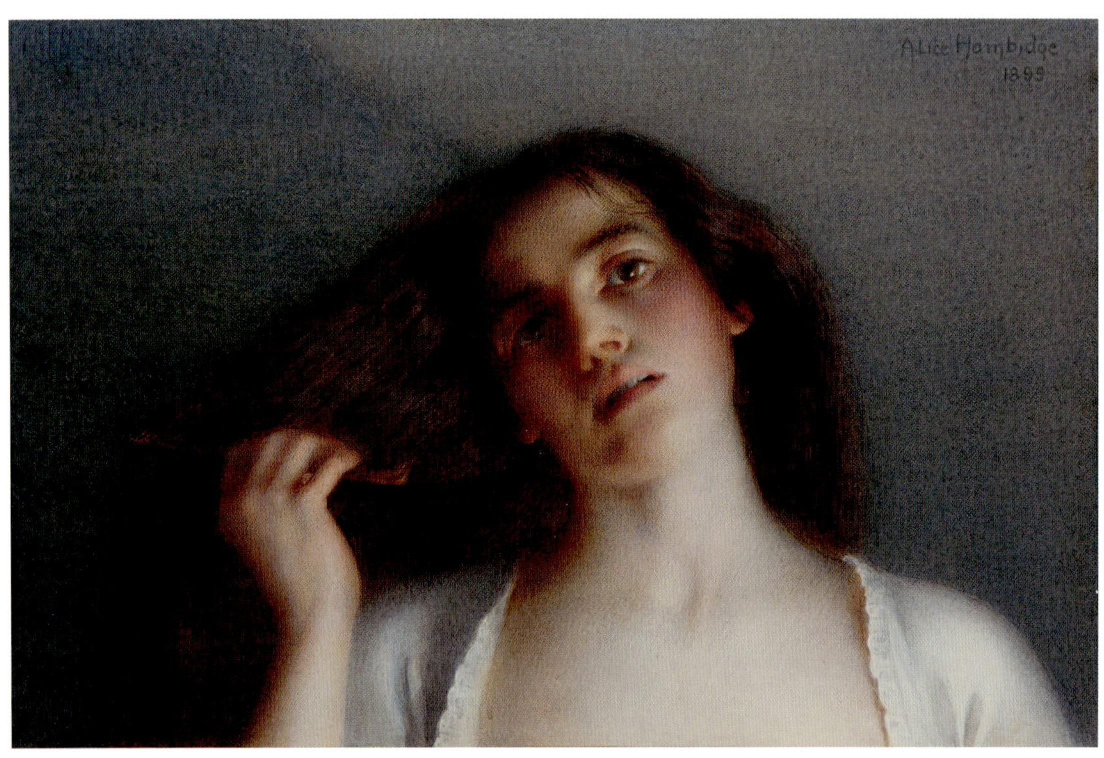

Alice Hambidge *By the light of the candle* 1899, watercolour on paper
Art Gallery of South Australia, Adelaide. Elder Bequest Fund 1899

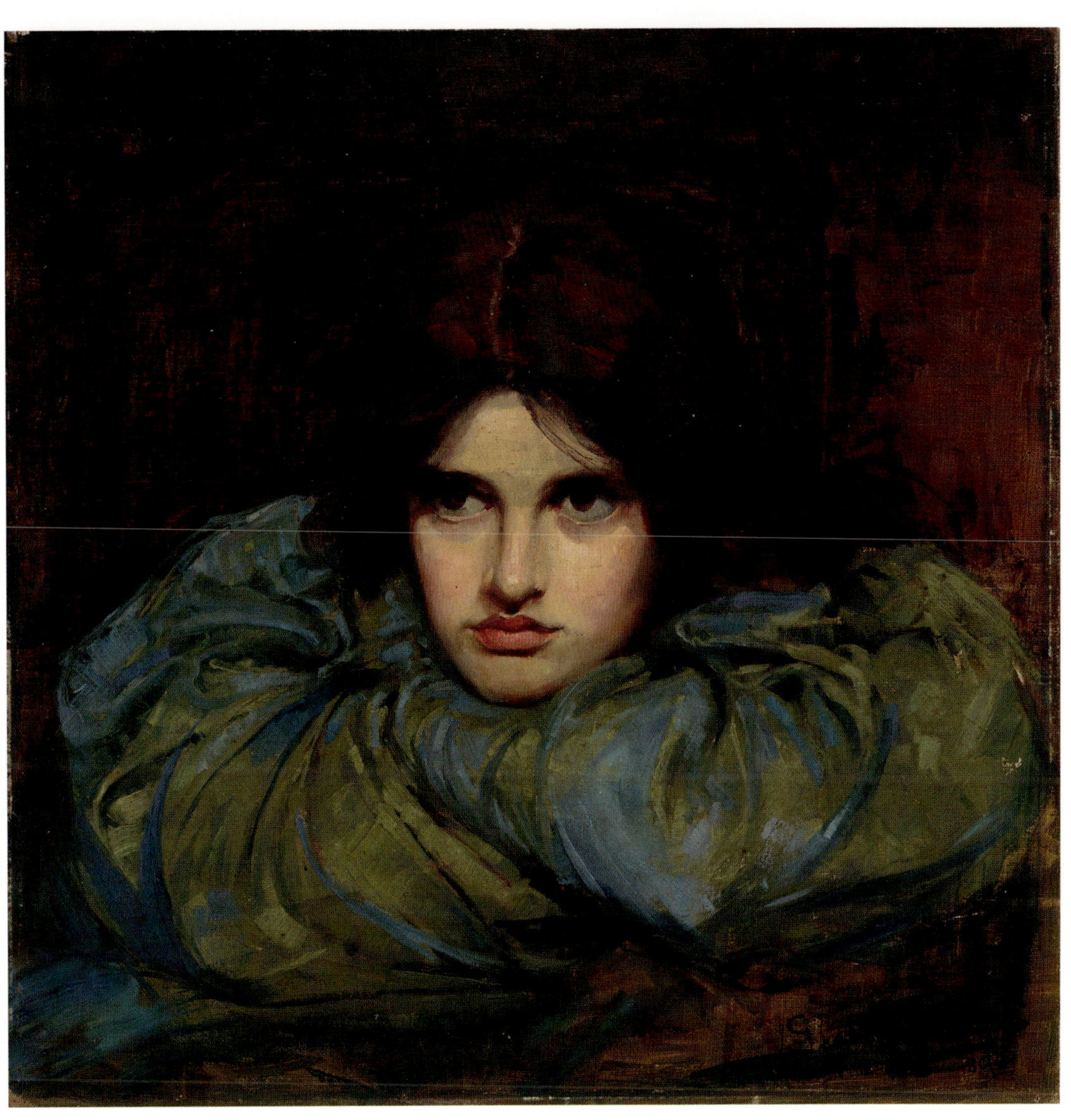

George Lambert *The serpent* 1898, oil on canvas
Private collection

forms – undoubtedly fuelled by his studio partner Sydney Long's enthusiasm
for such expression at the time. During his early years at the Julian Ashton Art
School in Sydney, Lambert painted portraits of 'his young girl friends ... with an
impressionistic flower silhouetted behind them suggesting their type', a practice
that implies his Aestheticisation of the figure.[50] This expansion of literal portraiture
was similarly developed in *The serpent* with the model's 'fierce, compelling' stare
being that of Lamia, the mythological femme fatale also known as the serpent.[51]
Lamia is a conflicted mythological being, known as both a demonic seducer and
as the victim of a sleepless grief resulting from the murder of her children, her wide
eyes the outward sign of her madness. Lambert emphasises the model's unblinkered
gaze in reference to Lamia's insanity. The work reveals Lambert on the cusp of
artistic maturity (he would produce his monumental homage to rural labour, *Across
the black soil plains*, the following year), applying colour in evocative combinations
and elaborating on the imaginative qualities of the figure in cautious curiosity
for the Symbolist genre. *The serpent* shows how the Symbolist woman had become
entrenched in Australia's artistic imagination by the end of the century, and how
young artists in search of psychologically charged subjects turned to it as an antidote
to a prosaic attachment to the life model.

Symbolism and Aesthetic beauty

The soulful, somnambulistic woman, whose mind is distanced by sleep or faraway
thoughts, was a paragon of beauty for the British Aesthetic movement. More of
a phenomena than a formal movement, Aestheticism pursued beauty in all its
artistic outlets – the visuals arts, craft, design, architecture and dress – in a cult-like
fashion.[52] In relation to painting, Aestheticism replaced the narrative tradition of
moral instruction in British Victorian art with opulent compositions intended to
appeal on both sensual and spiritual levels. Invested with the sensations of dreamy
atmospheres over didactic content, Aesthetic painting was in many respects aligned
with the character of Symbolist art.

The Adelaide-born and trained Alice Hambidge produced a number of distinctly
Aestheticist illustrations for the South Australian Society of Artists catalogues
from 1897 to 1898. Her adaption of these forms to service a strong introspective
positioning of the figure singles out the work *By the light of the candle* 1899
in her oeuvre. Hambidge worked primarily in watercolours and was traditional
in her methods, continuing the minutely detailed rendition of Victorian miniature
painting. *By the light of the candle* demonstrates how her meticulous technique and
delicate feel for tone came to serve a meditative mood and evoke the shimmering
ambience of candlelight. The work suggests the influence of Hambidge's teacher,
the English-born HP Gill. Trained at the Kensington School of Art in London

and appointed head of the School of Design in Adelaide in 1882, Gill was a prime promoter of Arts and Crafts and Aesthetic ideals in Adelaide as both a teacher and Honorary Curator at the Art Gallery of South Australia from 1892. His works, such as *Hera, wife of Zeus* 1894, provided Hambidge with a direct model for the Aesthetic terming of the figure in her preferred watercolour medium. Hambidge would have found reinforcement of Gill's Aesthetic practice in the examples of contemporary British painting that Gill had been instrumental in acquiring for the Art Gallery of South Australia.

In *By the light of the candle* Hambidge responds to the terms of Aestheticism as a sensuous and imaginative experience. The figure is presented in a tightly foreshortened perspective, directly confronting the viewer who is positioned as an implied mirror. Yet her gaze is focused elsewhere, beyond her reflection and into the distant, inner world of her thoughts. The subject is of a transitional world, located between the physical arena and the domain of inner being, suggestively half-lit by the ambience of candlelight. Hambidge's remote and soul-gazing woman appeals as the patent beauty of Aesthetic art and of the associated iconography of British Symbolism.[53] While Hambidge may have taken her artistic cues from such traditions, *By the light of the candle*, which has been claimed as a self-portrait, also strongly resonates as an intensely intimate portrayal of female subjectivity.

In Bernard Hall's *Sleep* c1906 the Aesthetic somnambulist subject is fashioned in direct relation to the example provided by British artists. The English-born Hall had studied at the National Art Training School in South Kensington between 1874 and 1878 under the direction of Edward Poynter, one of the early protagonists of Aesthetic painting in Britain. Hall continued his studies in Munich and Antwerp between 1878 and 1882. He arrived in Australia in 1892 to take up the position of Master of the National Gallery Schools (the job Loureiro had declined due to ill health) and Director of the National Gallery of Victoria. He remained at the helm of these institutions until his death in 1935. From this influential platform, Hall's promotion of Aesthetic values had a great impact. His views on the applied arts were derived from the philosophy of the Arts and Crafts Movement, which touted the life-enhancing benefits of design in the everyday environment. Hall's position was broadcast in both press publications and teaching practices.[54] As Director of the National Gallery of Victoria he acquired exemplary works for the state collection and, significantly, as a reflection of the Aesthetic movement's admiration for Eastern art, he also founded the Gallery's Asian collection.[55]

Hall's artistic accomplishments were realised in his development of a set of aesthetic formulas over stylistic innovations. In his teaching and studio work, Hall held to the credo that painting was a practice concerned more with perfecting technique through a process of continual refinement than it was with originality. In *Sleep*, a work

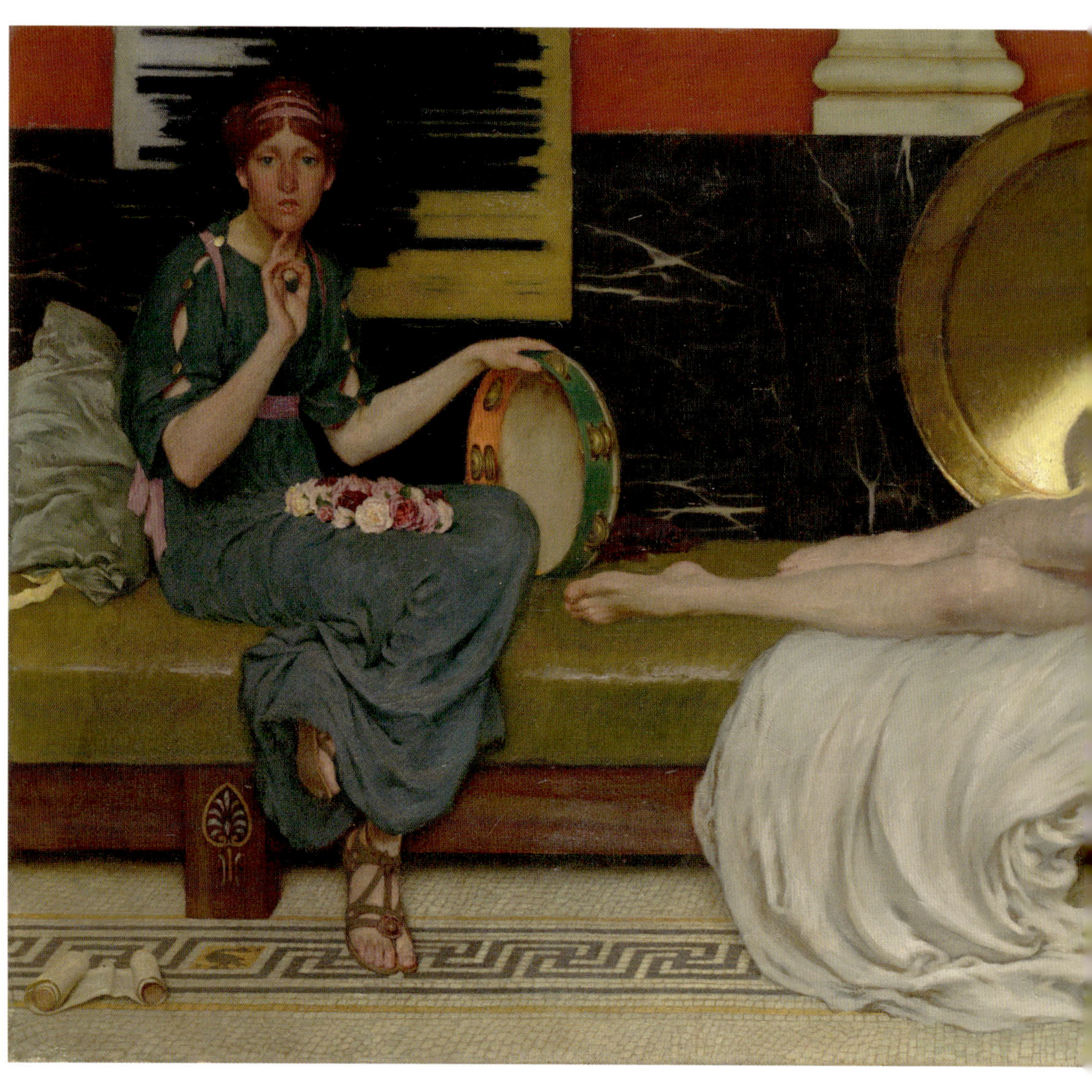

Bernard Hall *Sleep* c1906, oil on canvas
National Gallery of Victoria, Melbourne. Felton Bequest 1919

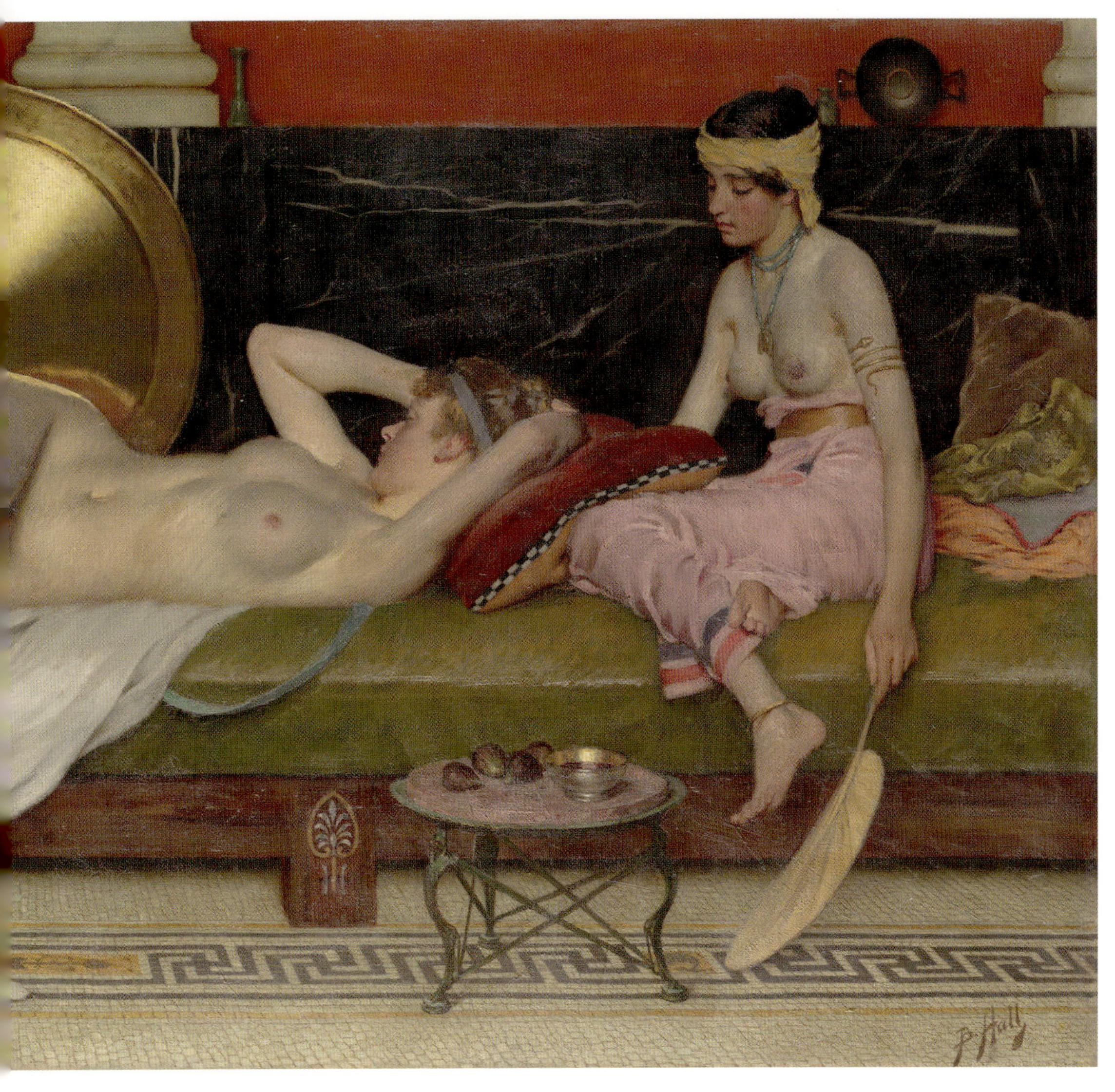

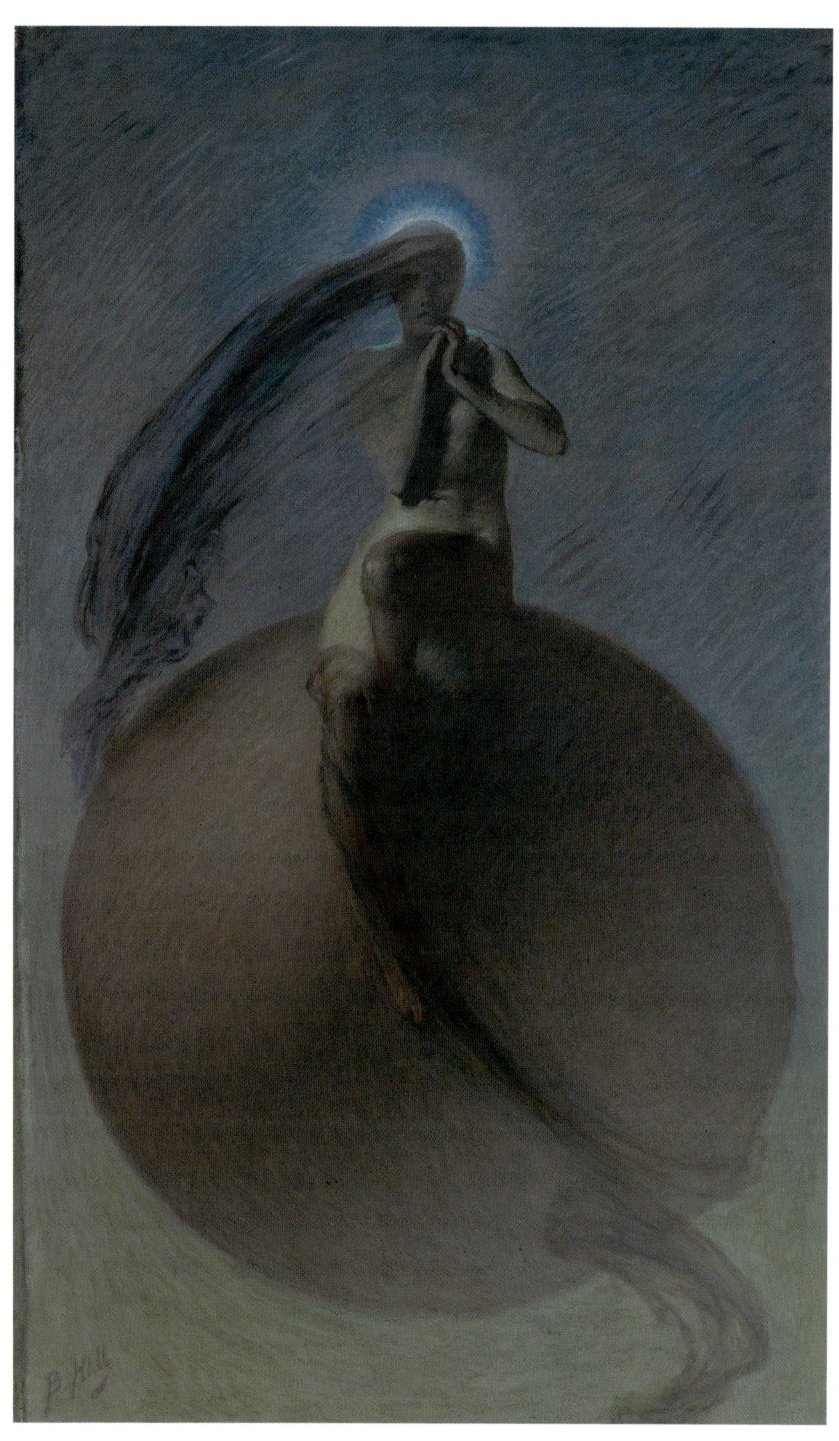

Bernard Hall *The quest* c1905, oil on canvas
National Gallery of Australia, Canberra. Purchased 1977

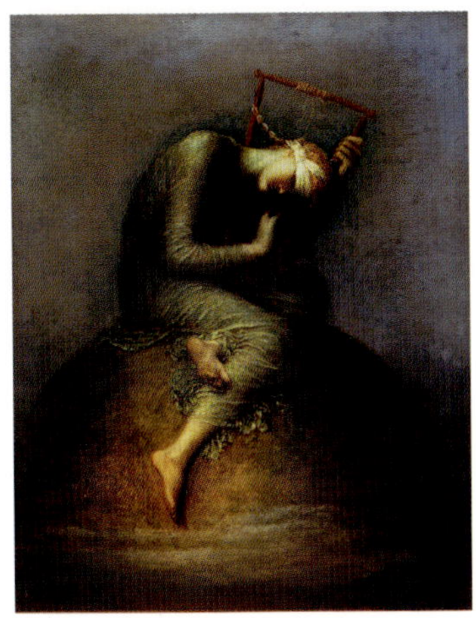 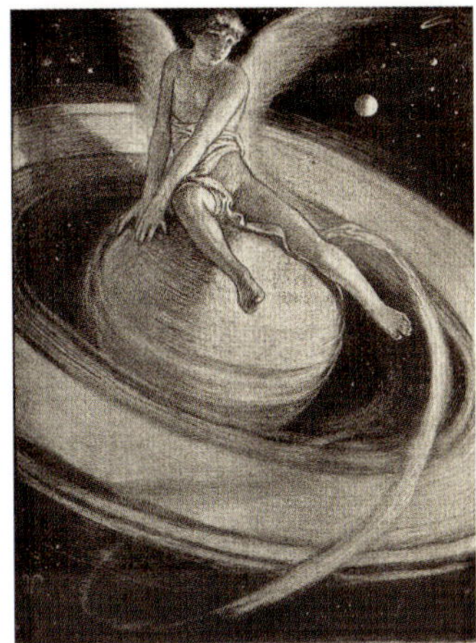

meticulously composed over a period of at least seven years, Hall grafts the model of Aesthetic painting that he had absorbed during his London years, especially from the Olympian group of painters including Albert Moore, Frederick Leighton and Edward Poynter. These artists had been inspired by the precision of classical art. They sought a clarified atmosphere that distilled painting into the essentials of sensualised forms that imbued their ancient references with a timeless quality. *Sleep* includes the hallmarks of this approach: objects, figures and design that infer an ancient past, and a stilled atmosphere and the eroticised contraposto of the sleeping nude reminiscent of Albert Moore's work.

While *Sleep* draws directly on examples from the Aesthetic movement, his *The quest* c1905 comes closer to the character of British Symbolism. The work is arguably the most successful of Hall's paintings and a key painting of Australian Symbolism. In the ensuing decade, Hall painted various versions of the work.[56] The features of the veiled figure in *The quest* are darkened by celestial shadow as she presides over the globe as a gatekeeper to a world of mystery. Rendered in Art-Nouveau line, her contraposto pose is similar to that of her counterpart in *Sleep*, providing eroticised overtones to the figure that fuel her enigmatic force.

The painting is indebted to George Frederic Watts's *Hope* 1886 , which Hall would have studied at the Tate Gallery in London. Watts's ambiguous allegory depicts a melancholic, harp-playing figure seated on a globe, and in *The quest* Hall emulates its blue tonality and Watts's use of sfumato effects to enhance the dream-like mood. However, when he first exhibited *The quest* in 1910, Hall reproduced lines from the twelfth-century mystical Persian poem, the *Rubáiyát of Omar Khayyám* (in both the catalogue and on a plaque on the work's frame): 'I sent my Soul through the Invisible, some letter of that After-life to spell: and after many days my Soul return'd and said

George Frederic Watts *Hope* 1886, oil on canvas, Tate Gallery, London, presented by George Frederic Watts 1897
(right) Elihu Vedder's *The throne of Saturn* from the *Rubáiyát of Omar Khayyám*, featured in *Magazine of Art* 1885

"behold myself and Heav'n and Hell."' *The quest* is also allied to the American Elihu Vedder's illustrations for Edward Fitzgerald's hugely popular English translation of the *Rubáiyát* in 1884. Indeed, there is a striking rapport between Hall's painting and Vedder's illustration for *The throne of Saturn*. The 'mood of psychological curiosity [and] delicate spiritualism' of Vedder's work influenced the way the *Rubáiyát* was understood by western readers and, like many painters of the late nineteenth century, was one that Hall drew on when seeking the crossover of poetic and visual forms in *The quest*.[57]

Charles Douglas Richardson: the Symbolist as the 'seeker of souls'[58]

There is little of the egoist to be found in Mr Richardson, whose attitude towards art and life has in it something of the mystic … he has never lost touch with the higher and more spiritual aspect, which has been the dominating influence in his art and life.[59]

Of the Australian artists who adopted Symbolist expression to define a spiritual dimension in art, none were as intently focused on the search for mystical meaning as Charles Douglas Richardson. The late-century revival of spiritual doctrines; the rise of Catholicism in Paris; and the broader development of esoteric faiths such as Spiritualism and Theosophy in western cultures, saw artists respond to concepts of religious mystery through Symbolist form in both avant-garde and academic practice.[60] In this sense the Symbolist era re-established a nexus of religious mystery and aesthetics in ways that informed a modern emphasis on the spirit in art. Richardson's preoccupation with mystical themes was related to aspects of the Spiritualist movement he followed in Melbourne.[61] While the context of belief conditioned the motivation and meaning of his works, Richardson's fundamental concerns were aesthetic. He produced what is perhaps one of the most varied oeuvres of Australian artists of his generation, encompassing painting, sculpture, decorative arts and design, as well as landscape, portrait, narrative and metaphysically oriented genres. By 1895 the consensus among critics was that if 'Richardson [was] a Frenchman he would be described as a Symbolist'.[62]

The English-born Richardson arrived in Melbourne at the age of five. He studied at the National Gallery School in the 1870s before returning to Europe in 1881. Settling in London, he shared a studio with his fellow students from Melbourne, Tom Roberts and Bertram Mackennal, from 1883. In London he enrolled at the Royal Academy Schools where, unlike Roberts and Mackennal who left the course for more progressive study, he remained from 1882 to 1886. By the time Richardson returned to Melbourne in 1889 he was exhibiting works of metaphysical subjects but, paradoxically, was staunchly committed to an art of meticulous observation. This commitment he had demonstrated from his early times in Melbourne as a vocal campaigner for the introduction of life-modelling classes at the National Gallery School. He also attended anatomy classes and witnessed operations in Melbourne Hospital in his quest for figural accuracy.[63] Thus while Richardson explored elements of the fantastic in his art, he was equally concerned with the prosaic treatment of such subjects. His painting practice was ultimately shaped by the fusion of these qualities.

Richardson left Melbourne in 1881 with the belief that 'artists should paint what is around them, and select incidents from Australian explorers and subjects of a local nature'.[64] By the time he returned to Australia, he had reoriented his art towards 'ideal subjects'.[65] The lessons he had learnt from British varieties of Symbolist art facilitated this transition. *The passing of Arthur* 1885, the first painting Richardson exhibited at the Royal Academy in 1885, adheres to the poetics of late Victorian painting. The spiritual quest of Arthurian legend is given impetus in a typically Victorian aestheticisation of death. Richardson's literary source for the mystic event of King Arthur's death was Alfred Lord Tennyson's poem *The passing of Arthur,* first published in 1842. Intangible elements of the narrative are conveyed by inference, through a composition of dramatic tonal shifts and blackened chromatic structure where enigmatic forms partially emerge from an ambience of dense obscurity, suggesting the presence of the supernatural. The white accents of the lilies on the water's surface echo the cosmic light that glimmers through the work. With its investigation of transcendental form, attention to colour as a means of defining supernatural elements, and mystical theme of the movement between life and death, *The passing of Arthur* established the parameters for Richardson's future work in Australia.

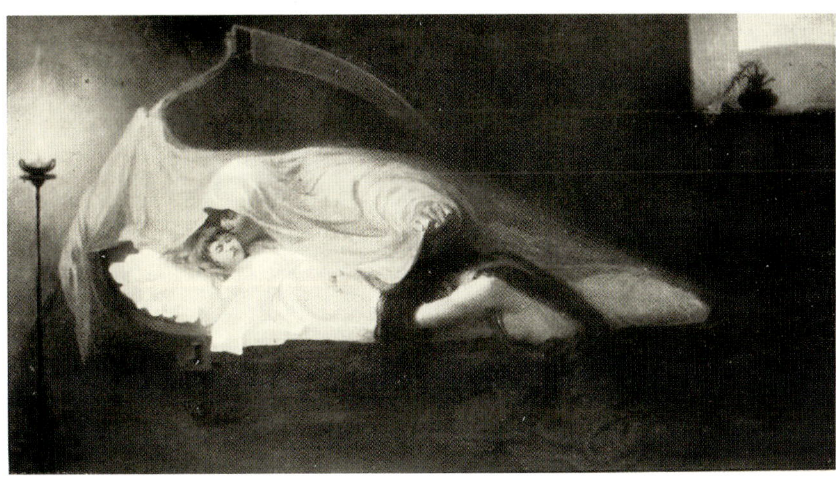

Charles Douglas Richardson's *The kiss of death* 1890, featured in *Magazine of Art* 1900

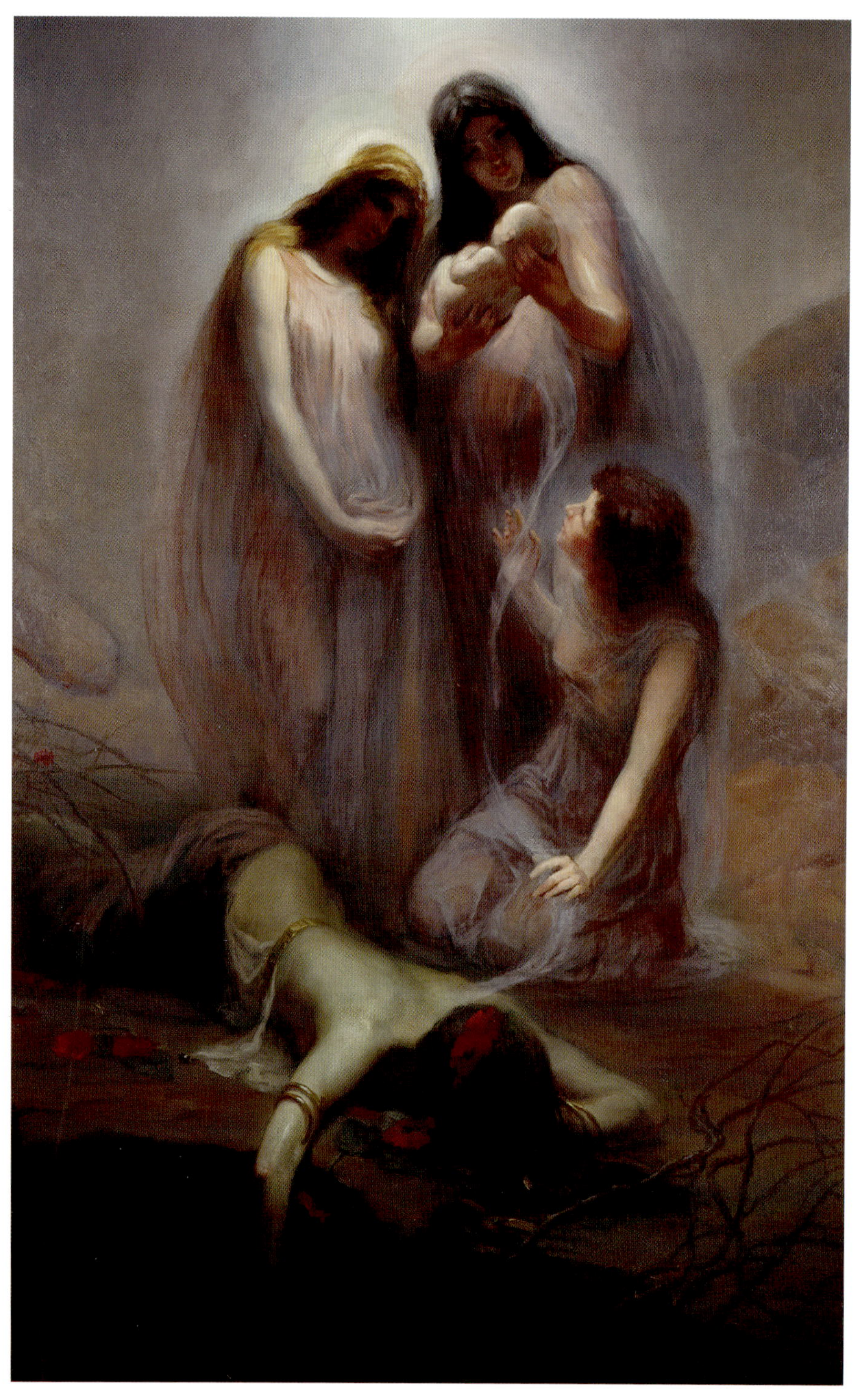

Charles Douglas Richardson *The undeveloped soul* 1901 (above) and *The passing of Arthur* 1885 (opposite) , oil on canvas

 Bayside City Council, Melbourne

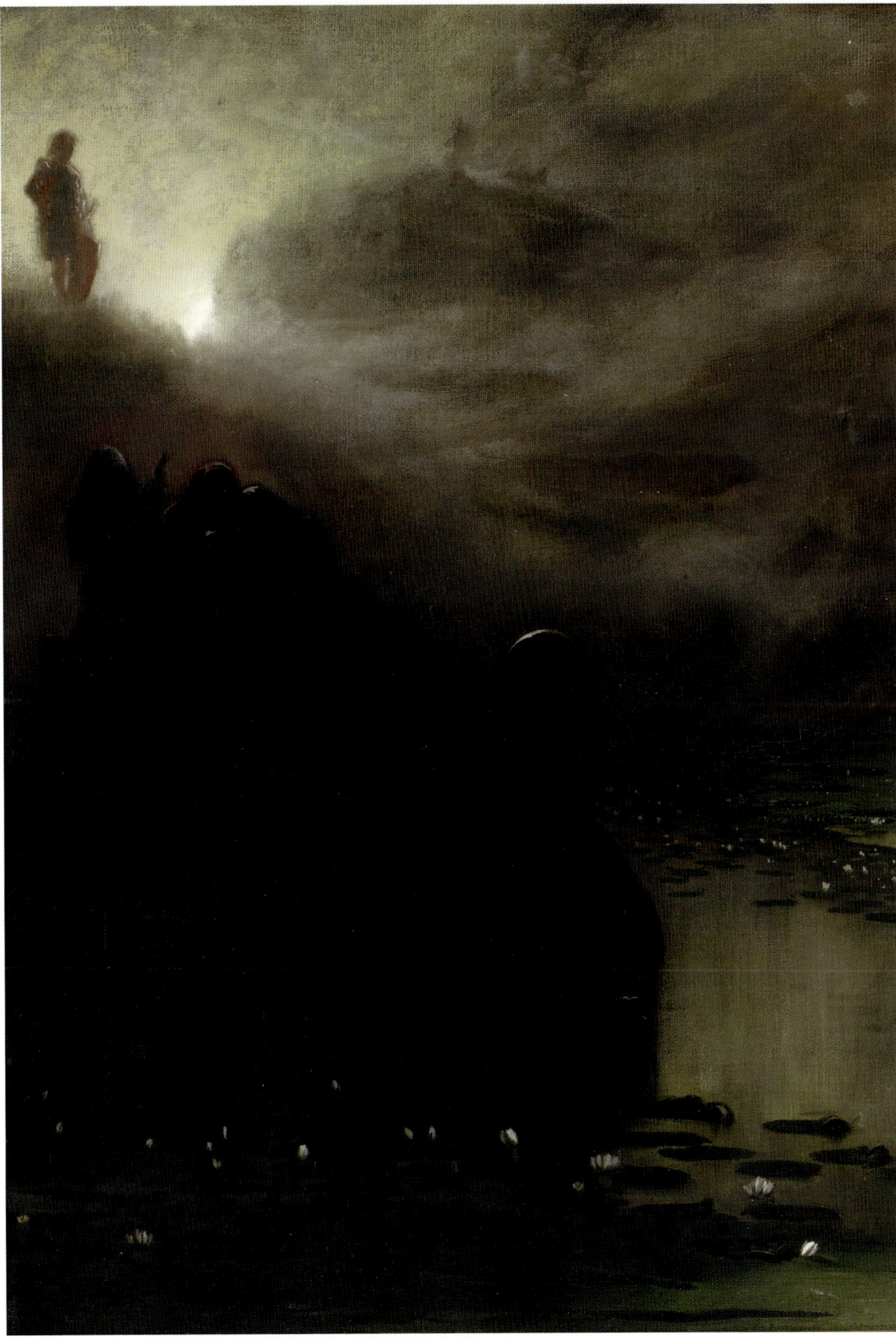

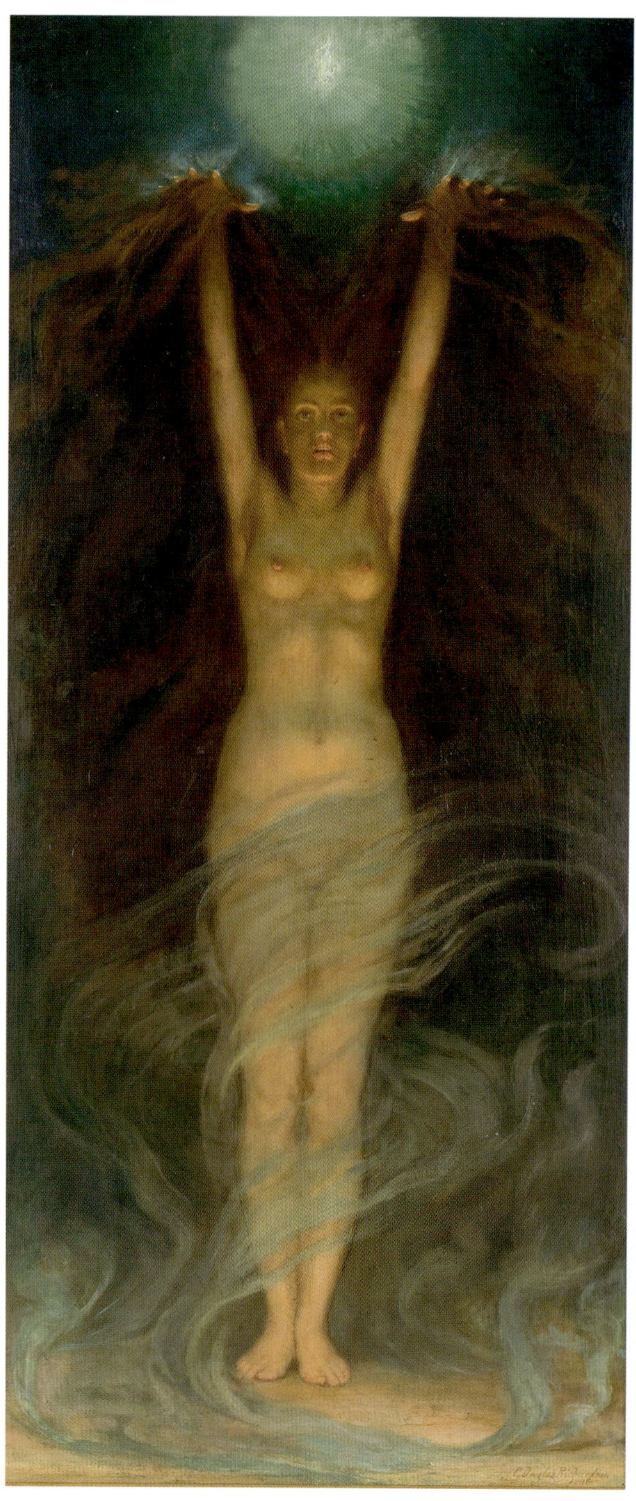

Charles Douglas Richardson *Casting the spell* 1896, oil on canvas
Art Gallery of Western Australia, Perth. Purchased with funds from the Great Australian Paintings Appeal 1992

In the 1890s Richardson developed a series of paintings based on supernatural apparitions and encounters with death. His focus on the expression of inner life earned him the label of 'Antipodean Watts'.[66] Despite his British grounding, Richardson's work became increasingly self-directed in Australia; he delved further into the mystical quest of the soul through life and death, and abandoned the literary sources that catalysed his art in England. He found a philosophical footing in the doctrines of the Spiritualist movement, which had attracted a significant following in Victoria by the 1880s. Originating in the movements that developed in America and northern Europe in the 1870s, Spiritualism prompted a critical reconsideration of orthodox Christianity, encouraging a more progressive reading of the bible by considering, for example, aspects of evolutionary science in relation to Christian teachings. Through a quasi-Darwinian understanding of a world in constant flux, the Spiritualist doctrine described 'man as an eternally progressive being' for whom the advent of death was merely one stage in their soul's evolution.[67] Despite the movement's complex belief system, it became notorious for attempts to communicate with the dead through mediums and séances – a preoccupation that catalysed the downfall of the movement at the turn of the century.

A sense of the mystical infuses Richardson's treatment of the figure in *The undeveloped soul* 1901. Through an arabesque, umbilical-like formation Richardson connects a lifeless woman (whose eternal sleep is signified by the poppies with which she is adorned) to a baby held by attendant angel-like beings. Colour again elaborates a sense of the fantastic. A diaphanous palette of evocative pale blues, pinks and mauves appears as a series of pigmented veils, enshrouding the figures in a softened focus and endowing them with transient qualities of the spiritual. *The undeveloped soul* is one of Richardson's most overtly Spiritualist works highlighting his strategies for the expression of intangible realms of being.[68]

The Art-Nouveau line defining the soul's extension in *The undeveloped soul* is a device that Richardson repeatedly used to infer the movements of inner life. The motif relates to the swirling pattern that Elihu Vedder created as a symbol for metaphysical motion in his illustrations for the *Rubáiyát*.[69] In Richardson's earlier *Casting the spell* 1896 the swirling forms denote the dynamic substance of supernatural energy. The declamatory gesture and nudity of Richardson's sorceress recalls Mackennal's *Circe*. But while coloured in unearthly green and dramatically lit, this sorceress is characteristic of Richardson's mystical being rather than the era's signature seductress.

While Richardson paid close attention to nature as a plein-air artist, his landscape paintings also revealed erosions of the real for the supra- or beyond real. *The hillside, Bacchus Marsh* 1899 depicts both a specific site and a symbolically transposed place. Richardson paints a brooding atmosphere and landscape that encapsulates the

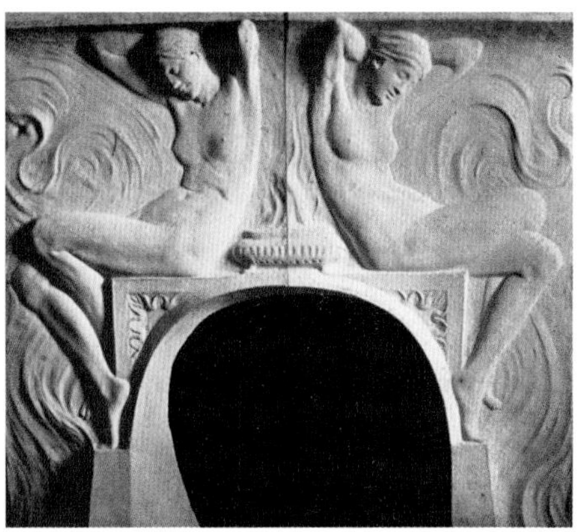

transitory conditions of nature: he portrays a world in flux. The sky shifts with an upward sweep of cloud, mirrored by thc downward slope of the hill dotted with cloud-like formations of shrubs and sheep. Sky and land are constructed as opposing elemental forces and nature as a spiritually driven force – the landscape is seen through the prism of a dream state.

It was as a sculptor that Richardson created his most inspired forms. While his commitment to the life model could tend towards a static treatment in his paintings, the floating arabesque he used to infer spiritual energy was used to greatest expressive effect in his sculpture. In *Memories* 1895 figurative forms seem to pulsate beneath the surface. The dynamic life of thoughts and memories is personified as youthful female figures, their movements constructed by the rhythms of sinuous line as the dreams that envelop the elderly central figure. Like Mackennal, Richardson's period as a student in London in the 1880s coincided with the heyday of the New Sculpture movement. Its impact is evident in the evocative surface forms of *Memories*, where the surfacing and swelling of figures also recall the rhythmic rise and fall of bodies in Rodin's *The gates of hell*. Exhibited in 1896, *Memories* testifies to Richardson's significance in broadening the parameters of sculptural practice in Australia at the turn of the century, providing an example to a new generation of sculptors of a modernised and psychologically nuanced set of concerns for their practice.

With *The cloud* 1900, Richardson confidently resolves the stylisation of British Aestheticism and Art-Nouveau design in sculptural form. *The cloud* was initially exhibited as a lifesize plaster model in 1901, intended for bronze casting on purchase.[70] Although Richardson's ambitions for the sale of the lifesize figure remained unfulfilled, he seized on its critical success and the appeal of its streamlined form and produced a more commercially viable statuette. Like Hall, Richardson was influenced by the Arts and Crafts movement and New Sculpture principles in his advocacy for domestically scaled, aesthetic and functional objects to adorn the home.[71] The figure of *The cloud* is similar to that in his *Design for a fireplace* c1900, which uses the body's curve to suggest the movement of billowing smoke and the figure of the dreamy female as decorative ornament. *The cloud* epitomises this model

    Charles Douglas Richardson's *Design for a fireplace* c1900, plaster model, featured in *Magazine of Art* 1900

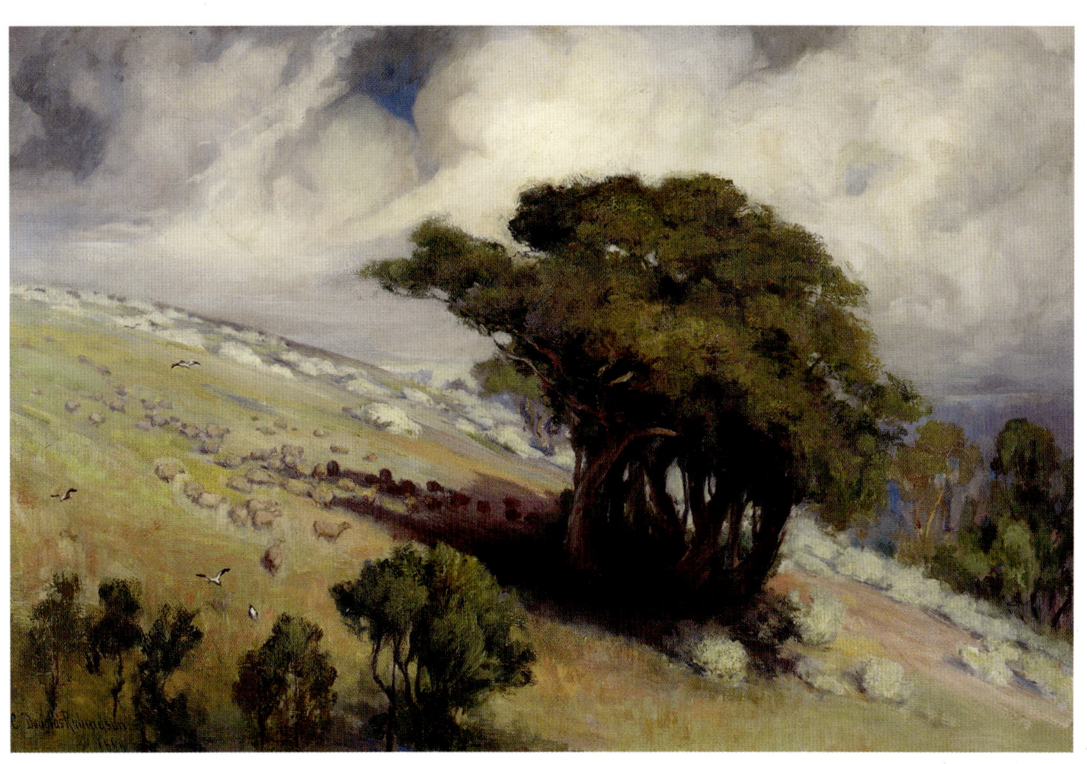

Charles Douglas Richardson *The hillside, Bacchus Marsh* **1899**, oil on canvas
Geelong Gallery, Victoria. Purchased with the generous assistance of the Friends of the Gallery and the JB Ryan Perpetual Trust 2008   63

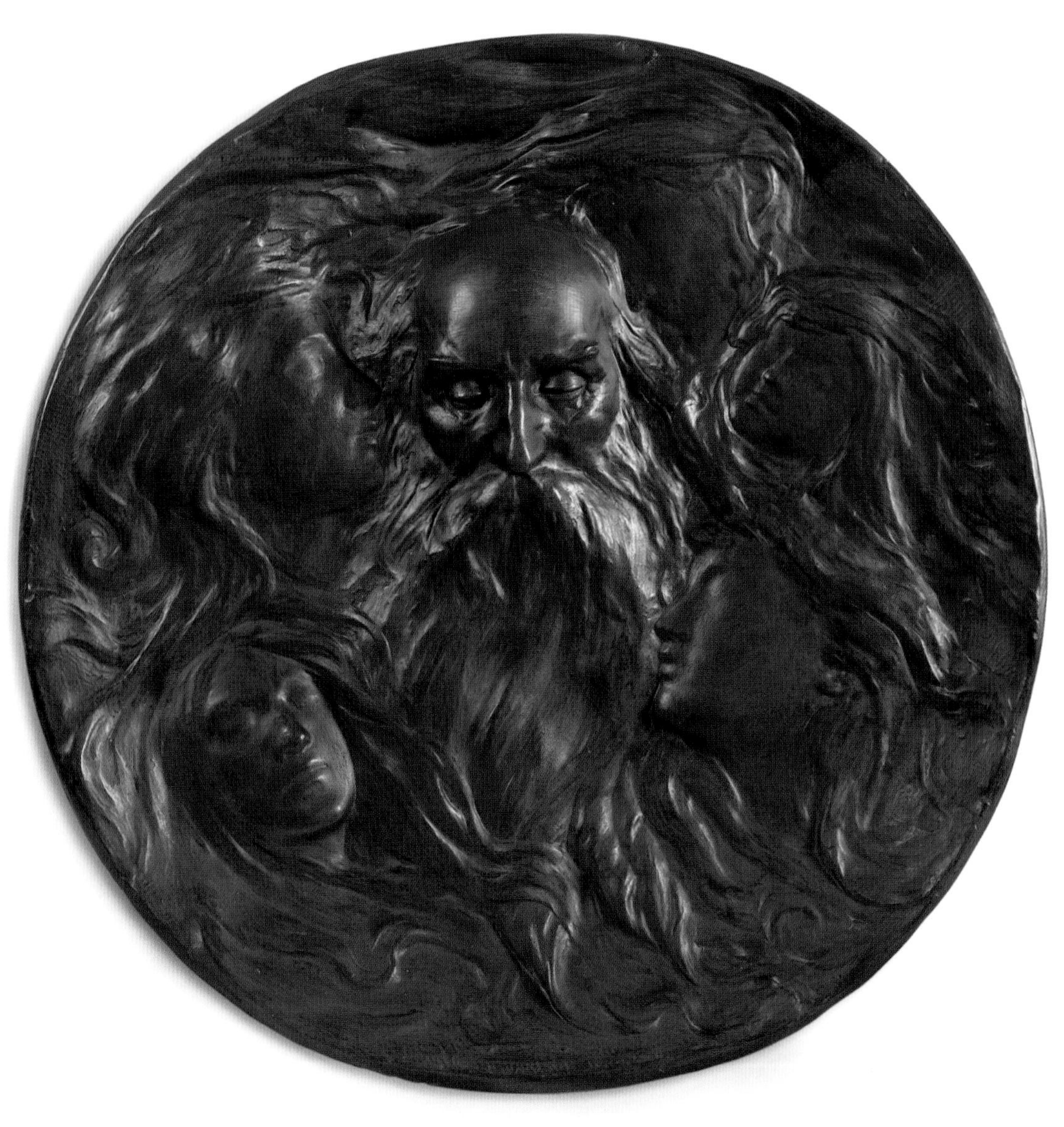

Charles Douglas Richardson *Memories* 1895, patinated plaster
 Bayside City Council, Melbourne

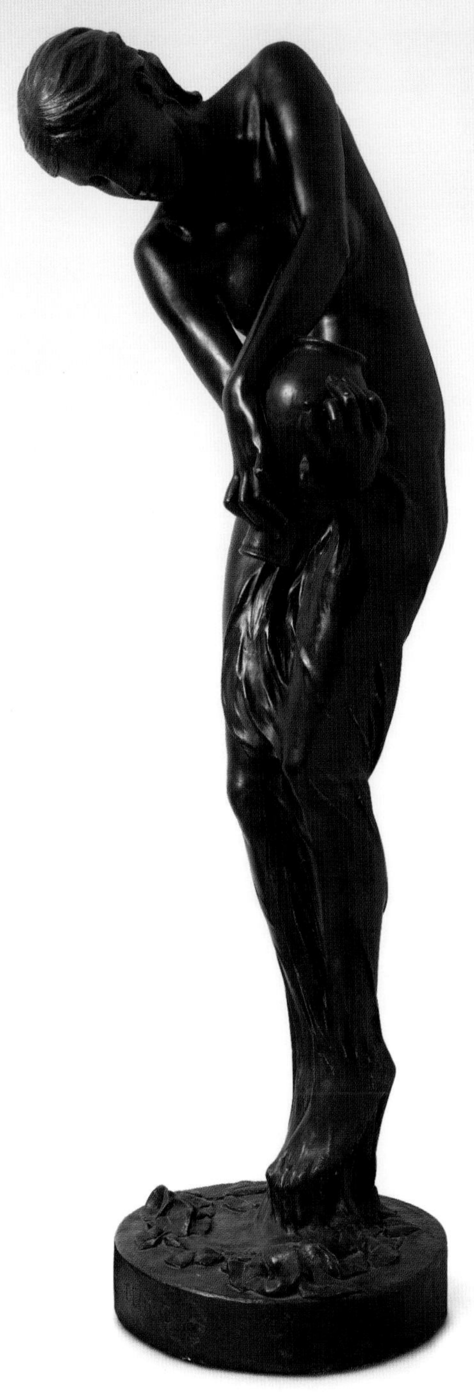

Charles Douglas Richardson *The cloud* 1900, patinated plaster
Bayside City Council, Melbourne

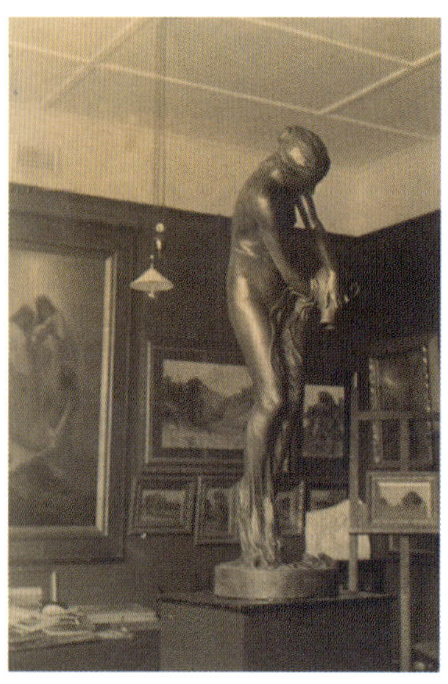

of classically informed beauty that Richardson held as his decorative ideal. The work is based on lines from Shelley's poem of the same name: 'I bring fresh showers for the thirsting flowers.'[72] Richardson began working with personifications of natural elements in 1889 (including the small wax models that were exhibited in the *9 by 5 impression* exhibition that year, see page 98) and developed this interest in a series of statuettes. Of these *The cloud* most readily demonstrates his capacity to extend from literal form into imaginative design. He presents the figure as a continuous Art-Nouveau contour, and with his spiritual emphasis on the serpentine motif he instils ethereal suggestion in physical form.

Death and angelic allusions

European Symbolist art generated images by means of the interplay of opposites. For every work depicting the terror of nightmares there were paintings of elated dreams; those of death, disease and madness were balanced by visions of an Arcadian, pastoral restoration; and in contrast to the demonic femme fatale there were chaste, angelic visions. *The cloud* stands as the polemically feminised other to *Circe*'s physical potency and the fin-de-siècle repertoire of Australian expatriates Rupert Bunny and Abbey Altson included images of women as angelic entities and as a mysterious source of beauty. In *(Burial of a saint)* c1887–90 Bunny uses the transient qualities of watercolour to imply the spiritual radiance of an angelic gathering. Bunny's admiration for Dante Gabriel Rossetti is evident in the flat, angular depiction of his figures and the colour scheme, which echoes Rossetti's *Ecce Ancilla Domini!* 1849–50 (Tate Gallery, London). The Pre-Raphaelite influence is also apparent in the subject of the poeticised encounter with death, which is echoed in Altson's *Fantasy – Angel drawing the cloth of the night* 1897. As a magazine illustrator in London in the 1890s Altson was preoccupied with angelic subjects.[73] In *Fantasy – Angel drawing the cloth of the night*, the eschatological theme unfolds in the Aesthetic context of Whistlerian twilight, depicting an angel gliding towards earth carrying a shroud as an emblem of death. In contrast to Bunny's weightless figures, Altson's angel is a more solidly symbolic object depicting death as a mysterious, eternally present force.

The late Victorian aestheticisation of death through the evocative symbol of the angel is epitomised in Paul Montford's *Memorial to youth* 1895. The English-born

Charles Douglas Richardson's *The cloud* in his studio with *The undeveloped soul* in the background c1920
Bayside City Council, Melbourne

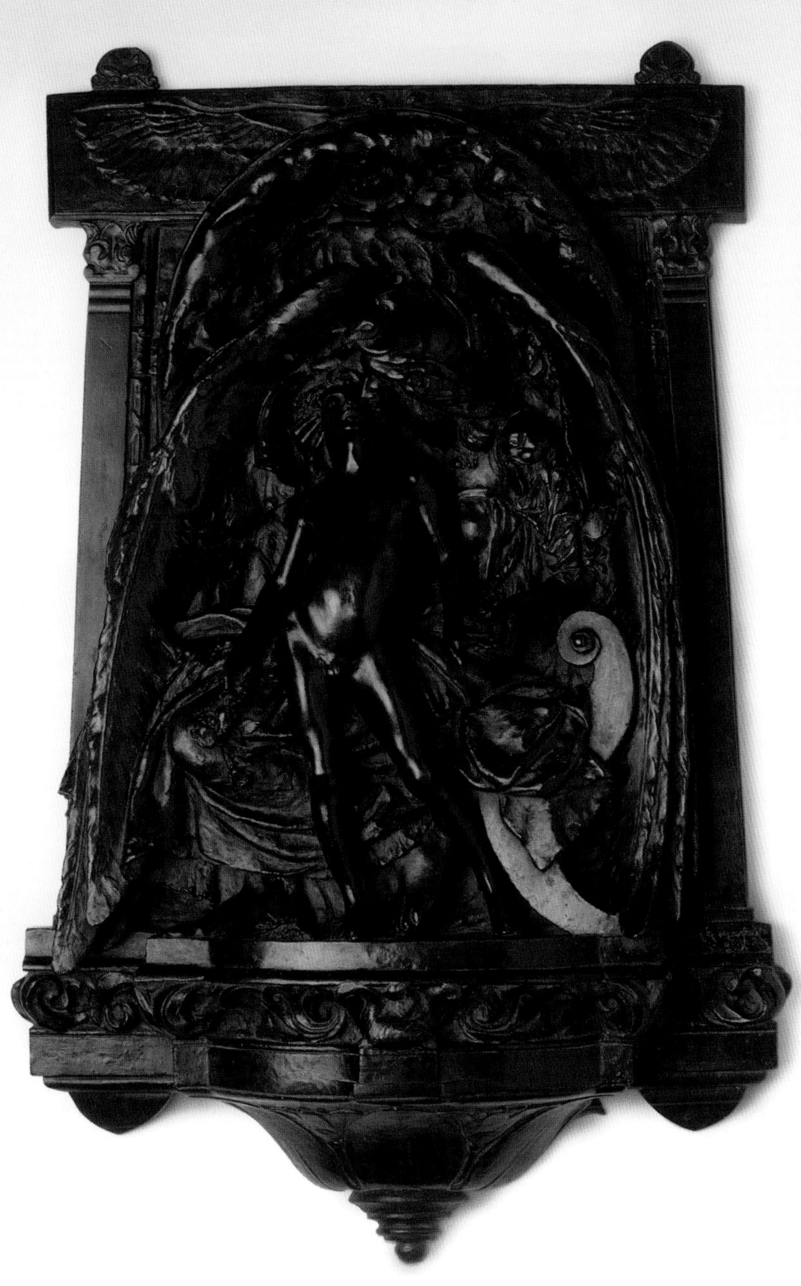

Paul Montford *Memorial to youth* 1895, bronze
National Gallery of Australia, Canberra. Purchased 1979

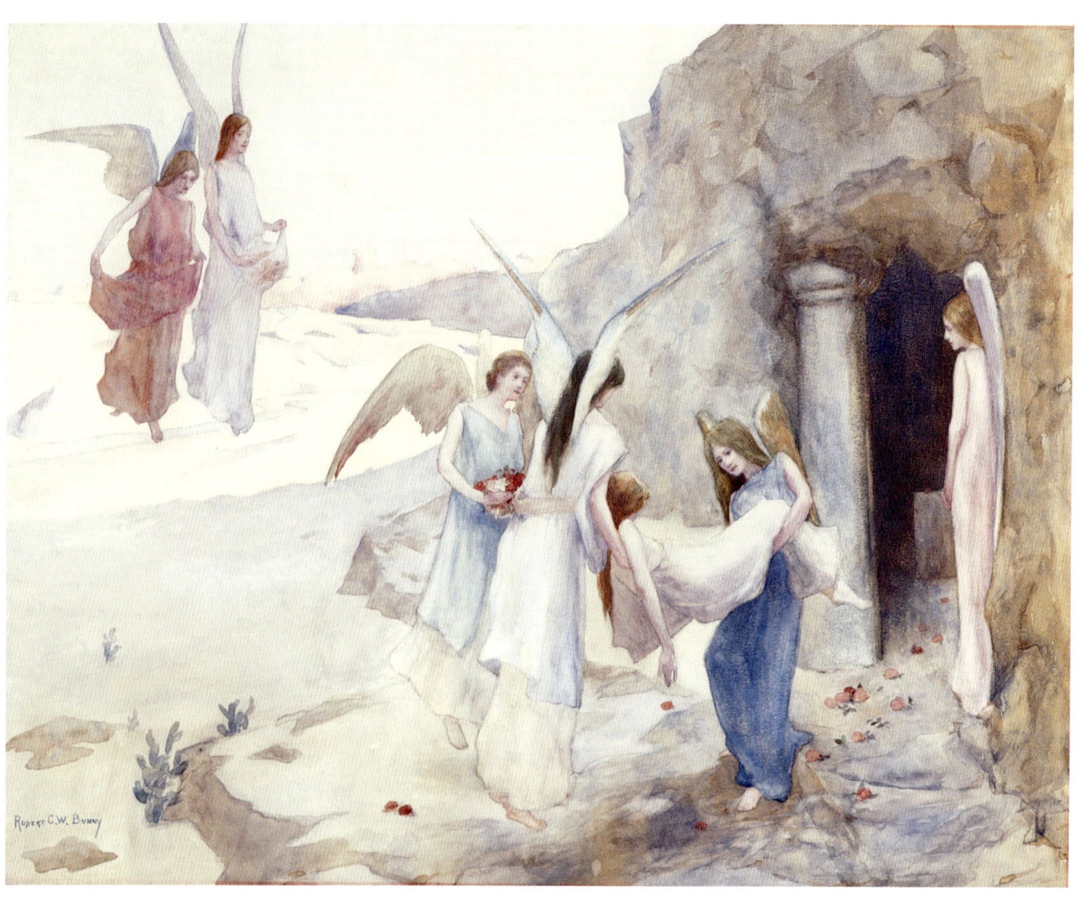

Rupert Bunny (*Burial of a saint*) c1887–90, watercolour over pencil on paper
Philip Bacon Collection, Brisbane

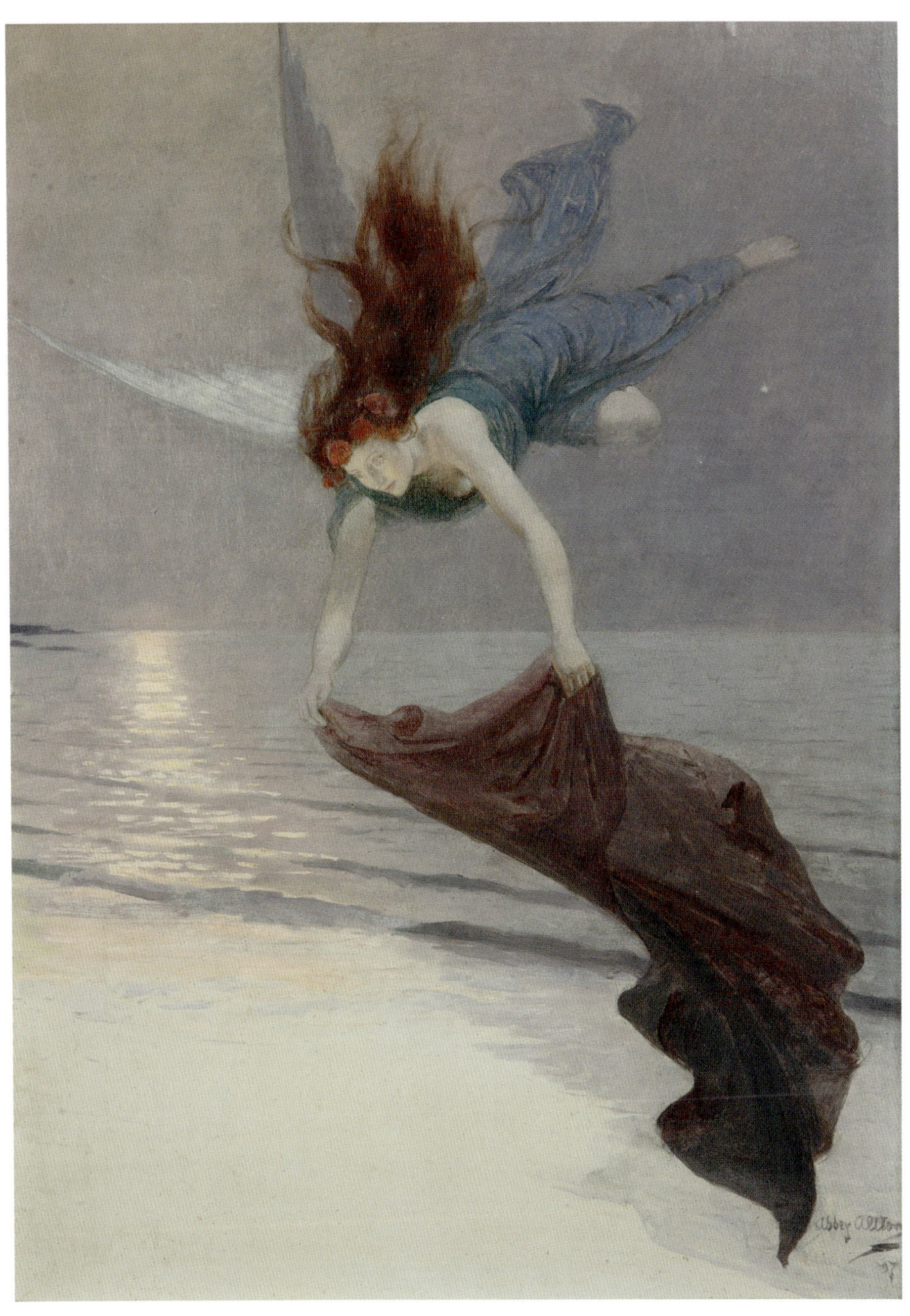

Abbey Altson *Fantasy – Angel drawing the cloth of the night* 1897, oil on academy board
Kerry Stokes Collection, Perth

Montford, who trained at the Royal Academy Schools (1887–91), established his reputation in Britain before arriving in Australia in 1923 where he became prominent as the creator of Victoria's First World War memorial, the Shrine of Remembrance. While his Aestheticist emphasis lessened in Australia, the memorialising aspect of Montford's sculpture was established early in his career. *Memorial to youth* allegorises death in dramatically embellished form, shifting between polished and encrusted surfaces that are indicative of the expressive ideal of the New Sculpture. In a format which implies an architectural setting, the erotic figure of youth as he is drawn into the powerful, encompassing embrace of the Angel of Death. The theme of death is elaborated through quintessential Victorian sentiment: via the imagery and symbols of love and sensualised youth, New Sculptural artifice, and with the Symbolist motif of the ethereal being.

Brittany and the Arcadian vision

You feel you are witnessing … a strange and happy encounter between very remote antiquity and naked modernity. Vincent van Gogh, 1882.[74]

In 1893 Rupert Bunny and Abbey Altson exhibited large Arcadian-themed canvases at the Paris Salon which earned each of them honourable mentions and the distinction of prominent placement in the exhibition. Bunny's *Pastoral* c1893 and Altson's *The Golden Age* 1893 both figure the 'strange and happy encounter' between an ancient Arcadian ideal, contemporary figures and a modern style that was suggested by van Gogh in relation to Pierre Puvis de Chavannes's widely admired painting *Pleasant land* 1882.[75] The Australians seized on the theme of Puvis's Arcady that had been a triumph at the Salon in 1882 in which he transformed a bucolic vision into a fin-de-siècle dream state.[76] While Puvis rejected the label of Symbolist painter, the self-proclaimed aim of his art – to distill complex emotional states into expressive form – was central to Symbolist aims. In the 1880s Puvis explored the concept of Arcady as an interior state. With a muralist's eye for composition, his simplified forms, flattened areas of muted colour and lulling rhythms became the qualities driving his design and the means by which he infused the classical ideal with a psychological paradigm of the modern age. When Bunny and Altson exhibited their 1893 Salon works, the attachment to Puvis was strongly implied. Both artists addressed the technical challenges of large-scale decorative painting and paired these elements with expressions of Arcadia as a state of inner being.

The fin-de-siècle pastoral unified classical ideals with Symbolist expression. Arcadia was envisaged as the state 'uncontaminated' by positivist doctrines of the material age and provided a link to the redemptive rhythms of nature, and pursued the quest for the spiritual in art. The nineteenth-century painter's experience of Paris generally

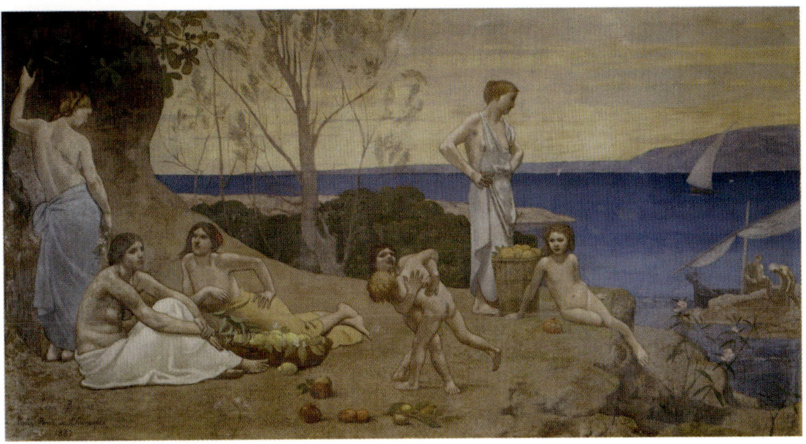

included summer retreats to the French coastline, which feature as the backdrop in many examples of these Arcadian visions. In 1887 Bunny made the first of what would become annual summer pilgrimages to the coastal villages of Brittany. The region's pristine landscape and traditional peasant population seemed completely isolated from modern urban life, and was part of the charm they held for artists who idealised rural Brittany as an untarnished world. Bunny tapped into this ideal, populating his Brittany landscapes with mythological characters in various early works, including *(Burial of a saint)* as well as *Pastoral*, where triton and pagan beings mingle with modern youths. *Pastoral* underlies Bunny's Symbolist affiliations. With a mood coloured by the encroaching twilight, he focuses on the inhabitants of the littoral zone between dark woodland and silvery sea who sit transfixed by strains of music. The correspondences between music and painting were emphasised in Symbolist art. As the most abstract of art forms, and as an expression registered primarily through the senses, music represented the condition aspired to by the Symbolists and became a recurring theme in their art. In *Pastoral*, music resonates as a timeless, powerful source. While referring to the ancient strains of Pan's piped reeds of Arcadian myth, Bunny also implies a Puvisian impression of deep silence, enveloping the figures in a trance-like state of inner momentum.

Altson's Arcadia, *The Golden Age*, has been considered the artist's nostalgic nod to an Australian sun-drenched atmosphere, although the source of the work was the remote Island of Noirmoutier, off the coast of Brittany, where he had painted studies of the nude immersed in summer light.[77] Altson arrived in Paris in 1891 as the recipient of the National Gallery Travelling Scholarship and following a successful studentship at the Gallery School between 1887 and 1890. *The Golden Age* is a demonstration of his European experiences, submitted to Melbourne's National Gallery as the final requirement as part of the conditions of his award. Like Bunny's *Pastoral*, Altson's

Pierre Puvis de Chavannes *Pleasant land* 1882, oil on canvas
Musée Bonnat, Bayonnne Photo ©RMN/René-Gabriel Odéja

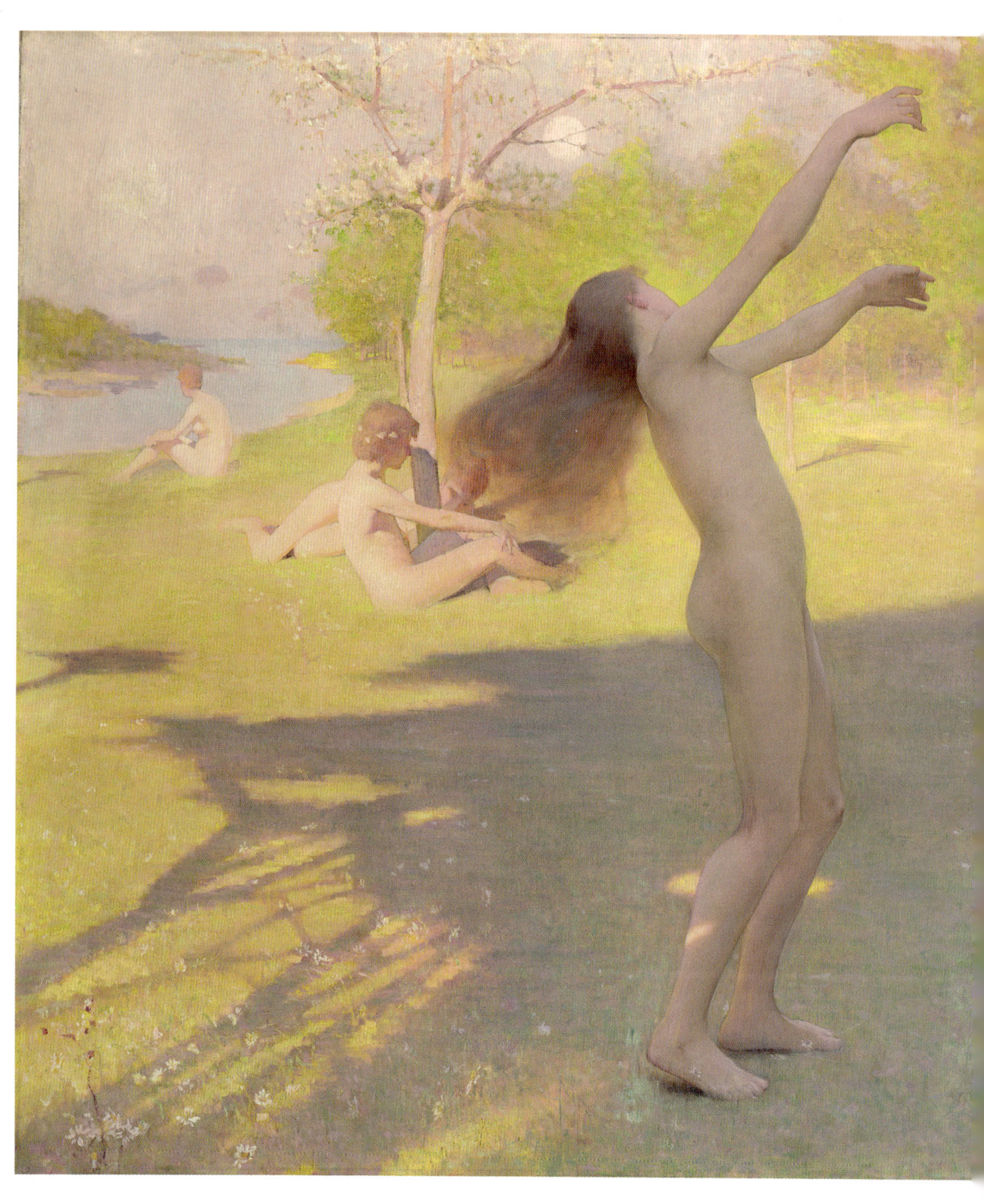

Abbey Altson *The Golden Age* **1893**, oil on canvas (see detail page 7)
National Gallery of Victoria, Melbourne. Presented by the artist under the terms ot the National Gallery of Victoria
Travelling Scholarship, 1895

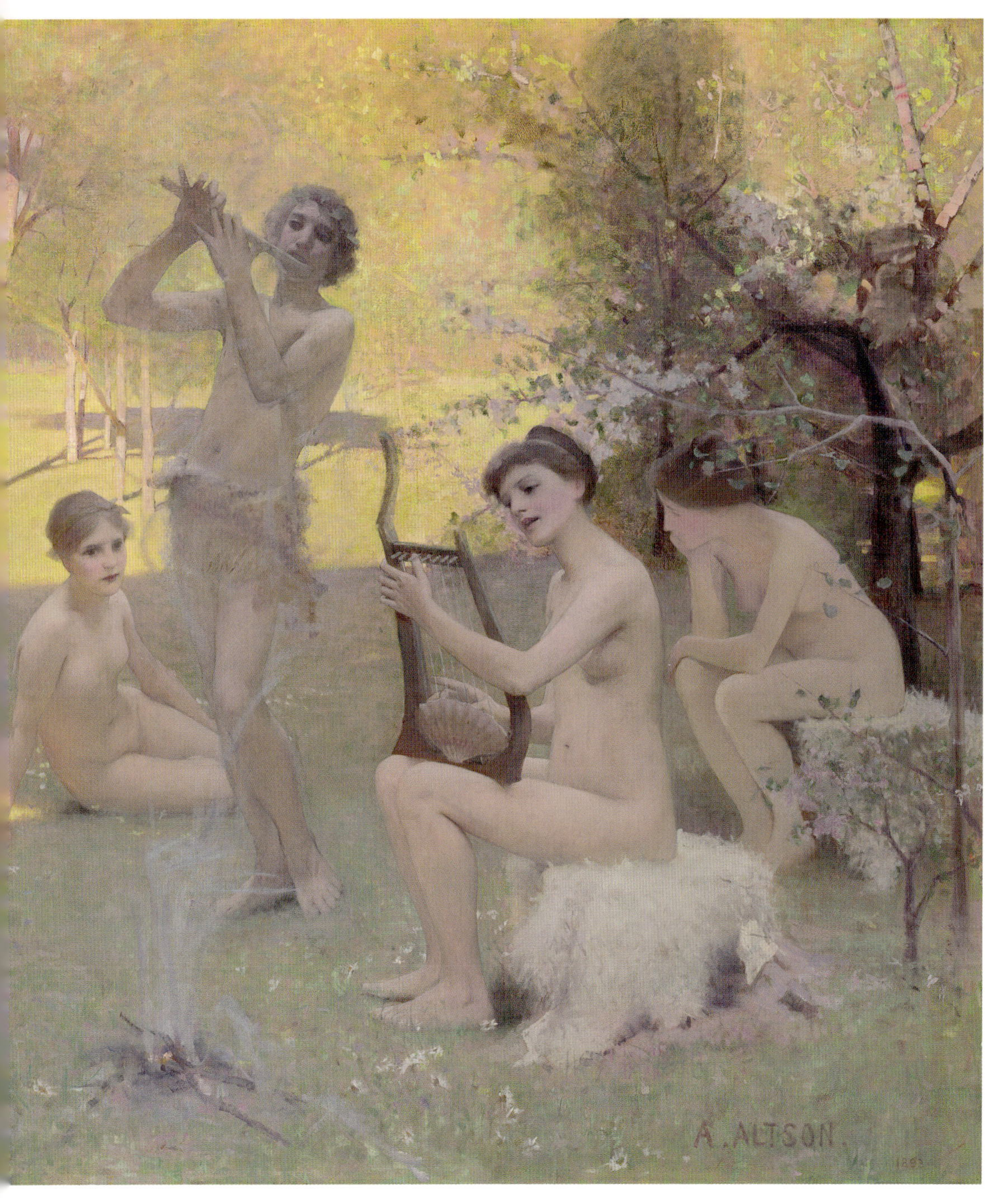

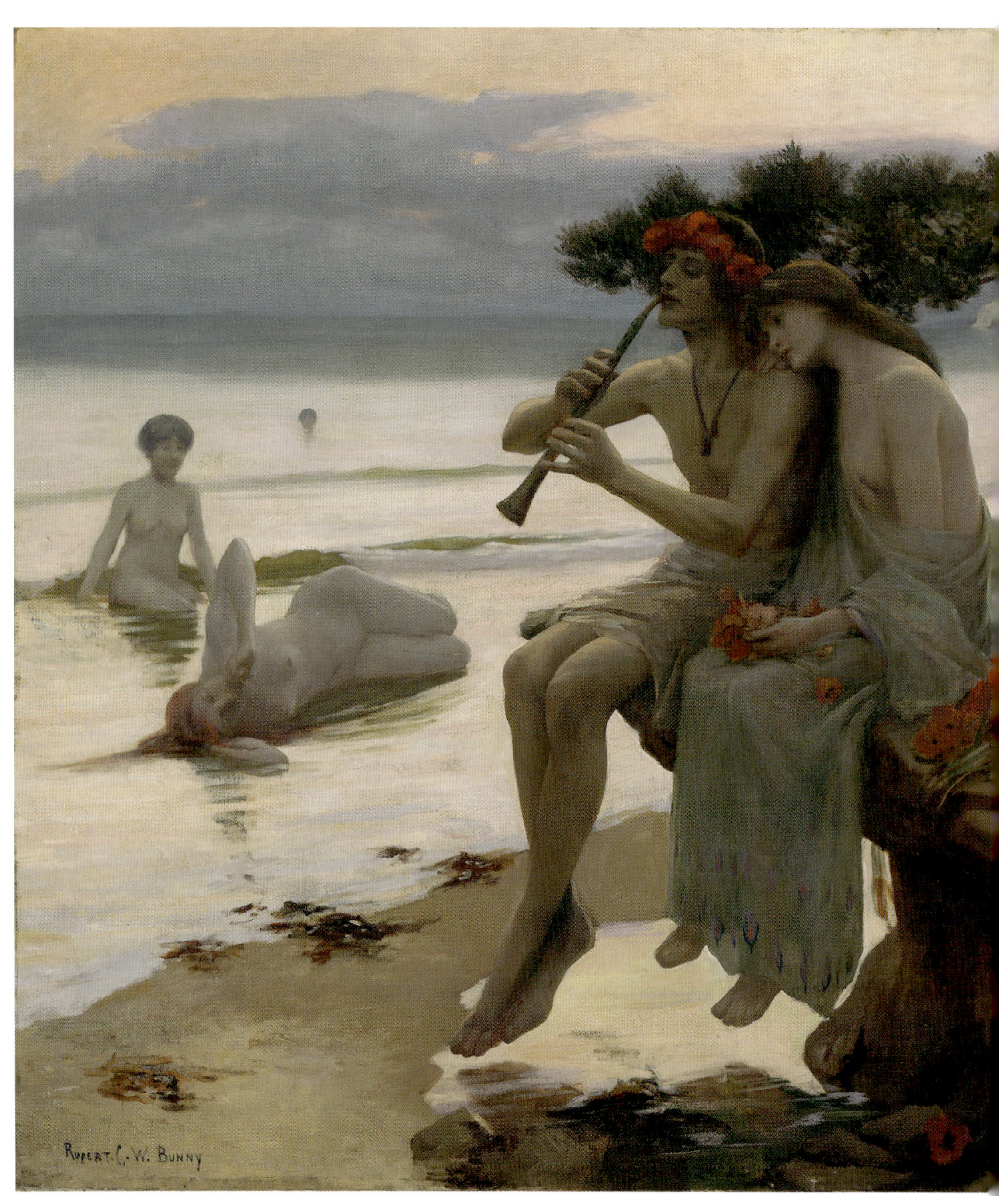

Rupert Bunny *Pastoral* c1893, oil on canvas (see details pages 4 and 151)
National Gallery of Australia, Canberra. Purchased 1969

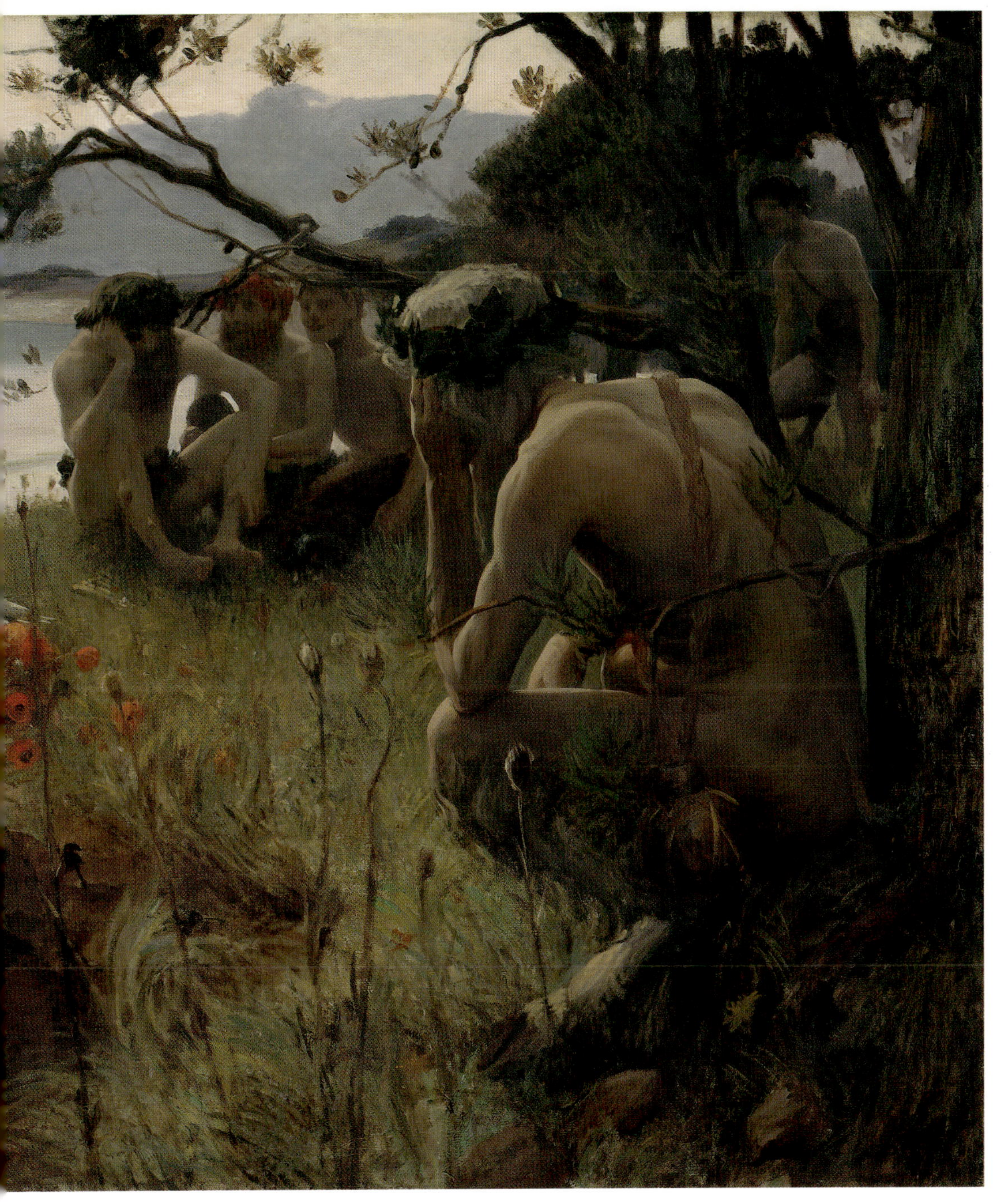

The Golden Age is a hybrid, blending observations of a Naturalist painter (honed from Altson's studies at the Académie Julian and in the ateliers of the painters Jean-Paul Laurens and Colarossi) and his expanded awareness of contemporary art. Altson grafts academic studies of the life model onto a composition that highlights a decorative unity. He applies aspects of Impressionist styling, the aesthetics of Japonisme and Puvis's flattened forms and, like Bunny, appropriates these decorative qualities of light and colour to enhance mood. While Bunny conveys soporific stillness through his cool palette and muted tones, Altson's saturated cadmium pigment imbues the work with a sunlit energy. The correlation between music and altered emotional states also underpins *The Golden Age*, and is used to envisage the figures in a lyrically infused state of abandon. Musically bound in a trance state, the youthful bodies of the work are streamlined into sensualised nudity, the eroticism of which is tempered to convey a sense of restored innocence.

After studying at the Académie Julian from 1887 to 1889 and immersing himself in the art of Paris, Emanuel Phillips Fox altered his expression of light as an element observed in nature to one that also symbolically enriched his subjects. In the summer of 1889 Fox produced a series of works portraying the Breton religious novice. Of these, *Sunlight effect* reduces naturalism for an emphasis on the communicant as a spiritual subject: the figure is backlit to imply her spiritual illumination and mystical reverie. His palette, aligned to that of Monet and Pissarro in the 1880s, amplifies the mystery of the figure. Like the Impressionists, Fox used prismatic hues, although with different outcome: here, the greens are infused with purples and pinks, offset by dappled yellows in an abstracted background that sets up a patterned glow around the figure. The modulations of whites from the shrouded figure are key to activating the intensity of colour. When Fox arrived in Paris in 1887 he reacted with distaste to Charles Douglas Richardson's paintings of idealised subjects, claiming that 'I think I belong to realism body and soul'.[78] Two years later in *Sunlight effect* he sidesteps realism, intersecting ambient colour with suggestive form, where the 'sunlight effect' of the title conveys a metaphysical outcome.

Fox painted *Sunlight effect* at Le Pouldu on the Breton coast in the same year that Paul Gauguin and his follower Paul Sérusier (who Fox had met at the Académie Julian) travelled to the region to paint. While no contact between the artists at Le Pouldu is documented, it is likely that Fox encountered Gauguin given that the village consisted of only four dwellings.[79] From 1886 to 1889, when Gauguin was living mainly at Pont-Aven, the Breton peasant became a key signifier of a Symbolist Arcadian vision in his art, as the object of a desired (and imagined) 'primitive' (in the sense of pre-modern) state. In 1888, Gauguin, with Émile Bernard, cemented a new pictorial style that broke with Impressionism in their desire to esablish correspondences between the pastoral ideal and simplified form. It was through a synthesis of subjective colour and rhythmic form that Gauguin produced his

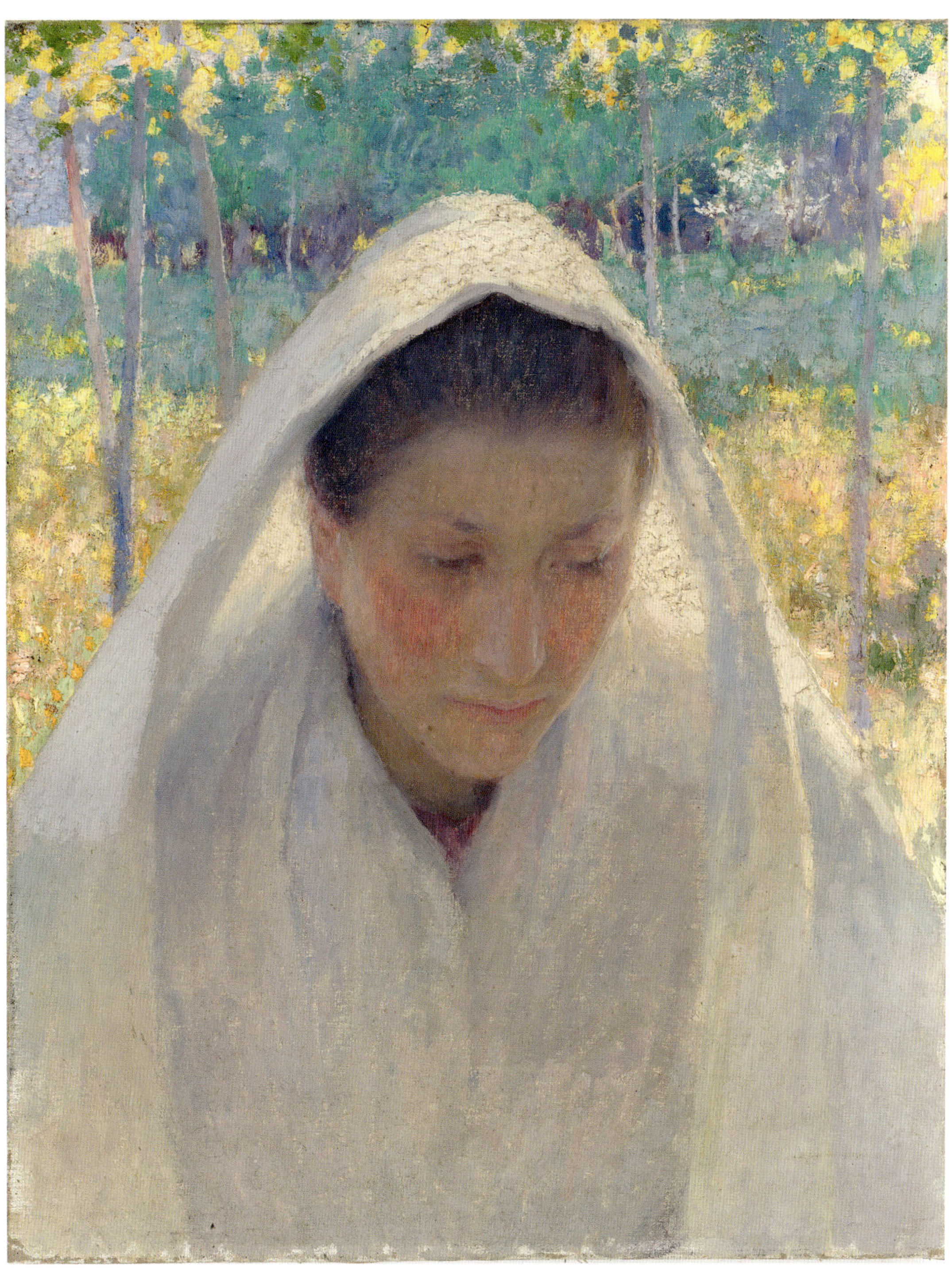

E Phillips Fox *Sunlight effect* c1889, oil on canvas
National Gallery of Australia, Canberra. Gift of the artist's nephew Len Fox in memory of his mother Irene Fox 1984

77

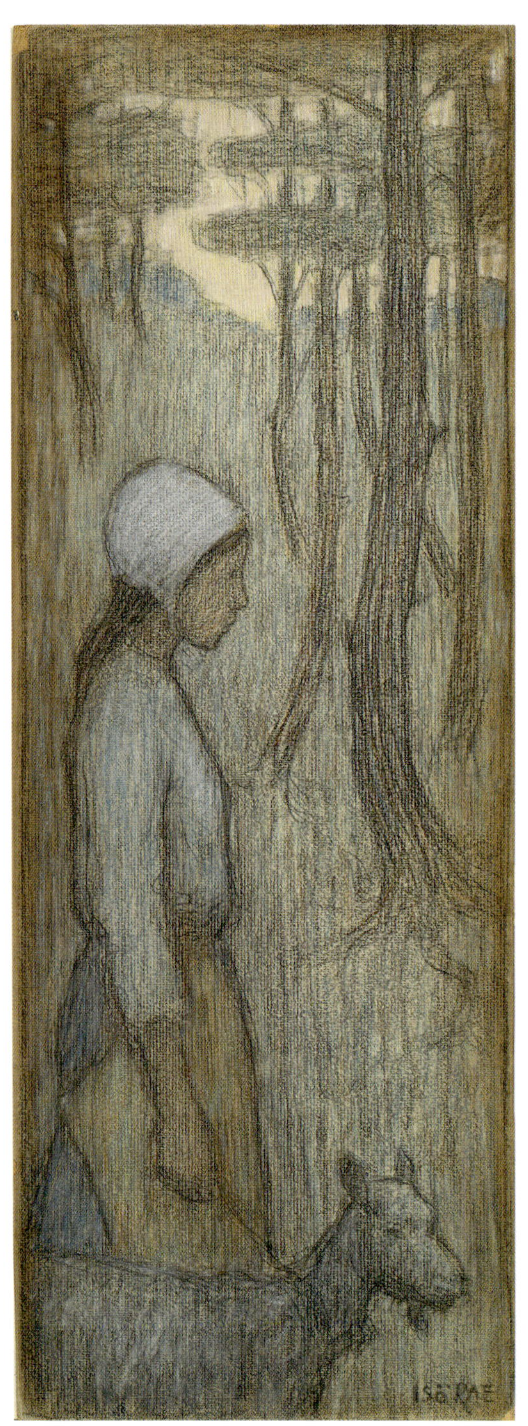

Iso Rae *(Breton girl with goat)* c1889, pastel on card
National Gallery of Victoria, Melbourne. Purchased with funds donated from the estate of Quida Marston 1940

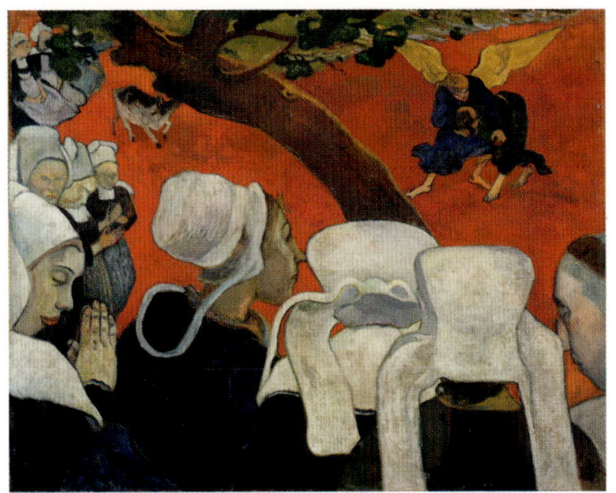

seminal Symbolist painting *Vision of the sermon (Jacob wrestling with the angel)* in 1888. Here his non-naturalistic style transposed the Breton religious ritual as an evocation of an otherworldly vision. In 1891 the critic George-Albert Aurier referred to the qualities of the work – an art of ideas expressed through a subjective decorative style – as a visual manifesto of the Symbolist movement.[80]

Iso Rae's *(Breton girl with goat)* c1889 signals the impact of the decorative aesthetic of Gauguin and his Pont-Aven School.[81] Rae began a decade of study at the National Gallery School in Melbourne in 1877 where her colleagues included Bunny, Mackennal and Richardson. On completing her studies she left permanently for France where she initially enrolled at Colarossi's, while maintaining contact with Australia as a newspaper correspondent detailing student life in Paris. She eventually settled in Etaples in northern France in 1893.

(Breton girl with goat) reveals Rae's exploration of Symbolist expression. The Breton subject is translated through Cloisonnism, the term coined by Édouard Dujardin in 1888 pertaining to certain artists' use of non-naturalistic colour in darkly outlined, flat shapes – analogous to (and influenced by) medieval stained glass windows and Japanese woodblock prints. These decorative features are overt in *(Breton girl with goat)* with its vertically condensed composition and strong dynamic of arabesque trees. Rae exhibited similarly themed works, including *Dan les bois* 1895 and the more emotively suggestive *La solitude* 1895, at the Société Nationale des Beaux-Arts. Yet in *(Breton girl with goat)* she emulates Gauguin's poetically simplified form and his use of the peasant as a symbol to convey the subtle mystery of this solitary woodland encounter.

(Breton girl with goat) is distinct among the work of expatriate Australians in its espousal of avant-garde aesthetics. The art of the expatriates was driven by a quest to succeed in the cultural centres of Europe in establishment terms and, accordingly, their responses to Symbolism were largely content driven, matched by moderated shifts in representation. By contrast, and while maintaining qualities that are the artist's own, *(Breton girl with goat)* responds to Gauguin's intent of rejecting the pictorial conventions of realism to instead 'bring out the feeling of things [and their] ... intimate reality'.[82]

Paul Gauguin *Vision of the sermon (Jacob wrestling with the angel)* **1888**, oil on canvas
Scottish National Gallery

Chapter 2

DREAMS OF AN ANTIPODEAN ARCADY

The sunny south: the landscape as Aesthetic ideal

While Australian expatriates in France painted Brittany idylls as dreams
of a modern Arcadia, in around 1887 Tom Roberts created an Antipodean
counterpart with *The sunny south*. The painting is a voyeuristic glimpse at a group
of male bathers in a shady grove of banksias during a moment's respite from the sun.
The style is naturalistic; Roberts attends to the qualities of light and heat, and the
different pigments of coastal foliage set against the brilliant water. Nonetheless, the
work is not an entirely factual account of place. The figures are rhythmically dispersed
among the patterns of trees, the branches echoing the posture of their bodies. The
nudity of the central figure is emphasised as if to stress the sensation of sun on skin.
Crouching beneath the trees is a semi-clothed figure who could be mistaken for Pan,
the forest deity who presided over Virgil's classical Arcadia and the traditional
intermediary between the forces of nature and culture.

More than a decade later Roberts's nymph-like creature would become a faun
when Sydney Long painted a squatting Pan in the mythical boundaries of an

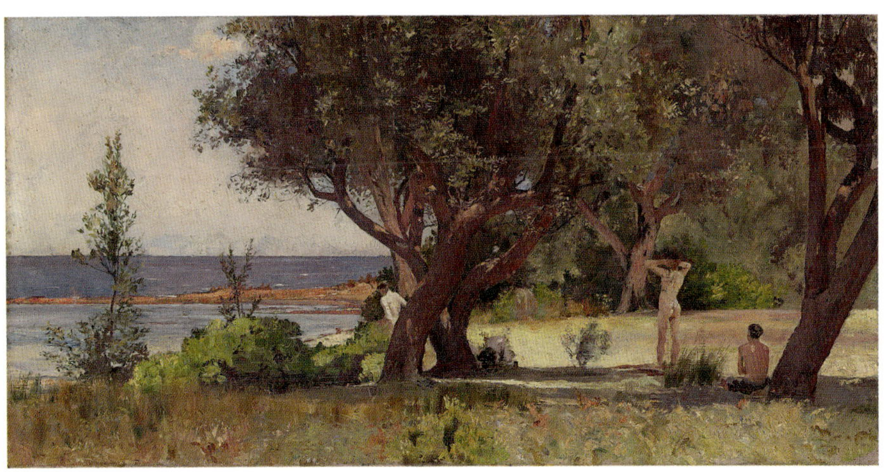

Tom Roberts *The sunny south* c1887, oil on canvas
National Gallery of Victoria, Melbourne. Felton Bequest 1940

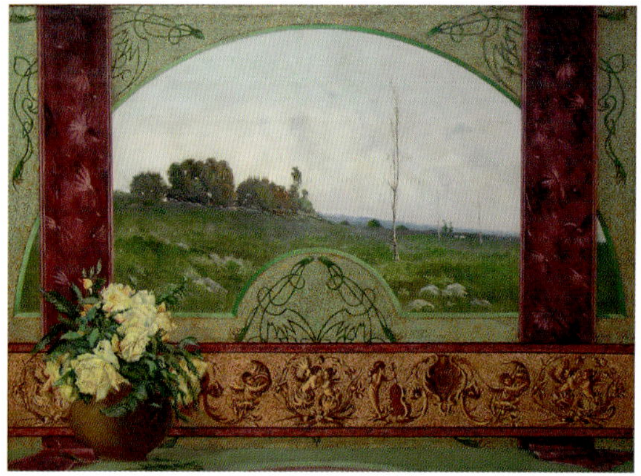

Art-Nouveau gum-tree landscape. Through Symbolist ambience, Long translates the sentiments of Roberts's idyllic sunny south into a decoratively enhanced arena of sensation and emotion. The rapid social transformations in Europe's urban centres in the latter part of the nineteenth century led to a widespread belief that society was in a downward spiral. While these cultural anxieties of fin-de-siècle Europe were channelled into apocalyptic and decadent imagery, with Arcadia serving as an artistic refuge, Australians were painting the landscape as the ideal of a new modern state. Here, as art historian Virginia Spate has noted, their 'personal response to a particular scene [was] infused by a wider optimism, the confidence in Australia as a new arcadia'.[1] Symbolist practices in Australia provided cultural reinforcement for this vision.

In 1889, the year he returned to Melbourne from England, Charles Douglas Richardson produced a painting that is indicative of the period's cultural packaging of the landscape. In *(Aesthetic landscape and interior)* Richardson depicts an outdoor setting framed by an ornamental fan design, juxtaposing a view of the natural world with the artificially constructed features through which we see it. The work can be viewed as an arresting nineteenth-century counterpart to the late twentieth-century conceptual works of Ian Burn such as *Value added landscapes* 1993, in which Burn explored the notion of place as it is superimposed by cultural and critical assumptions. In Richardson's work the 'value added' markers are those of European aesthetic design and potted roses as cultivated cultural symbols. Richardson's work implies how Aesthetic taste – the British cult for beautiful objects, which had become a popular fashion in Australia by the 1880s – was informing a creative worldview. *(Aesthetic landscape and interior)* is an almost literal demonstration of how Aesthetic features shaped the landscape as a Symbolist object.

The novelist Ada Cambridge noted that after the 1880 Melbourne International Exhibition, which had included a Japanese court of ornamental objects and design, Victoria's middle classes became 'rapidly Aesthetic'.[2] Australians followed the British vogue for Japanese-inspired fashion, which by the late 1880s had developed into a

Charles Douglas Richardson *(Aesthetic landscape and interior)* 1889, oil on canvas
Private collection

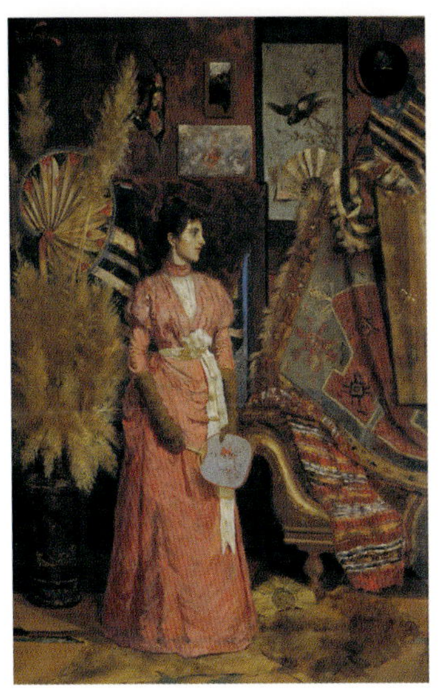

broader appreciation of 'exotic' ornament and design. This trend, adapted from Whistler's Aesthetic philosophy with its 'art for art's sake' creed, created an environment which integrated the fine arts, music, decoration and design. In Sydney, the British artist, teacher and designer Constance Roth, who had arrived in Australia in 1884, was significant in promoting the ideals of the movement as the basis for bohemian identity. Roth's studio, which became a hub for artists, musicians and 'bohemian types', exuded an Aesthetic atmosphere with its décor of oriental carpets, drapery and screens, and brightly coloured fabrics. It was here that Charles Conder reputedly met Tom Roberts in 1887 – an encounter that would eventually deliver the younger Conder to Melbourne.[3]

The artistically immersive environment of Roth's salon-style gatherings may have prompted Roberts's subsequent *conversazione* evenings at his Melbourne studio, where discussions were based on the 'latest French and other journals' that attendees were asked to bring.[4] The Aesthetic phenomena provided a cosmopolitan environment conducive to artistic formulation and the exchange of ideas that had particular currency in the colony's bourgeoning cities. By the late 1880s the Aesthetic interior was seen as an extension of the creative personality and became a standard design feature of artists' studios.[5] Accumulated Aesthetic ornaments feature in Girolamo Nerli's *The sitting* 1889, for example, where they submerge the portrait subject who appears part of the decorative tableau. The work suggests Aestheticism as a crossover trend between artful fashion and artistic strategy.

Constance Roth exhibited works in Melbourne and Sydney which combined qualities of painting with ornamental design, although few are known to have survived. *Apples* 1890, a painting on cedar wood panel, reveals the impact of Japanese art on Roth's Aesthetic practice, with its condensed composition and cropped focus on a lyrical bend of fruit and foliage. The example of Roth's practice may have been one impetus for the *9 by 5 impression* exhibition held in Melbourne in 1889 (although Whistler provided the template). Her influence is detected in the panel format of the works in the *9 by 5* show, as well as in her philosophy of providing domestically scaled and priced paintings, which paralleled the aims of the exhibition's organisers.[6] Roth's work appealed directly to Arthur Streeton and Conder and provided a local example of certain principles of Whistler's art

Girolamo Nerli *The sitting* 1889, oil on canvas
Queensland Art Gallery, Brisbane. Purchased 1997 with funds raised by Louis Vuitton Australia Pty Ltd and donations from James Fairfax AO, Philip Bacon and Wayne Kratzmann through and with the assistance of the Queensland Art Gallery Foundation

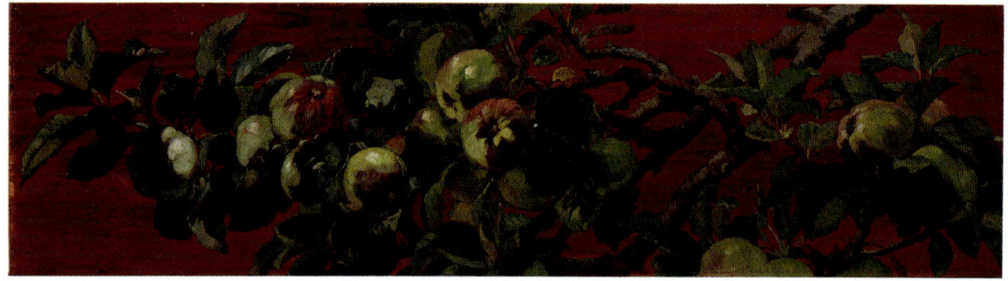

that had been enthusiastically espoused by Roberts on his return from his
European sojourn of 1885. Streeton produced a series of Roth-like 'decorations':
Bananas 1890 (University of Queensland Collection) and in around 1890 *The
flight of summer*, a lyrical tribute to the season's end which Streeton dedicated to
his sweetheart, the 'syren Florrie Walker'.[7] Streeton spent the spring and summer
of 1889 at Heidelberg where he painted some of the defining landscapes of the era.
Yet in *The flight of summer* he conjures the dreamy sentiments of a transitional
world through symbolically charged Aesthetic design and Japanese-inspired form
and colour. Eliminating narrative elements for the values of a decorative artistic
language, *The flight of summer* demonstrates the significance of Aesthetic painting
in implementing Symbolist expression, even if, in Streeton's case, such works were
a footnote to the main focus of his practice.

The Aesthetic influence on landscape painting is evident in a series of nocturnes
that distill the evocative atmosphere of twilight into symbolically enhanced images.
The motif of moonlight was common in Europe: a British reviewer of an exhibition
at the Grosvenor Gallery (London's temple of Aesthetic art) noted in 1889 that
'this is a year of moons in landscape ... she rises or sets in all galleries'.[8] While
Streeton inscribed the Australian twilight with the sentiments of romantic poetry,
his plein-air practice was focused on the tonal effects of light on the landscape,
albeit within the context of the moon's mood lighting.[9] Other artists, including
David Davies, Emanuel Phillips Fox and Conder, produced works more closely
related to Whistler's sense of the nocturne as a state in which the natural world was
diminished in favour of the atmosphere of twilight, conveyed through decorative
colour arrangements and a Japanese emphasis on reduced compositions.

While Davies's *Moonrise* 1894 (National Gallery of Victoria) monumentalises the
moonlit landscape under the terms of naturalism, his earlier and smaller *Moonrise*
1893 emphasises crepuscular effects through colour harmonies and design. Davies
had studied in Paris at the Académie Julian and at Jean-Paul Laurens's atelier from
1890 and at the plein-air colonies of Cornwall in England prior to returning to
Australia in 1893 to embark on a signature series of moonlit Victorian landscapes.

Constance Roth *Apples* 1890, oil on cedar panel
Art Gallery of New South Wales. Purchased 1890

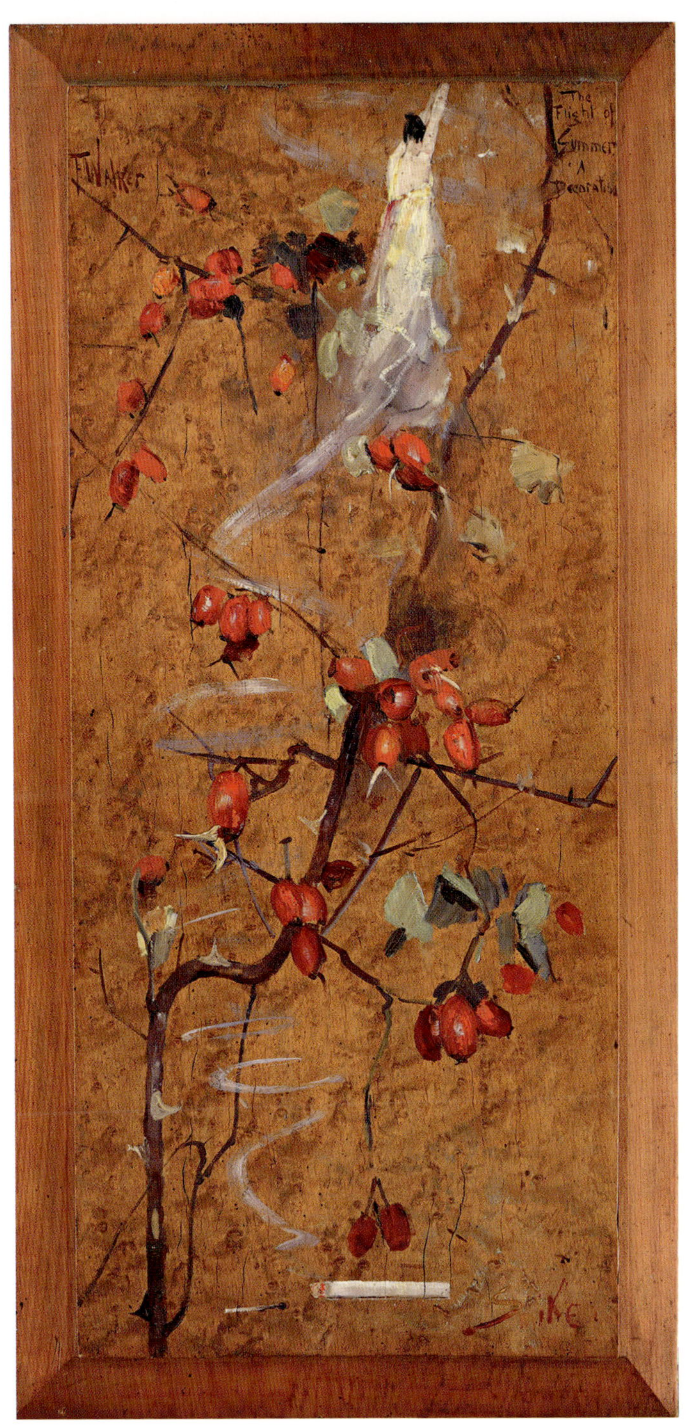

Arthur Streeton *The flight of summer* c1890, oil on panel
Private collection

Moonrise 1893 may have derived from his practice of observing nature but is ultimately composed as a decorative gesture. Swift, broken brushwork loosely defines form in a composition simplified for poetic impact. The raised horizon, twisting pathway and lilting grass lead the eye towards the moon. The palette is muted with a blue glow and the subtlest hint of red blossom from a staccato brush. With its sparse areas of paint and incised detail, *Moonrise* has an intentional 'coarseness' that enhances its emotional impact.

Such loose handling is also evident in Conder's *Moonlight* 1889. Referring to the same poetics of nightfall, Conder uses fluid paintwork to capture the moon's glowing highlights on a patterned silhouette of trees. Conder could not have studied Whistler's work directly at this stage, but it is possible that Davies, while overseas, noted the 'articulate surfaces' of Whistler's 1880s nocturnes: paintings in which Whistler incorporated the 'physical materiality of brushmarks [and canvas textures to] interrupt the mimetic aspects' of his work.[10] Davies would 'polish' such effects in his larger *Moonrise* of 1894. Yet his earlier composition, like that of Conder's, employs these techniques to heighten the expressive outcome of decorative form.

Emanuel Phillips Fox's *Moonrise, Heidelberg* 1900 is one of several versions of a painting where the title specifies a twilight Australian landscape but which Fox intended for an international arena. *Moonrise, Heidelberg*, the second of a number of versions of the work, was commenced in Melbourne and completed in London after 1901.[11] It was exhibited at the Royal Academy in 1903 and at the Paris Salon in 1910. Comparing this version to the original work, DH Souter described the decorative enhancements, noting that 'now the tones are fuller and richer, the masses broader and stronger, the technique bold in its masterly confidence'.[12] Although the textured brushwork suggests the Impressionists' shimmer of low light, it is the elaboration of colour – the viridian keynote and its analogous shifts towards the purples and blues of its spectrum – that shapes the dramatic strangeness of a landscape veiled in an emerald glow. While considered as antidotes to the sun-drenched imagery of Heidelberg's 'golden summer', nocturnes such as those by Fox, Davies and Conder veer towards the Symbolist ambience of a transitory state. Demonstrating the Aesthetic movement's crossover of art and craft forms, where the precepts of artistic beauty informed elements of design, the imagery of the moonlit landscape was similarly adopted by the English-born James WR Linton in *Australian landscape casket*. As the motif here is enhanced by its ornamental placement, so too do these nocturne paintings feature as products of Aesthetic design.

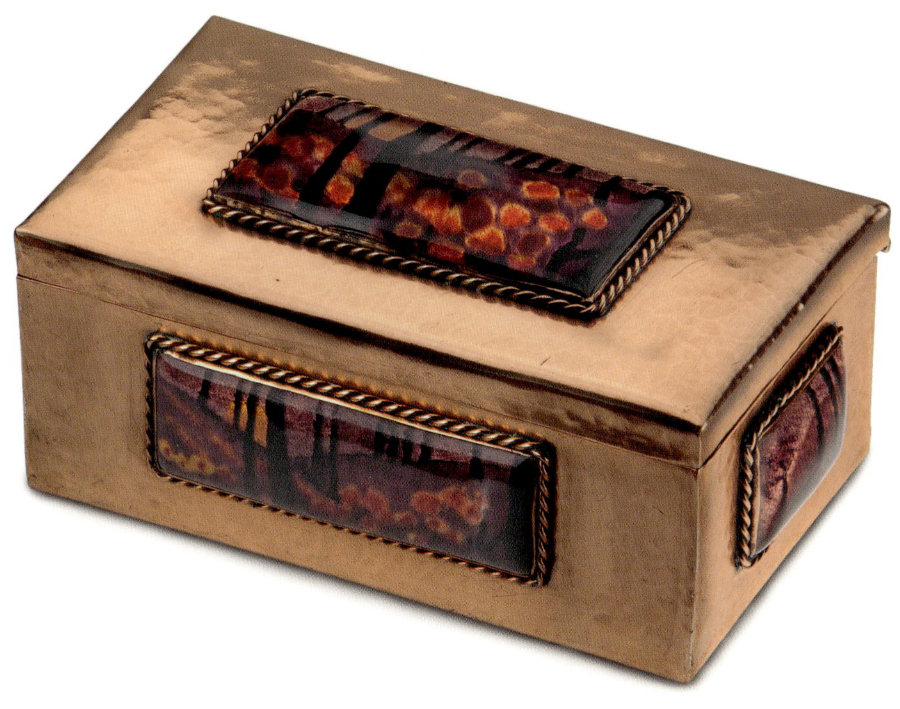

James WR Linton *Australian landscape casket* c1910, copper, enamel on copper
Art Gallery of South Australia, Adelaide. South Australia Government Grant 1985

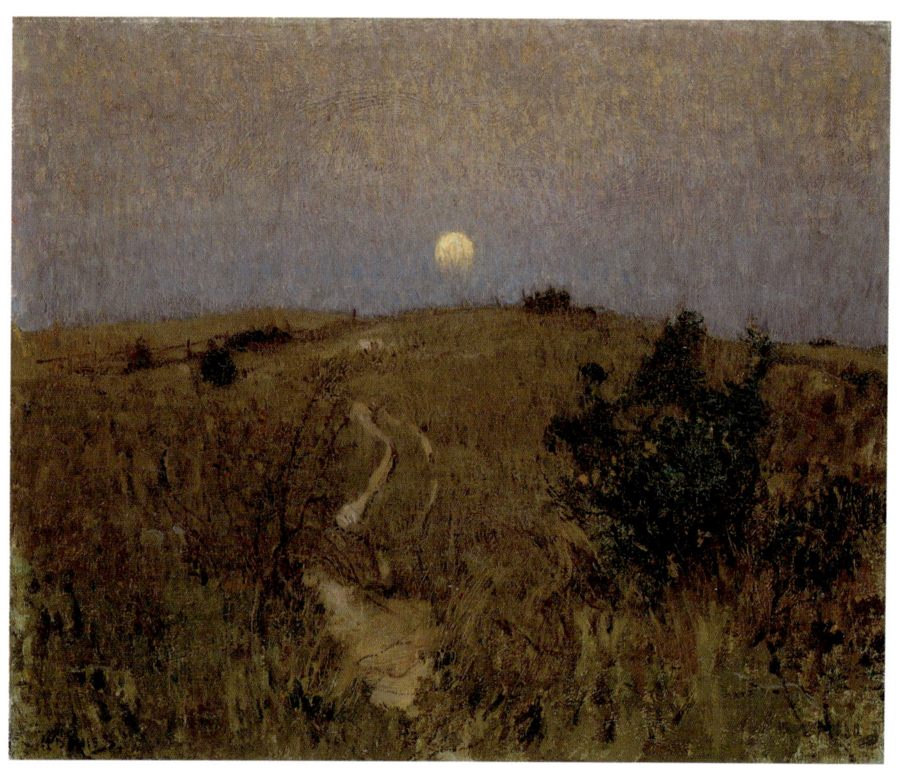

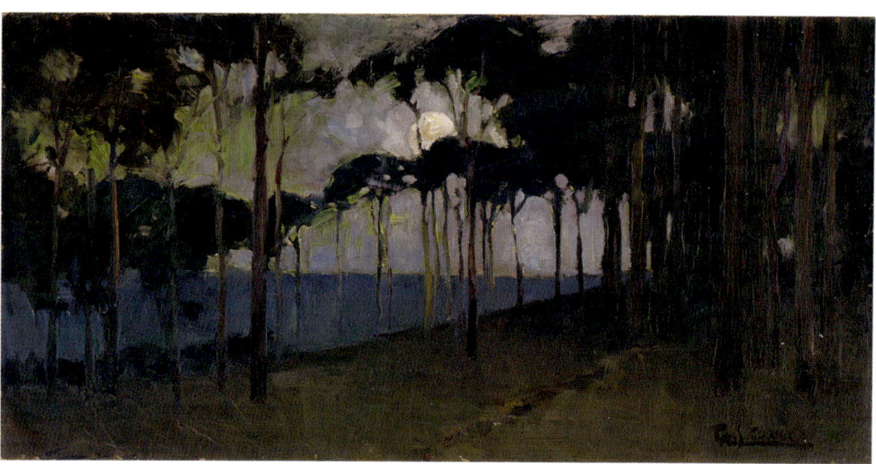

(top) **David Davies** *Moonrise* 1893, oil on canvas
Art Gallery of South Australia, Adelaide. Elder Bequest Fund 1947

(above) **Charles Conder** *Moonlight* 1889, oil on canvas on board
Bastiaan Collection

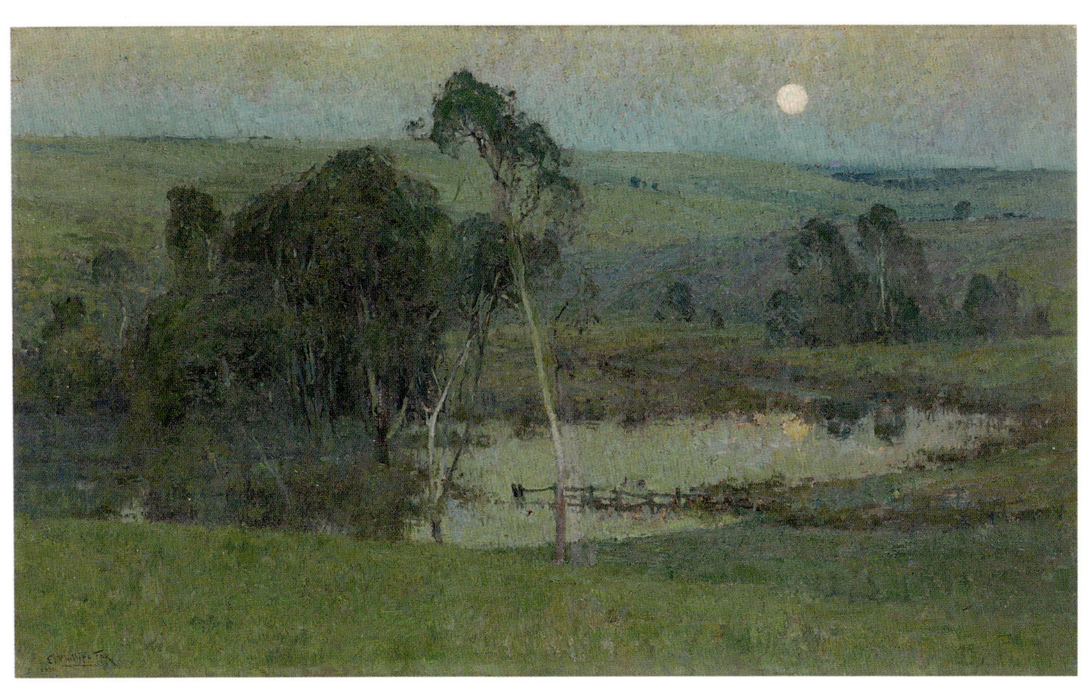

E Phillips Fox *Moonrise, Heidelberg* **1900**, oil on canvas
National Gallery of Victoria, Melbourne. Purchased 1948

Dreams of the bohemian idyll: Charles Conder and his impact

Never did Conder 'polish up an idea and so leave no suggestion'; he suggests a theme and allows the spectator to embody it according to his fancy.[13]

If the decadent styling of its bohemian followers shaped the character of French Symbolism, then it was the peripatetic Charles Conder who best fits such a description in this country, even though he can only be claimed as an Australian for six formative years of his practice. Conder travelled to Melbourne from Sydney in 1888 equipped with the reputation of a young painter of note, given that the Art Gallery of New South Wales had purchased his Aesthetic cityscape *Departure of the Orient – Circular Quay* 1888 earlier that year. It was an impressive artistic debut for a twenty-year-old who had little time for the methodical study of art and relied instead on his 'curious moods of abstraction' to fuel his artistic drive. Often referred to as an artist who was 'dreamy' in character, it was in Sydney, where Conder's chaotic studio dwelling in Darlinghurst paralleled an equally disordered life, that he was first noted as a living embodiment of 'one of the heroes of his favourite reading at the time', Henry Murger's *La vie de bohème* (1851).[14] Literary sources ultimately served as the inspiration for Conder's art. The work of Browning and Herrick, in particular, informed his imagination.[15] Conder's painting was most practically directed by the artists around him – AJ Daplyn, Girolamo Nerli, Julian Ashton and Constance Roth, as well as his later associations with the artistic fraternities of Melbourne. His dual ambitions as a painter and bohemian lured him to Melbourne, a city that offered artistic camaraderie and a greater emphasis on cultural practices.[16] He had connected with Roberts in Sydney through a common conviction, also shared by Arthur Streeton, that art was as much about a way of life as it was about painting.[17] Although he had previously complained about 'the heat, the dust, the flies, the mosquitoes' on his plein-air painting expeditions with Ashton in the New South Wales countryside, Conder seized the opportunity of living out Roberts's gospel of Impressionism when Streeton invited the pair to join him on a now legendary painting camp on a rambling estate at Eaglemont.[18] Here Conder lived out a bohemian idyll in a bushland setting, one that he would later nostalgically recall from another life, when he could be found hovering as a figure in the background of Henri de Toulouse-Lautrec's seedy visions of Paris nightlife.[19]

The shift from Impressionist to Symbolist inclinations in Conder's work is hinted at in an early series of plein-air paintings that enigmatically mark the landscape with the recurring presence of women carrying red parasols, or the allegorical rendering of Melbourne's middle class in *A holiday at Mentone* 1888 (Art Gallery

of South Australia). In 1889, when Conder exhibited *Hot wind* with the now
lost *Victorian idyll* (depicting a red-robed goddess of summer), suggestions
of a Symbolist practice were cemented with his shift in subject matter. Despite
the considerable interest that these works elicited, Conder voiced frustration
at the lack of a deeper understanding of his modern subjects, lamenting that:

> My 'Orient leaving' [*Departure of the Orient*] was liked at once because people understood
> it at once. With few exceptions outside artistic people I found my 'Hot wind' which
> is a much better work less appreciated. Although there was a picture before them they
> wouldn't take the trouble to look for the sentiment or motif.[20]

If the complexities of Conder's paintings were not appreciated on a wider level,
his artistic circle became his discerning public.[21] While Conder's relationship
with Roberts and Streeton is well documented, his associations in Melbourne
at this time also included a broader group of artists connected to the Victorian
Artists' Society, who were similarly pursuing Symbolist-inspired visions. Conder
is known to have visited Arthur Loureiro's studio and would have undoubtedly
seen his work *Study for 'The spirit of the new moon'*, which Loureiro kept until he
returned to Portugal in 1901. Conder was also aware of the Symbolist overtones in
the art of Charles Douglas Richardson who had returned to Melbourne to exhibit
works in 1889, including the Pre-Raphaelite-inspired *Arcasia or The enchanted
bower* 1889 (Art Gallery of South Australia) and the nymph-like figure in
Early sympathy c1889 (not located), in the same year as Conder's *Hot wind*.
Jane Sutherland's allegory of spring from the same year (not located) with
'accessories of the painting [that] bear out the idea' would have also been noted.[22]
The literary allusions in Conder's art were sustained through his association with
the Melbourne-based writer Kathleen Mannington Caffyn who he initially met
in Sydney. Caffyn, like Constance Roth, struck Conder as the epitome of the New
Woman: professional, creatively ambitious and self-reliant. Her impact on Conder
was considerable. Through her guidance he became keenly interested in Spiritualist
practices (a subject he no doubt also discussed with Richardson) and his attention
to alternative beliefs contributed to his artistic exploration of Symbolist imagery.
Conder produced a portrait of Caffyn in 1889 and she was subsequently noted
posing for him 'as a dryad'.[23] She may have been the model for *Hot wind*, draped
with the props that she had lent Conder for his studio.[24] Caffyn would later return
the creative gesture when she based the character of the young Aesthetic artist
in her major Symbolist novel *A yellow aster* (1894) on Conder. While Conder
may have looked towards the seductive, fictionalised beings of European literature,
he also drew on his awareness of politically emancipated women in his art. Like
Bertram Mackennal's encounters with Sarah Bernhardt, Conder used such figures
to shape the empowered, poeticised, anti-heroines of his art.

Echoing the sentiments of *Hot wind*, Conder rendered a forceful female spirit in the watercolour *Mirage* c1889. The work portrays a fiery nymph striding through an Australian landscape seen through the lens of Japanese *ukiyo-e* design. Colour washes delicately infuse the lightly inscribed linear form, concocting a dreamy vision, the sensuous appeal of which masks the threatening presence of the spirit who is about to ignite the bleached land. The work served as an example for Conder's artistic colleagues. Conder presented it to Roberts, who preserved it safely in his sketchbook and emulated its composition in a 1890s bookplate design.[25]

Conder's nymph reappears in oil and watercolour versions of Arthur Streeton's *The spirit of the drought* 1896.[26] These sketchy, experimental compositions are the most overtly Symbolist of Streeton's works, and reveal Conder as a direct conduit for such influences. As in *Mirage*, Streeton depicts the nymph in his painting *The spirit of the drought* descending from a parched hilltop, using the palette of *Hot wind* to highlight fire with rose madder reds and the intense gold tones of the land. With a mask-like face, she administers her powers of destruction as she hovers over the bones of her victims. Stripped of the seductive appeal of Conder's *Hot wind*, Streeton's figure is a more menacing drought spirit. His watercolours follow the composition of the oil, but extend the spirit's presence threefold as a ubiquitous landscape being who delivers a mocking dance of devastation. Streeton would return to the subject of bush spirits. In *A bush idyll* 1896, for example, a group of nymphs are linked in an Arcadian dance at twilight. Here they resonate as the spirits of pastoral traditions embodying the idyllic inflections of place. Like Conder, Streeton used such figures to depict the landscape as a place where dreams reside.

The exchange of imagery and free flow of experimental ideas in Melbourne's artistic community at this time is also evidenced by Charles Douglas Richardson's *Wind* 1889, one of the 'decidedly novel' wax-model sculptures portraying nature that the artist contributed to the *9 by 5 impression* exhibition.[27] The female figure in this work is abbreviated, rendered featureless like Streeton's spirit forms, but her bent body and flowing hair conform to the expression of her elemental being. Conder's contribution to this exhibition included *A dream of Handel's Largo* 1889. This work is a somewhat lighthearted reference to Roberts's rehearsal of Handel's Largo (without great effect) for the opening of the *9 by 5* exhibition.[28] Conder transforms the scene into a mini fin-de-siècle *Gesamtkunstwerk* (total work of art) where a lyrical sweep of figures unfolds with the quality of a musical crescendo.[29] Like the *9 by 5* 'impressions' of landscape, Conder here produces a sketch of the Symbolist imagination incorporating elements of music and dreams in enigmatic figurative form.

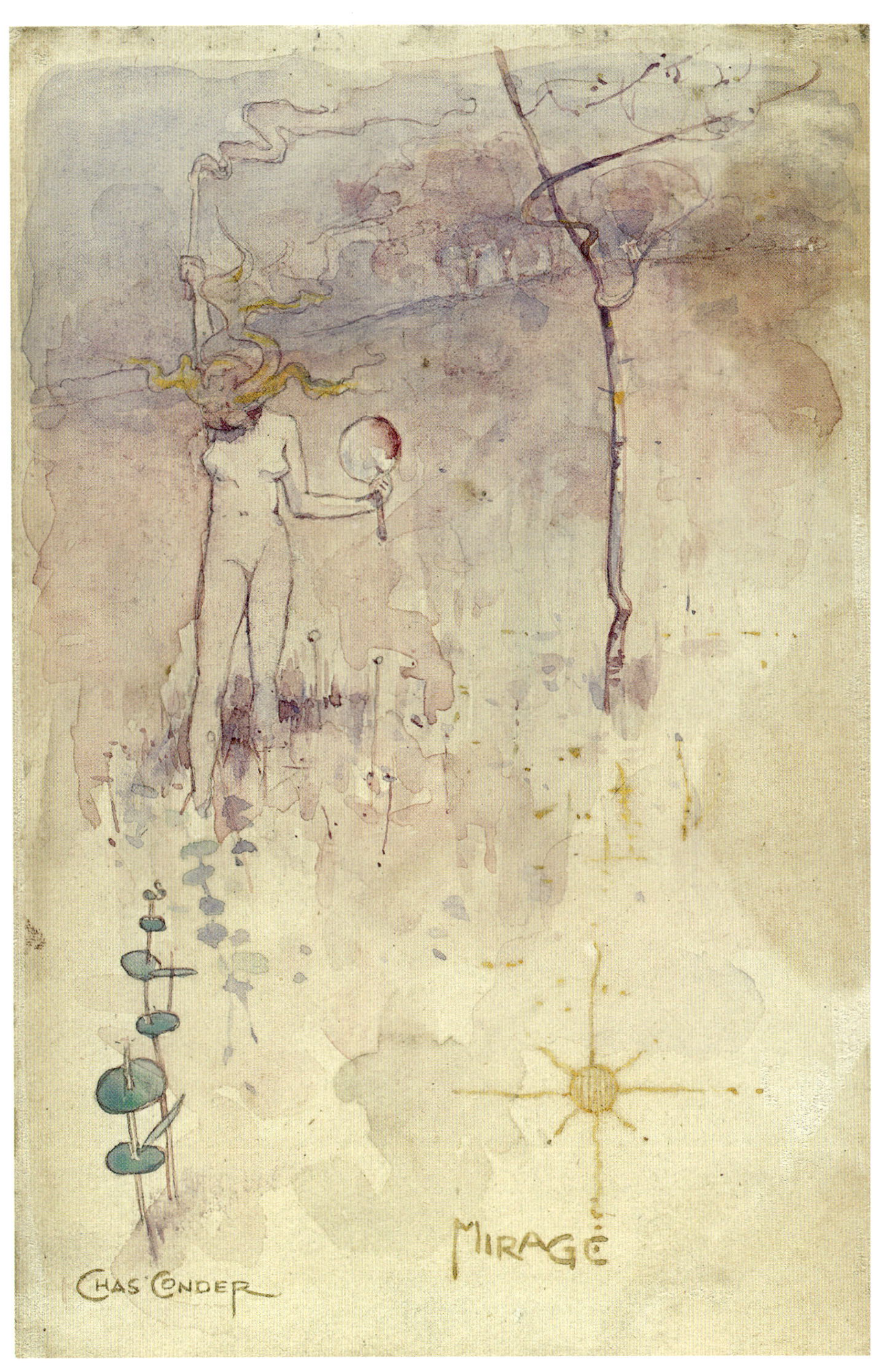

Charles Conder *Mirage* c1889, watercolour
National Gallery of Victoria, Melbourne. Purchased 1976

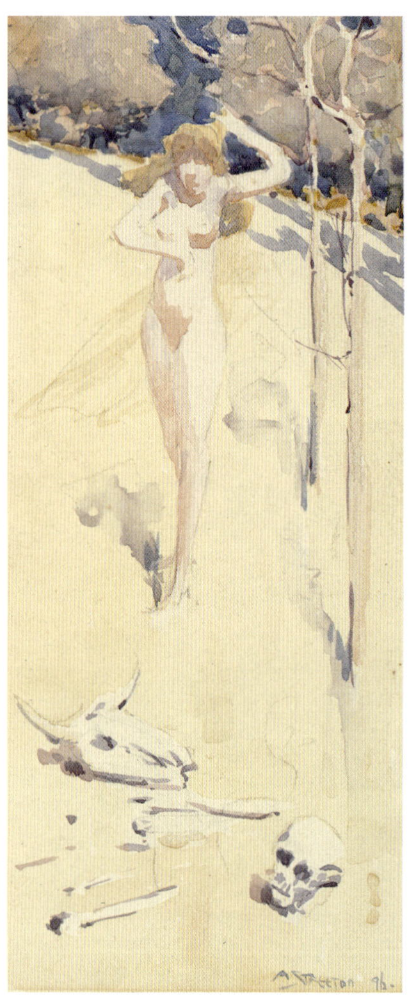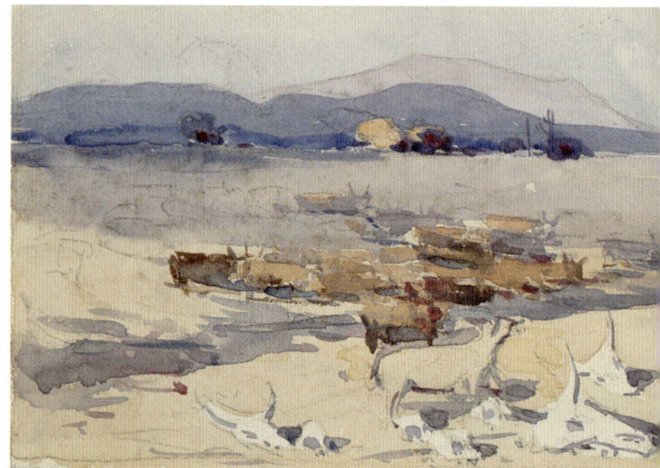

Arthur Streeton *The spirit of the drought* 1896, triptych, watercolour
Private collection

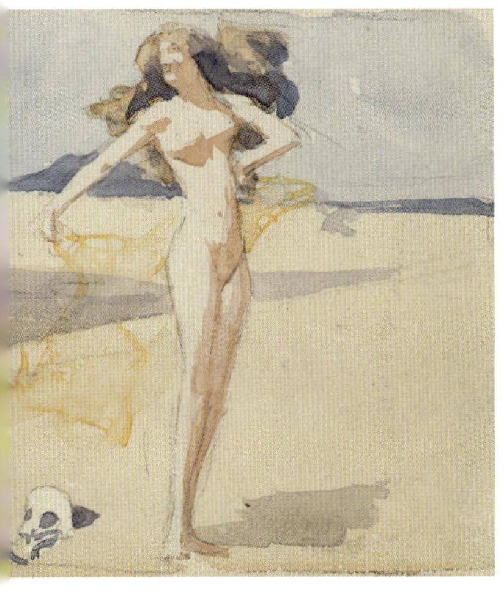

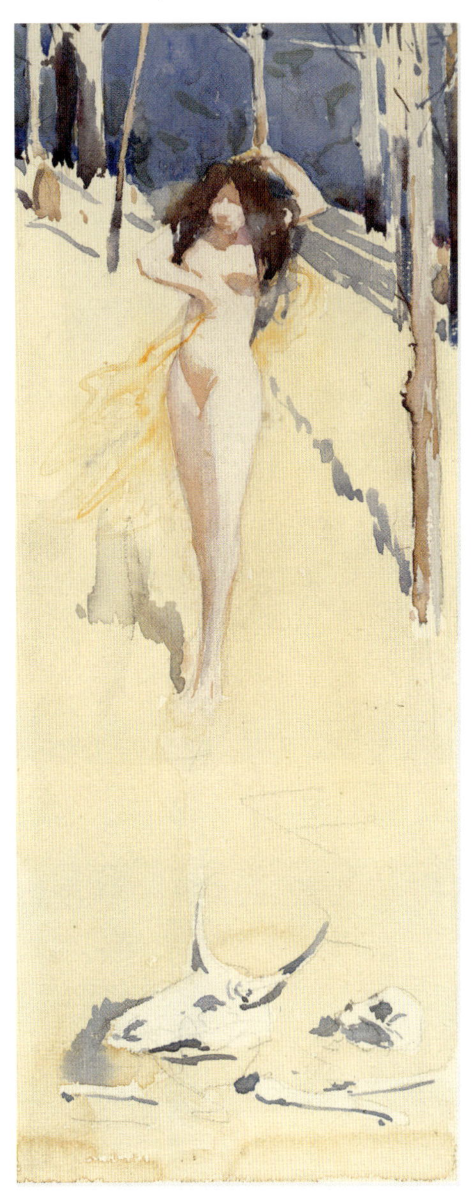

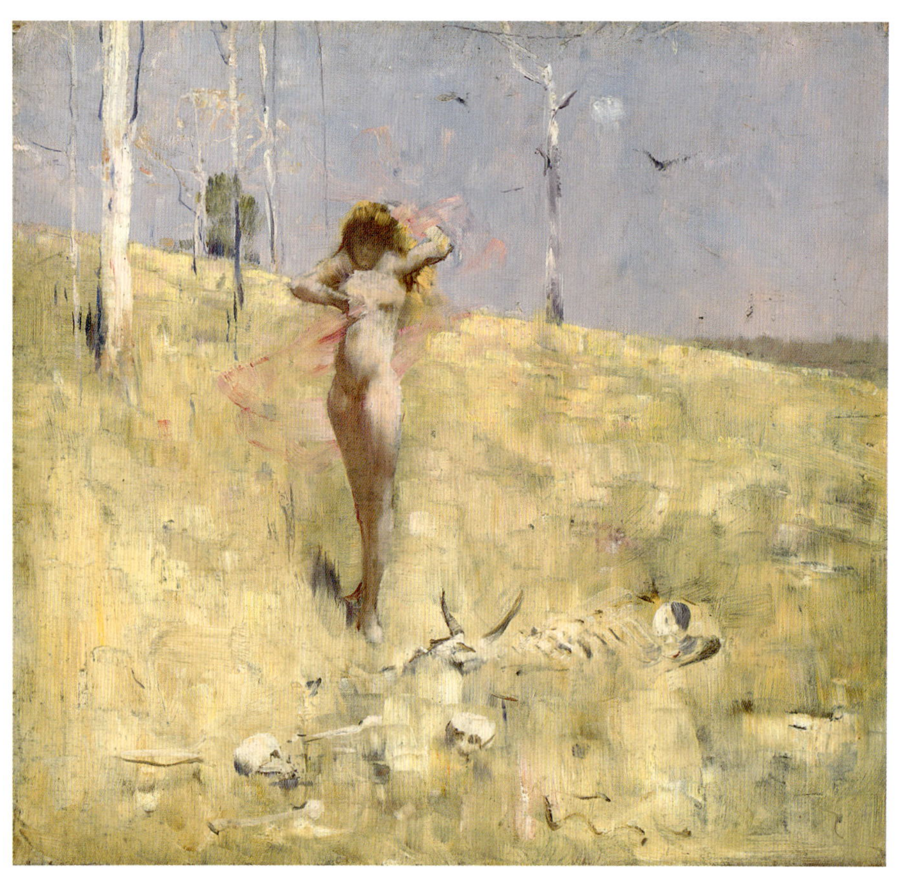

Arthur Streeton *The spirit of the drought* c1896, oil on wood panel
National Gallery of Australia, Canberra. Joseph Brown Fund

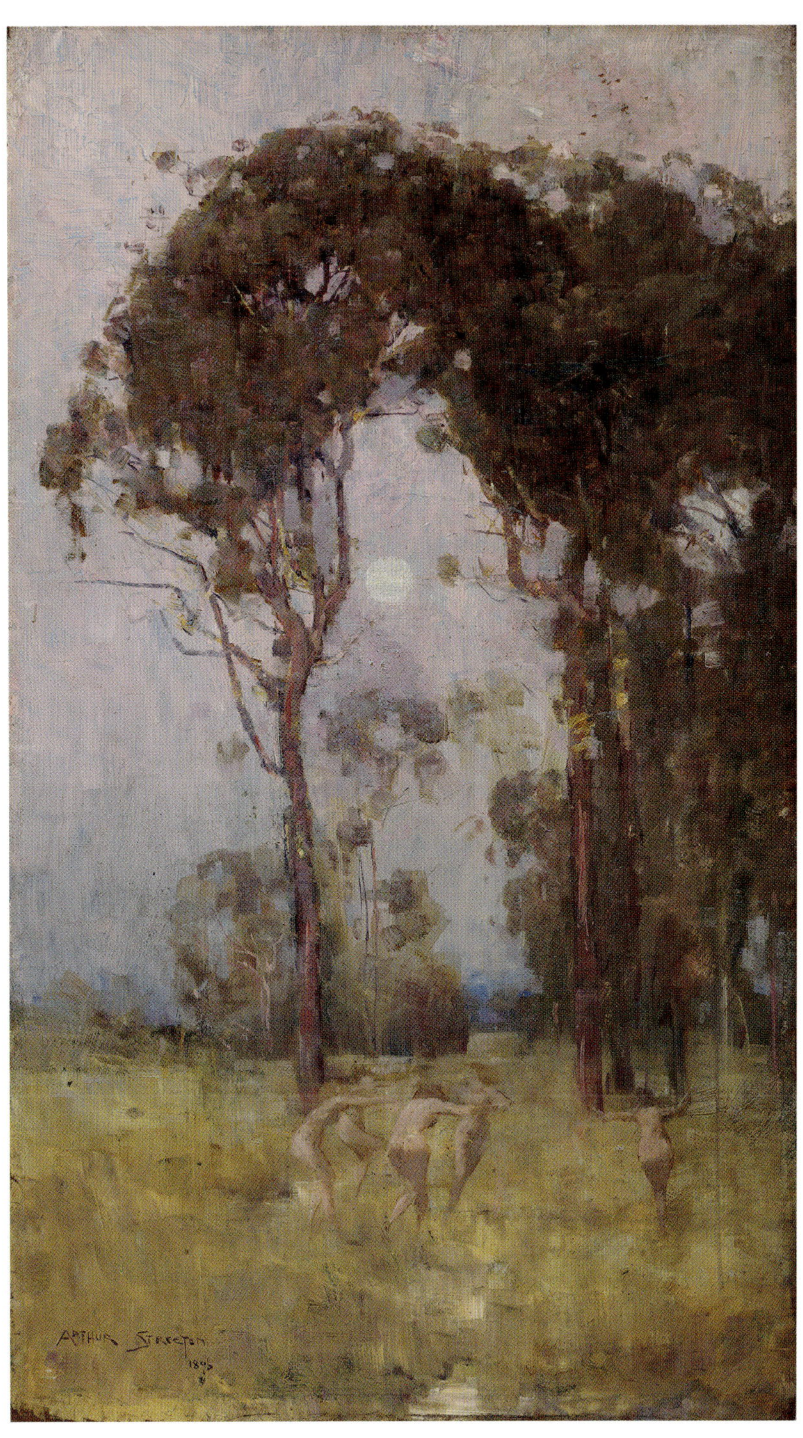

Arthur Streeton *A bush idyll* **1896,** oil on wood panel (see detail page 9)
Art Gallery of New South Wales. Gift of Dr Joseph Brown 1991

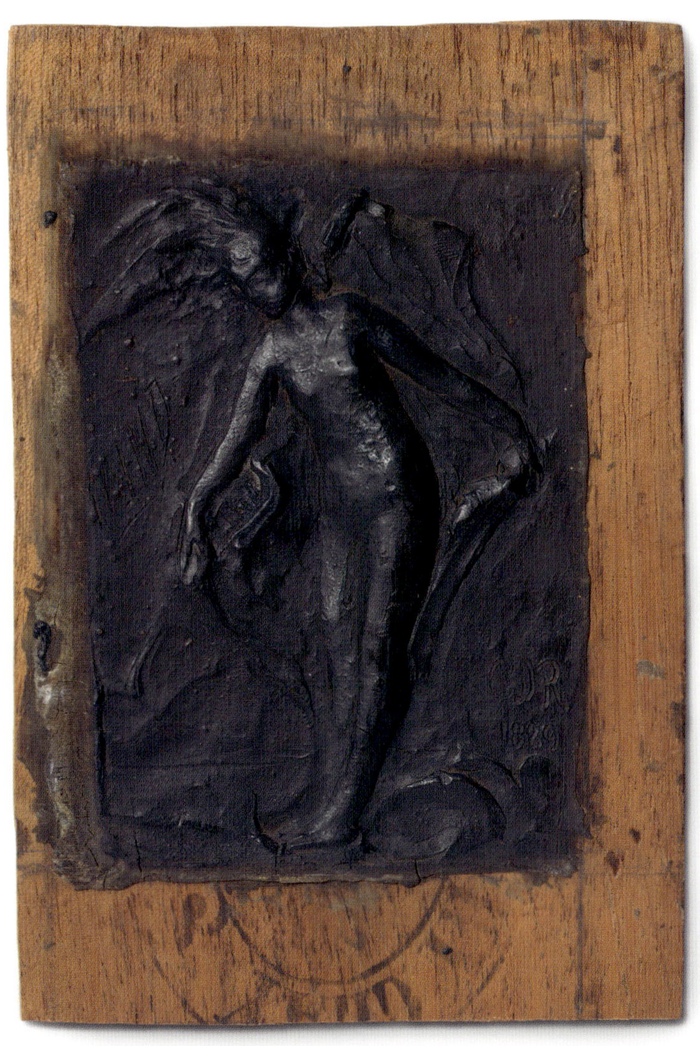

Charles Douglas Richardson *Wind* 1889, wax carved and modelled
National Gallery of Australia, Canberra. Rudy Komon Fund 1981

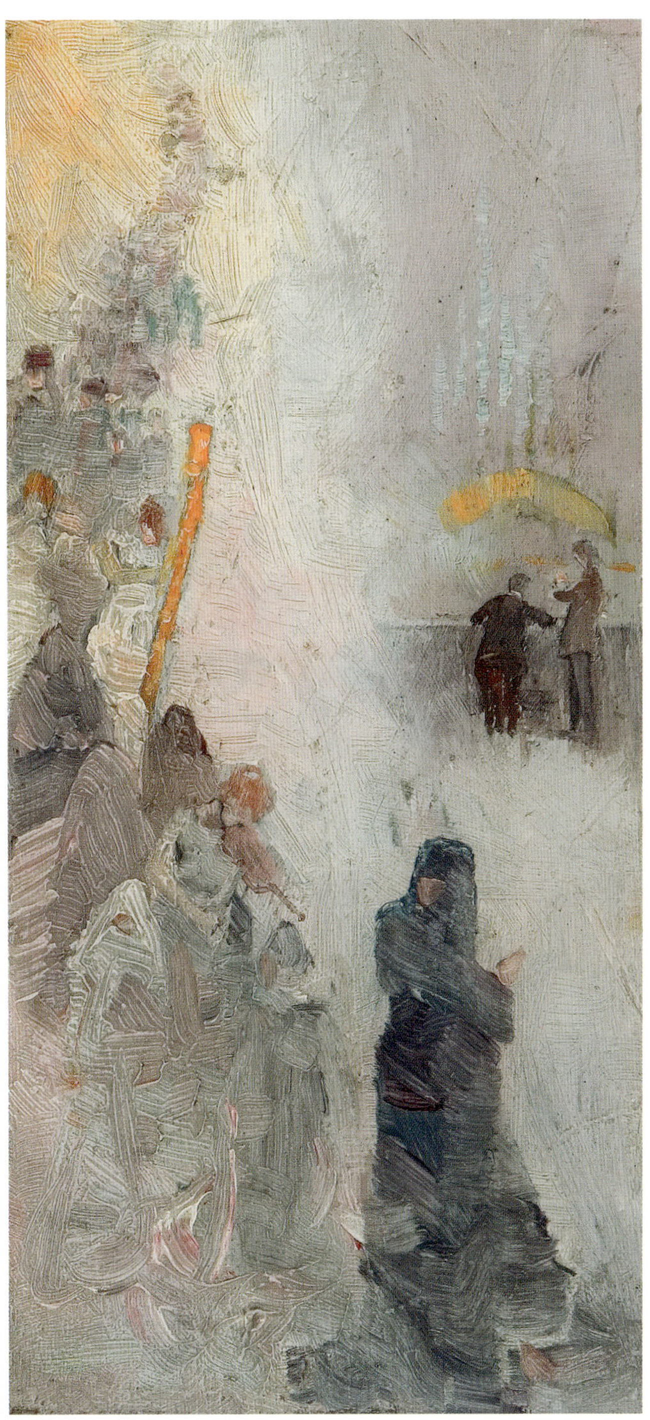

Charles Conder *A dream of Handel's Largo* 1889, oil on wood panel
Art Gallery of South Australia, Adelaide. On loan from the MJM Carter AO Collection

The hot sands, Mustapha, Algiers 1891 and *Moonlight at Mustapha* 1892 are two of the most evocative statements of Conder's Symbolist oeuvre. They were painted after Conder had left Australia for Paris in April 1890, and when, at the end of 1891, he was convalescing from a serious illness on a friend's estate near Mustapha. It was in Algiers, through the artist's perceived exotic poetry of place and in an atmosphere that nostalgically revived his feel for the Australian summer, that Conder painted these powerful allusions to the transience of life. The Mustapha works invoke the visionary Symbolist poetics of Paul Verlaine – his 'cult of faded things', where outer landscapes tell of inner mood (the soul becomes 'an exquisite landscape'), the vocabulary of which is formed by suggestion and instilled by the character of colour.[30] Both paintings figure symbolic presences to insinuate disintegrating or unstable realities. In *The hot sands, Mustapha, Algiers* rose petals fall from a wilting flower in a vase foregrounded against an expansive terrace. A distant figure looking towards the sea in a gesture of withdrawal echoes the sentiments visualised in the flowers. The poetic metaphor is heightened through the sensuous suggestions of the fragrance of flowers and the heat of the sun through a rose-tinted white palette, and the respite of the background water and invading violet shadows. While the work's title references the ambient qualities of place, the overall tone of the painting is the melancholic mood of departure.

Moonlight at Mustapha, the nocturnal counterpart to *The hot sands*, is similarly composed of fleeting appearances. The white, moon-washed terrace, where a shrouded figure hovers among unweighted pillars, is tempered by a vibrant cobalt night sky. Earlier in the year Conder had explored the expressive powers of a white palette in his paintings of Yport's cliffs, but here the pallid tone instils a mood of mystery. The poet WB Yeats referred to the 'faint mixed tints of Conder' and '*Mayday*' 1892, a work produced on Conder's return to France, is another of these fading images, in which a figure taking in the fragrance of blossoms is barely registered in the hazy, allusive landscape.[31] It has been noted that Conder's artistic vision (although not his style) had already matured by the time he left Australia for Paris.[32] In this context the image of the landscape's oblivion in *Hot wind* is reinforced in these three works, where reality softly dissolves into a dream state.

An example of the enduring influence of Conder's work on his colleagues can be witnessed in a handful of paintings by Streeton in the 1890s which present the female as a Symbolist subject. *Scheherazade* 1895 depicts a haloed but lasciviously draped nude as a mystical femme fatale. In *Ariadne* 1895, with its local rendition of light and colour (including Streeton's signature Sydney ocean blue) the abandoned Ariadne is almost overlooked in her Arcadian setting, as her drapery merges with the white sand. Yet on closer inspection, the mournful figure transposes the mood of her sun-filled surroundings through the enigma of her intense loneliness. This

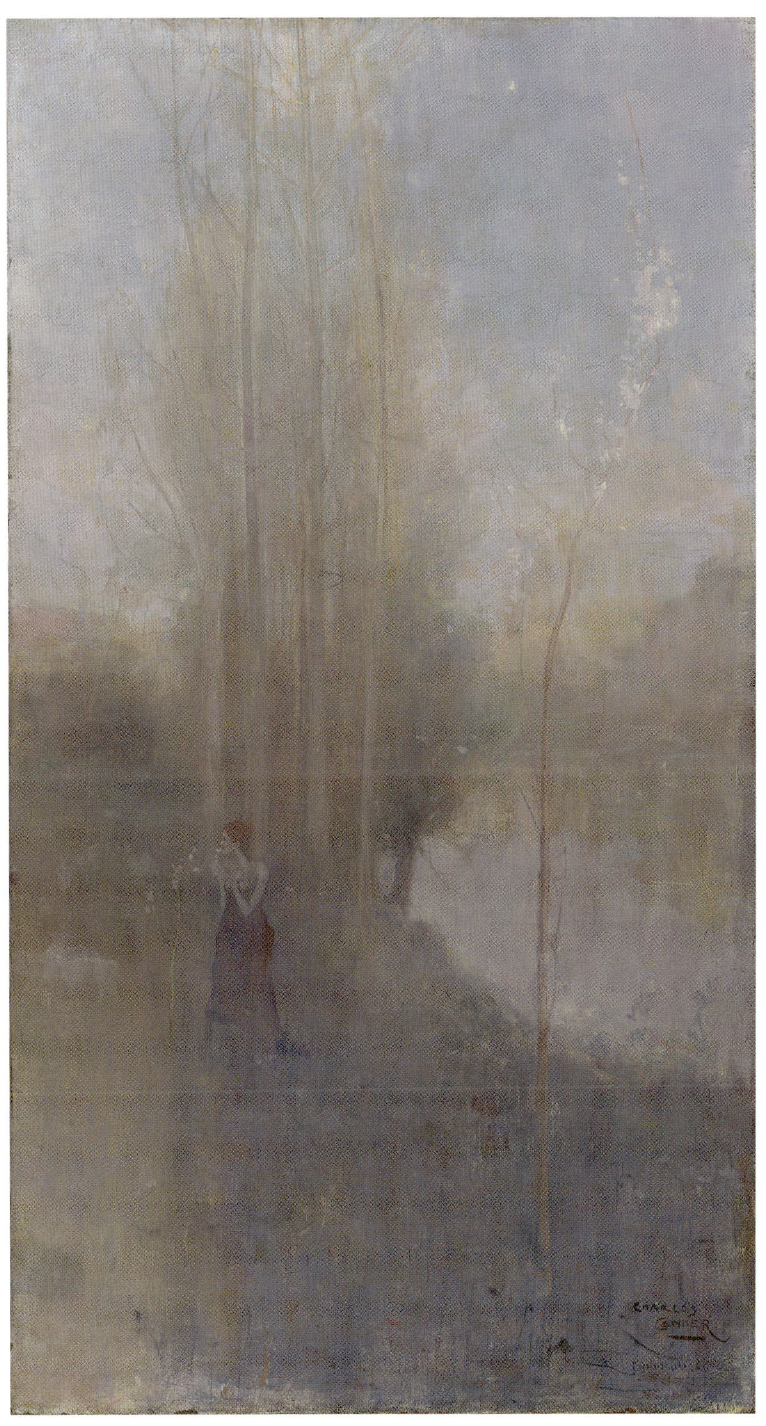

Charles Conder *'Mayday'* 1892, oil on canvas
National Gallery of Australia, Canberra. Purchased 1978

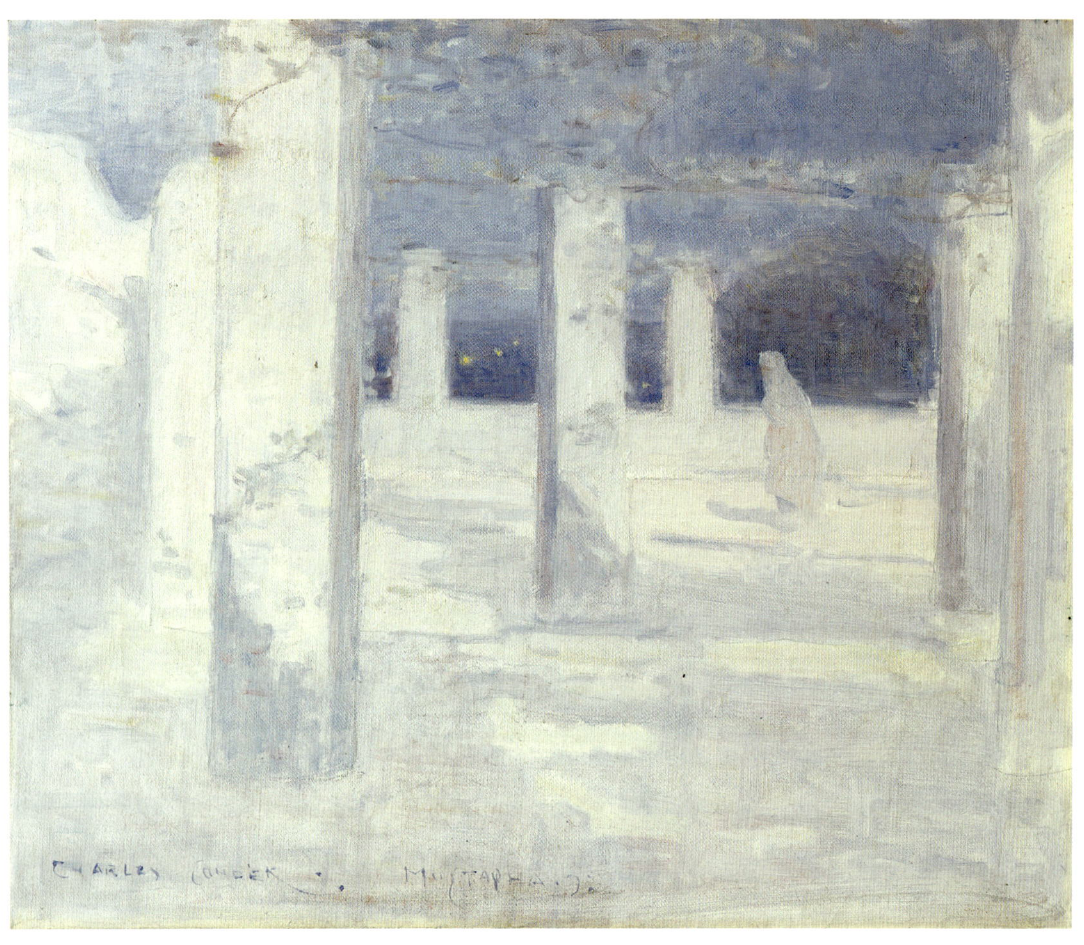

Charles Conder *Moonlight at Mustapha* 1892, oil on canvas

 Philip Bacon Collection, Brisbane

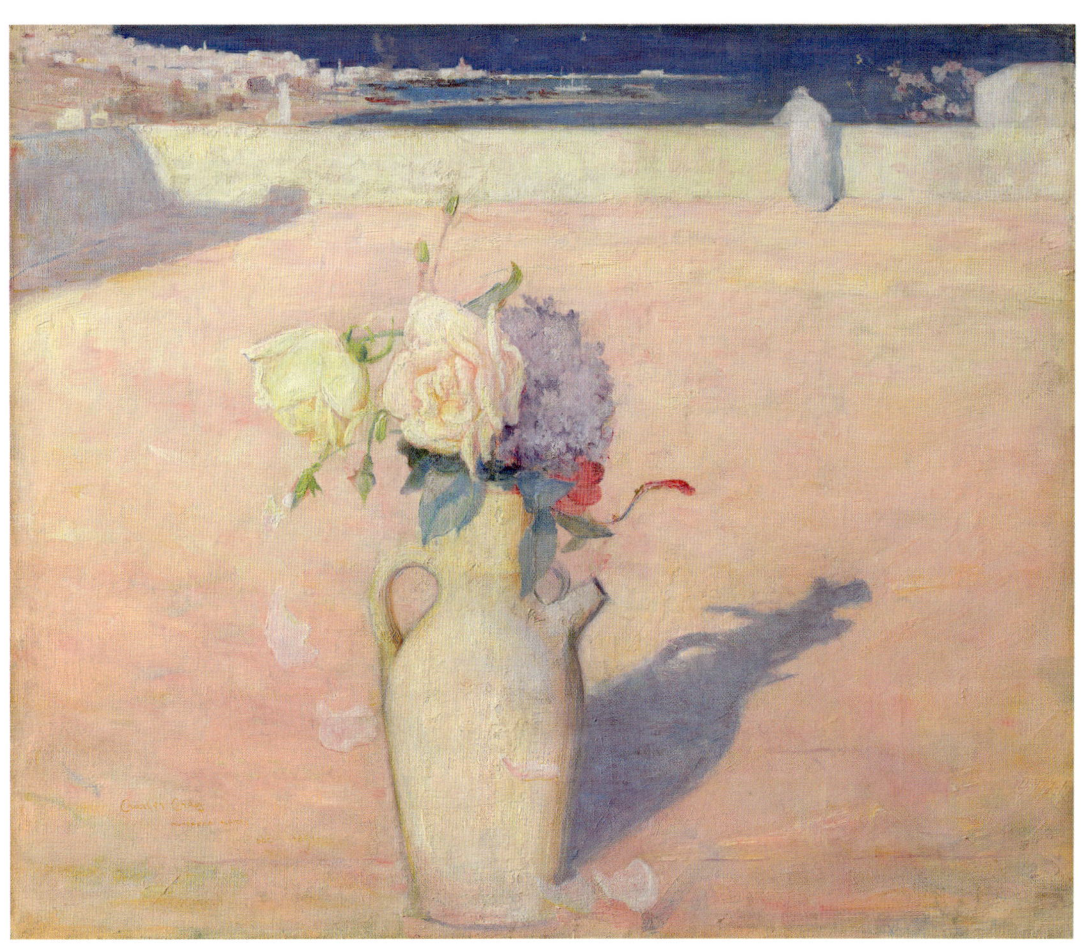

Charles Conder *The hot sands, Mustapha, Algiers* 1891, oil on canvas
Art Gallery of New South Wales. Purchased with assistance from Katies 1982

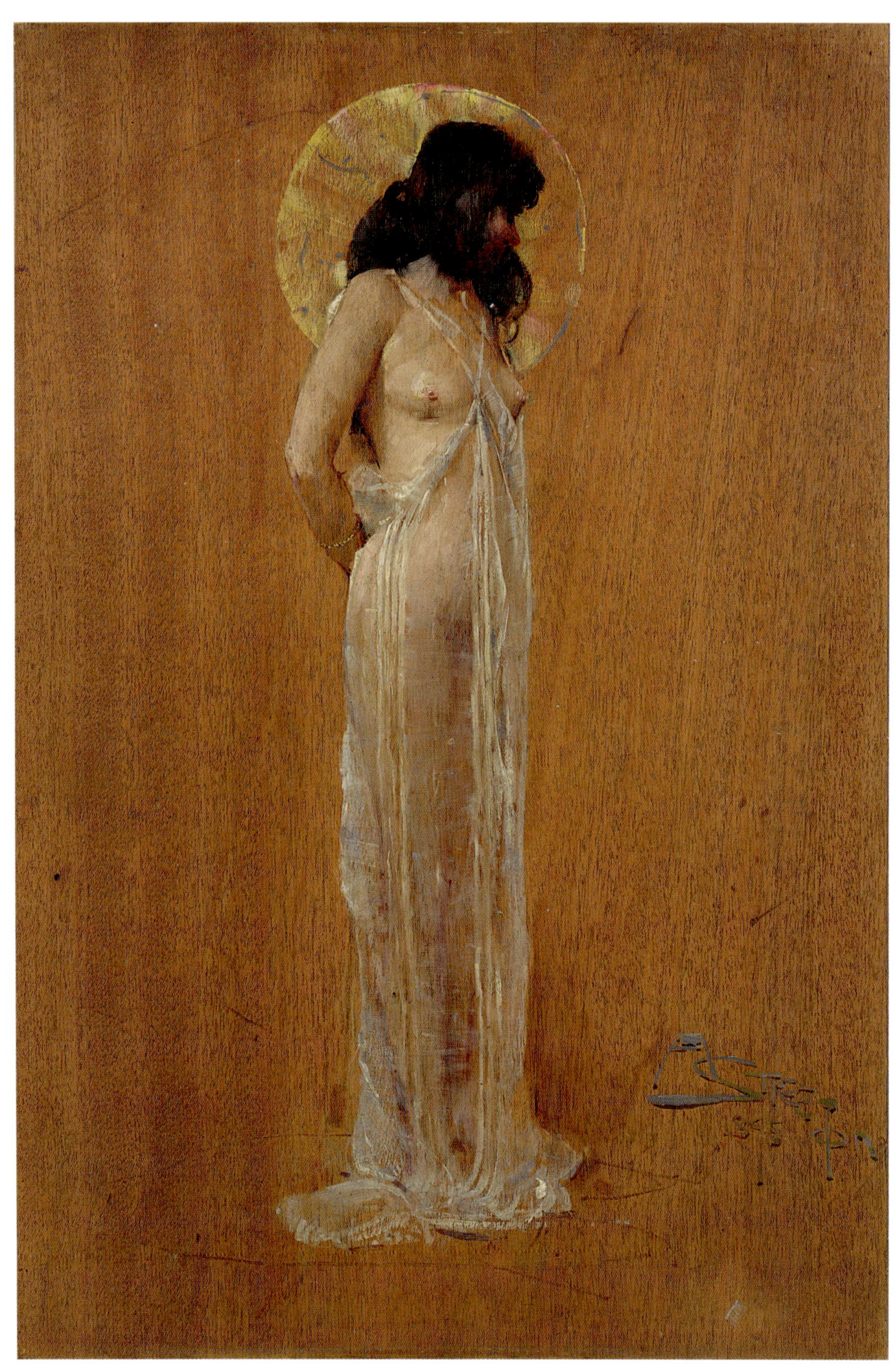

Arthur Streeton *Scheherazade* 1895, oil on cedar panel
National Gallery of Victoria, Melbourne. The Joseph Brown Collection, presented through the NGV Foundation by
Dr Joseph Brown AO OBE, Honorary Life Benefactor, 2004

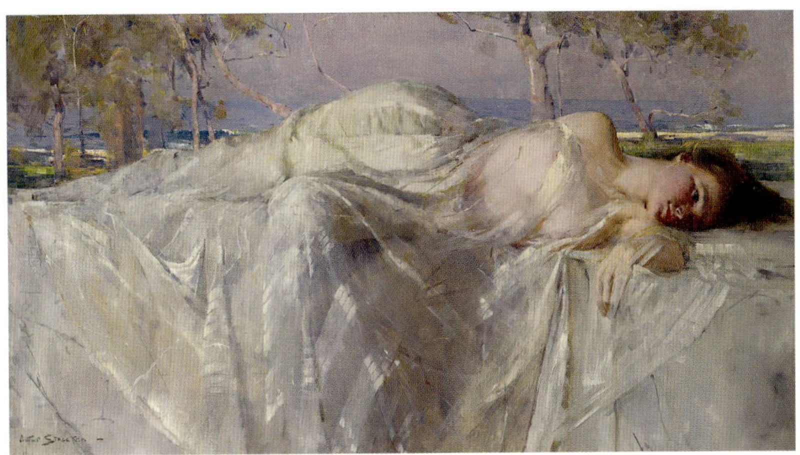

disjuncture between figure and place is also evident in *Oblivion* 1895 (based on Alfred Tennyson's poem *The lotus-eaters*) in which a woman appearing as if under hypnotic spell is set against a backdrop of the Australian coastline. The foreshortened perspective renders the figure's light-infused dream-state as monumental. Such paintings reveal how Streeton held to literal form, which was somewhat at odds with Symbolist emphasis, but applied the expressive suggestion of the female figure to elaborate on the poetry of place.

Tom Roberts produced a handful of paintings in the late 1890s that similarly position female figures in poetic states. In works such as *Jealousy* 1889 (Art Gallery of New South Wales) or *Mrs LA Abrahams* 1888 (National Gallery of Victoria), Roberts refers to the Aesthetic ornaments of his studio as fashionable interior décor. In *A study of Jephthah's daughter* 1899, he emphasised Aesthetic design to reinforce the exotic orientation of the figure. *A study of Jephthah's daughter* was exhibited at the Society of Artists exhibition in Sydney in 1899 along with *A Circe* (now lost) and *Adagio* c1893. These paintings represent the sum of Roberts's late attention to Symbolist form. *Adagio* is the inspired climax of a series of female profile portraits that essentialised the poetic features of the subject. In *Adagio*, Roberts elaborates on the figure through the Symbolist correlation between music, emotion and suggestive visual form. The evocative backdrop of a sublimely coloured sunset and darkened landscape alludes to the mysterious, emotional force of slow-turning music. The space of the work is radically condensed between figure and backdrop. With a cropped composition that prefigures the framing of modernist photography, the figure is depicted with intimate closeness while appearing psychologically remote.[33] Roberts's association with the bohemian

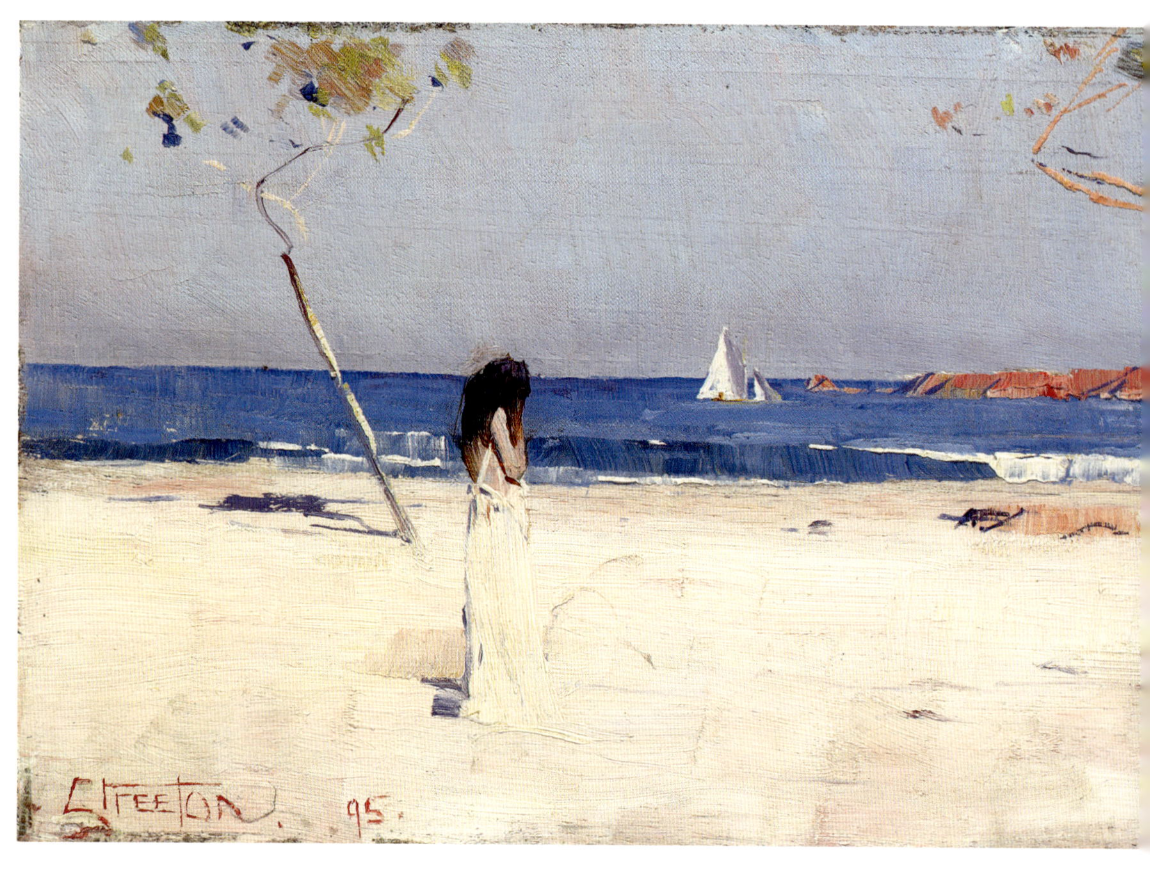

Arthur Streeton *Ariadne* **1895**, oil on wood panel
The estate of the late Stuart Johnston, Sydney

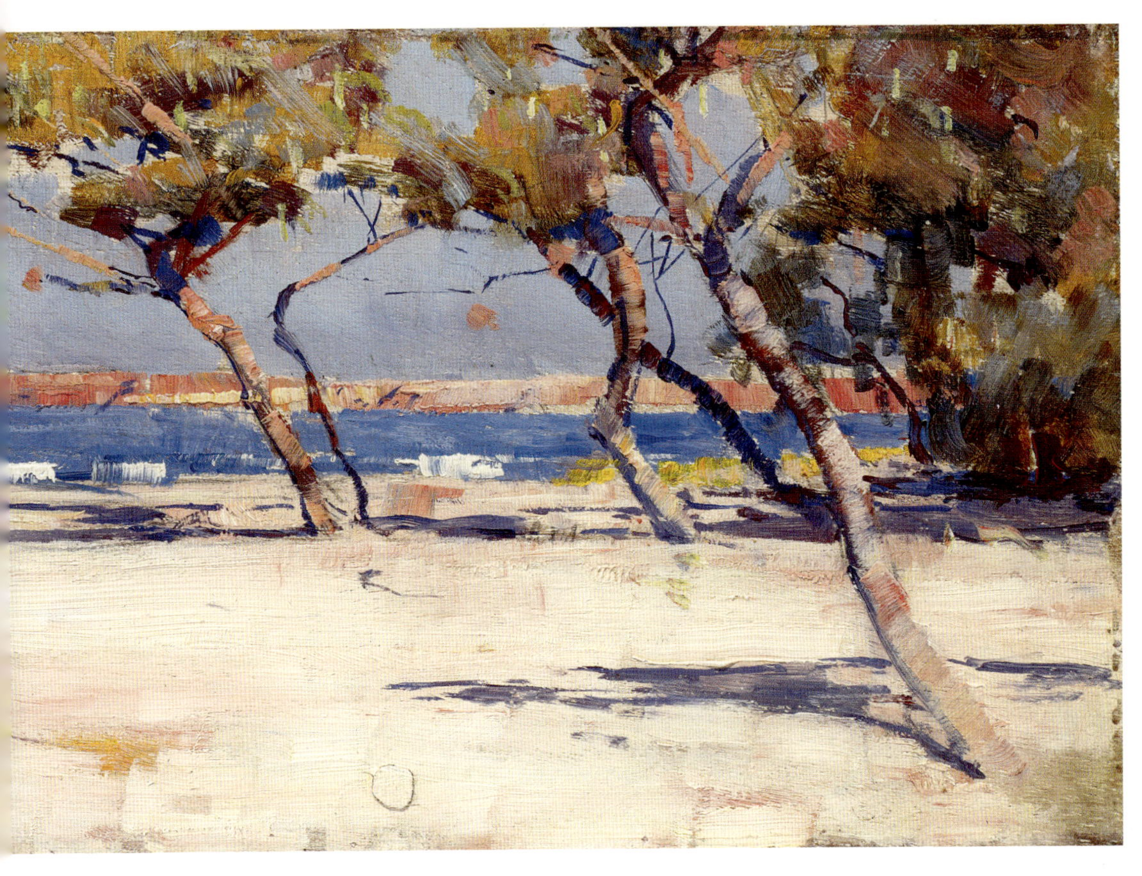

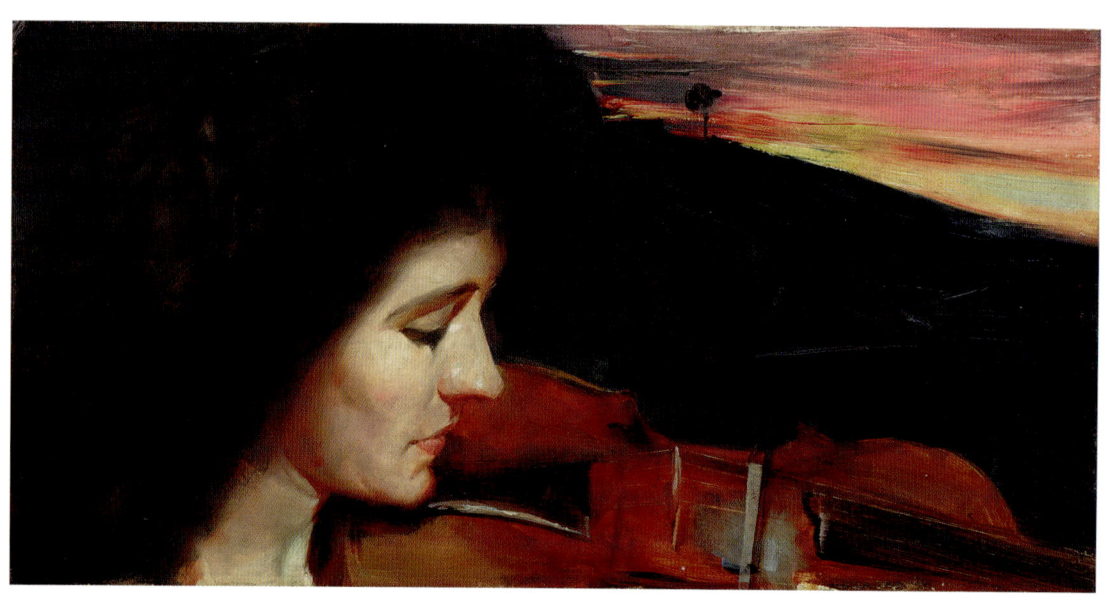

(above) **Tom Roberts** *Adagio* c1893, oil on paperboard
Art Gallery of New South Wales. Purchased 1947

(opposite) **Tom Roberts** *A study of Jephthah's daughter* 1899, oil on canvas
Art Gallery of New South Wales. Purchased 1899

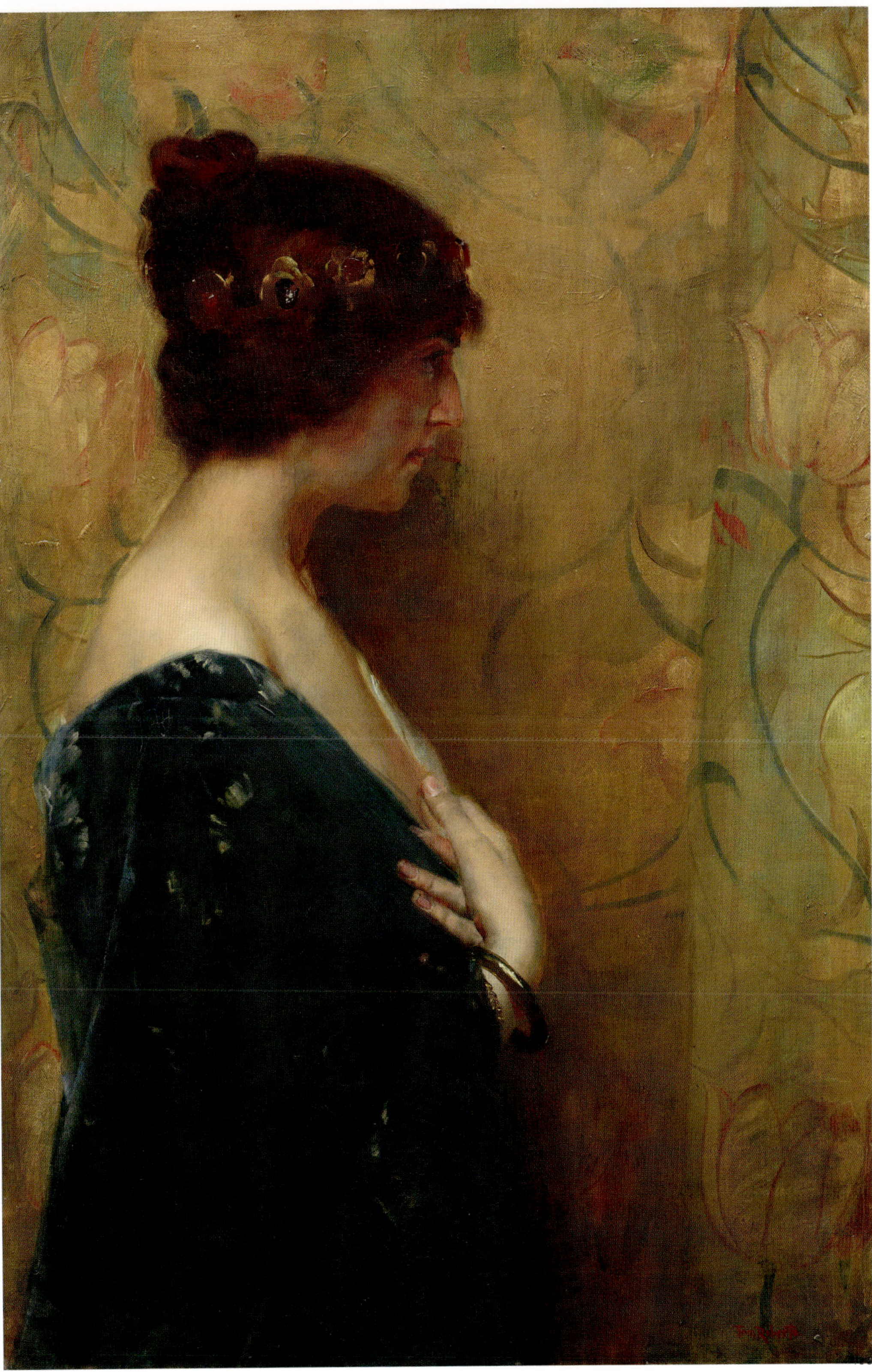

composer George Marshall-Hall may have encouraged this leap into imaginative rendering of musically inspired form. *Adagio* is distinct in Roberts's oeuvre, in which the depiction of the landscape is momentarily transformed to reference the intensity of a state of mind.

Sydney Long: Arcadian myth and the decorative landscape

In Sydney in the 1890s Sydney Long produced a series of works that use Art-Nouveau stylisation to create an emotionally charged and mythologically enhanced Australian environment. Long was the leading artist in the shift towards a decorative vision of landscape in Australian painting.[34] Praised locally, he was also recognised by the British Symbolist-oriented journal *Studio* as a painter of 'imaginative design', distinct in Australian art.[35] Long's practice reflected the journal's endorsement of Art Nouveau as a style that emerged from Symbolist thought and the principles of the Arts and Crafts Movement as an expression of the modern age. The articles and reproductions in *Studio* were an influential stimulus for Symbolist practices in the 1890s. Along with the example lent by artists returning from overseas, *Studio* was a crucial source for Long, given that he had not travelled outside New South Wales at a time when his works resonated with internationally dispersed contemporary practices. By the end of the century Long's search for modern forms of expression to envisage localised experience resulted in some of the key achievements of Symbolist expression in Australia.

Although Long absorbed the lessons of naturalism and plein-air painting at the Julian Ashton Art School in the early 1890s, his previous artistic training remained entrenched in his maturing artistic vision. In his hometown of Goulburn in the 1880s, Long had trained in decorative design, painting 'pretty things on satin'. His subsequent forays into painting focused on enigmatic lighting, including the early gothically illuminated *The river house* 1888 (private collection) and the atmospheric nocturnal scene *Circular Quay by moonlight* c1890 (not located).[36] *By tranquil waters*, Long's successful artistic debut at the Art Society of NSW in 1894, merged the principles of his Ashton School-training with his own mood-driven expression of place.[37] Long used the decorative dimensions of an Impressionist language to emphasise an idyllic space and otherworldly mood. His 1897 masterpiece *Spirit of the plains* established his Symbolist vision of landscape, one no doubt inspired in part by his association with Symbolist poet Christopher Brennan in Sydney.[38] Long's art had shifted to mythological terrain, portraying a female nymph piping a chorus of dancing brolgas through a golden landscape, the shimmering tones of which colour the mystical moment. The Art-Nouveau rhythm of the trees reinforces the birds' graceful, sensuous dance. In the synthesis of visual

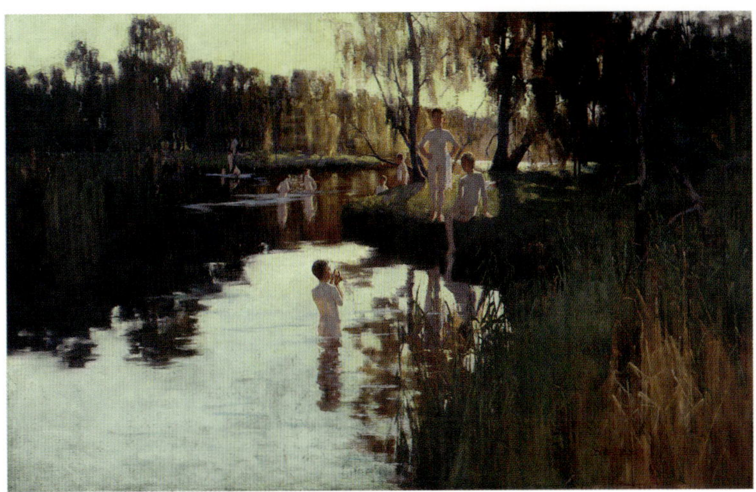

form and musical allusion, Long likens the horizontal sweep of rising birds
to a musical score imprinted on the landscape.

In *Pan* 1898, Long's sequel to *Spirit of the plains*, the bush spirit is replaced by
the pipe-playing god of Arcadia. Long specifically aligns the reference of natural
abundance and liberating abandon of Classical Arcadia with the Australian
landscape. *Pan* can be seen in the context of nationalist rhetoric equating the
Federated nation with a modern Utopia. However, Long later claimed the source
for the painting to be Elizabeth Barrett Browning's poem *A musical instrument*
1860, in which Pan creates his reed pipes at the expense of nature, suggesting a
metaphor for the artist's aesthetic alteration of the environment in the creative
process.[39] Consequently, *Pan* is a landscape of artistic transformation – an image
not of the landscape itself, but of the creative forces shaping it. Musical references
again shape the gum trees in their linear patterning, echoed in the curves and crooks
of the dancing bodies. The work is aligned with the spirit of Stéphane Mallarmé's
faun; the Symbolist poetic embodiment of bucolic liberty and erotic frisson
that saw Pan and his pagan flock recur as fin-de-siècle emblems in both art and
magazines like *Studio*. *Pan*, along with *Spirit of the plains*, signalled a clear aesthetic
and thematic shift in Long's practice which by the century's end was categorised in
Symbolist terms as 'contemplative, philosophic and a trifle metaphysical [dealing]
more with the abstract than the concrete side of things'.[40]

The valley 1898, a work exhibited with *Pan* in 1898, highlights the qualities of
Long's abstraction in panoramic form. It is composed of broad, flattened areas of
decoratively enhanced colour, including modulating mauves and blues that invoke

Sydney Long *By tranquil waters* 1894, oil on canvas
Art Gallery of New South Wales. Purchased 1894

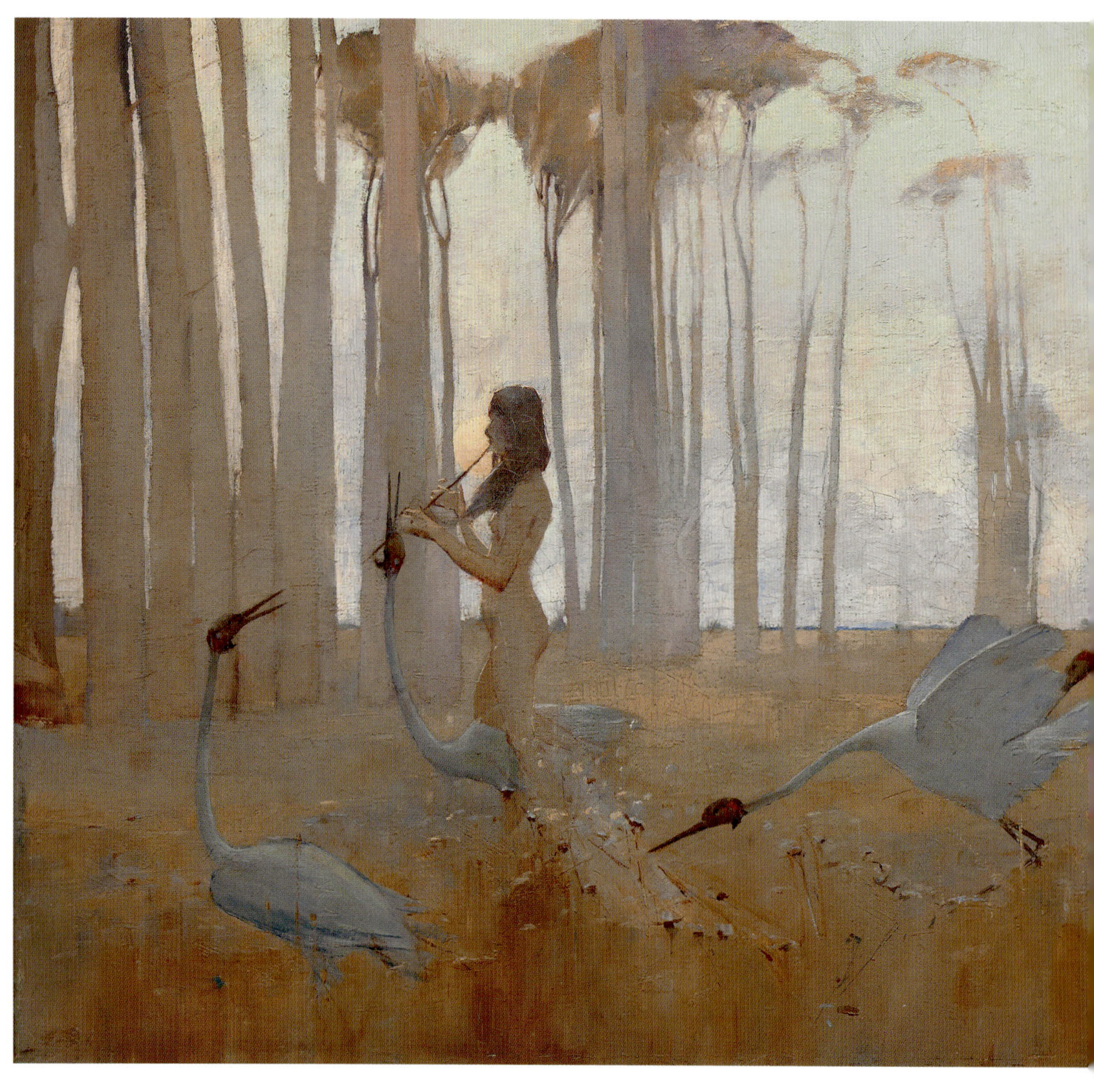

Sydney Long *Spirit of the plains* **1897,** oil on canvas on wood (see detail pages 2–3)
Queensland Art Gallery, Brisbane. Gift of William Howard-Smith in memory of his grandfather Ormond Charles Smith 1940

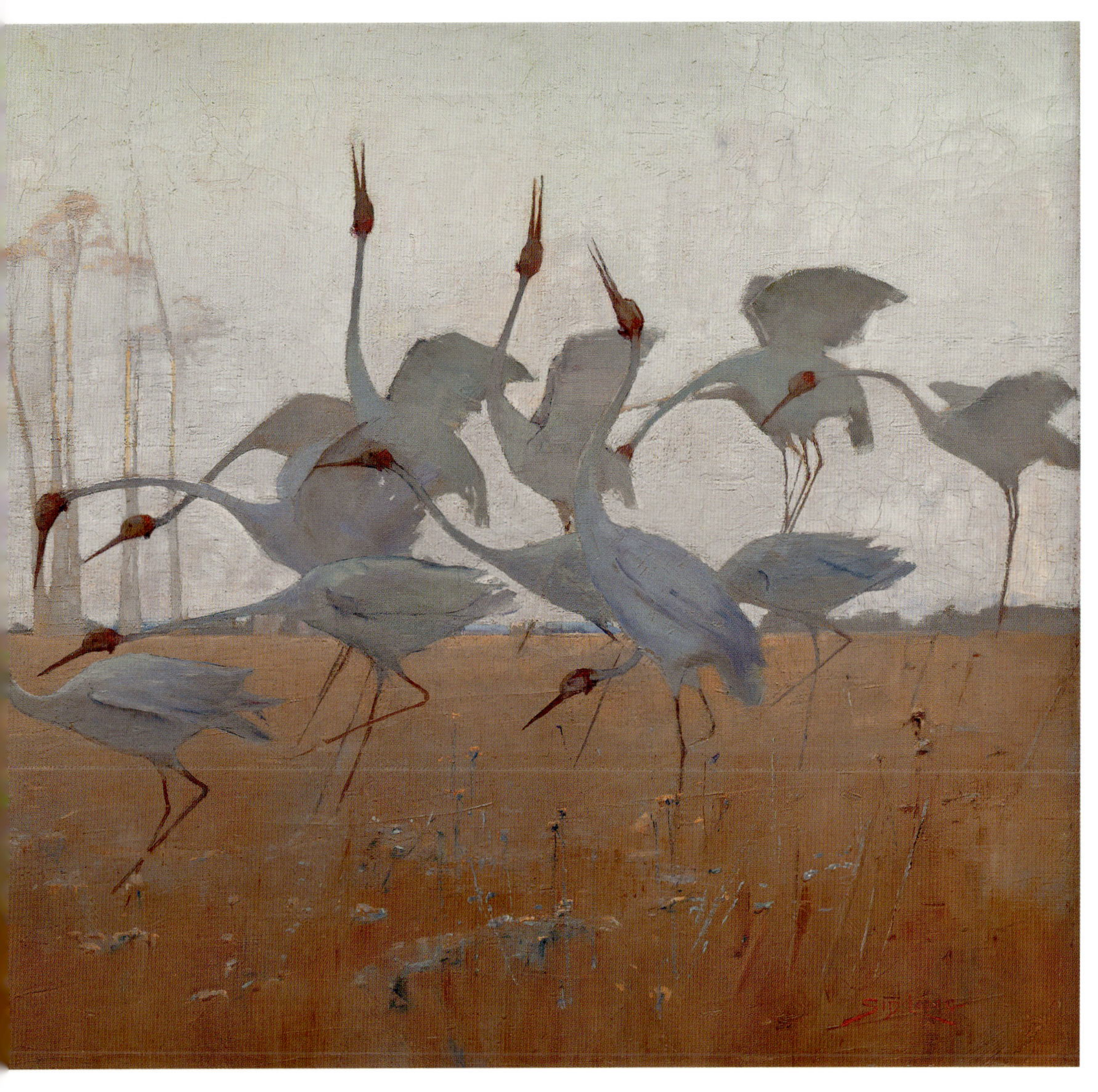

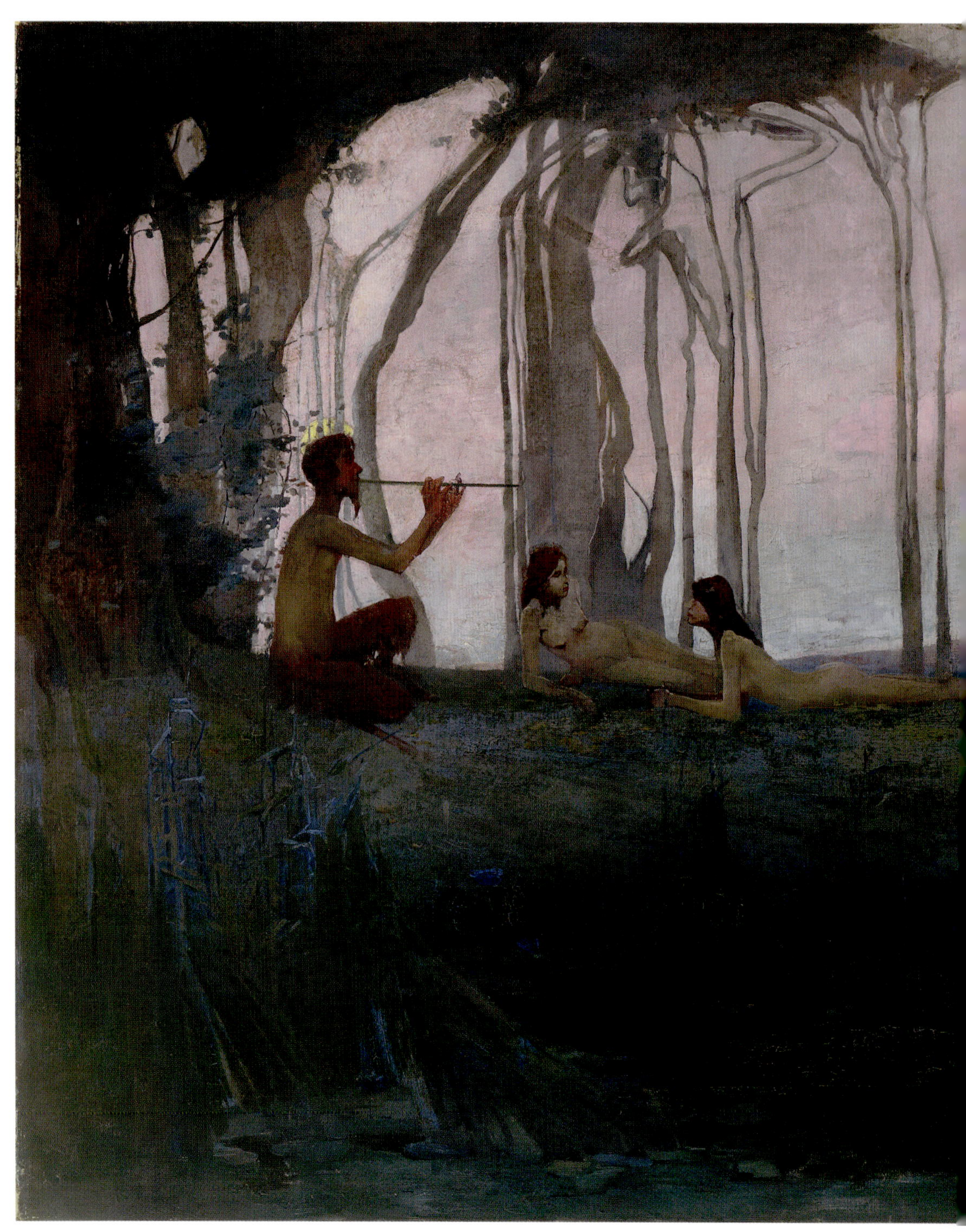

Sydney Long *Pan* **1898**, oil on canvas (see detail page 153)
Art Gallery of New South Wales. Gift of JR McGregor 1943

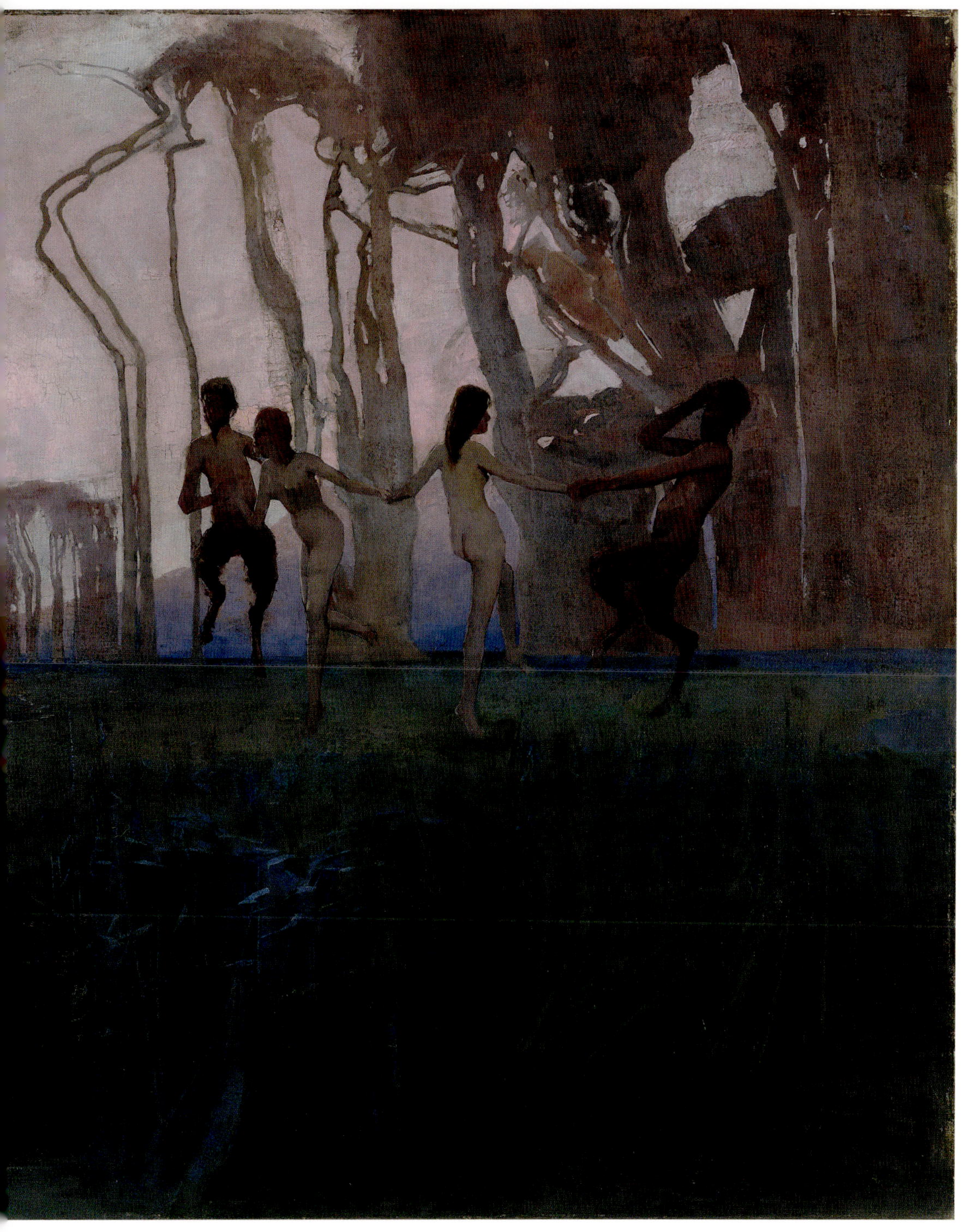

the enchantment of twilight. This sweeping decorative vision is prefaced by a cluster of Long's signature arabesque gum trees, set in the foreground's lilting slope. In *(Landscape with irises)* c1898 Long condenses these same elements into a Japanese-style microcosmic view of nature. Using the iris as an Aesthetic emblem, the image of which is superimposed with paper fragments of literary verse, the painting elucidates Long's Symbolist conception of landscape as one of decorative, poetic formulation.

The stylistic innovations of Art Nouveau developed in France with the aim of investing the private sphere of the home with ornaments of emotionally and imaginatively driven design.[41] Art Nouveau endowed craft and design objects with patterns based on nature's organic sweep as well as being emblematic of the movements of the psyche. Long would have witnessed the style's application through the Arts and Crafts Movement and commercial design in Australia, with objects such as Amy Vale's *Bowl with lillypilly design* c1897, Ada Newman's *Jug with solanum design* c1897 and Mildred Creed's later *Gumleaf pendant and chain* c1914. Art Nouveau also became a feature of artists' book designs; illustrations by Reginald Ward Sturgess and Violet Teague evidence how this style visually extended the dream worlds of texts that are removed from the everyday world, creating books as gem-like personalised objects.

In the new century, when Long's attention to experimental art forms diminished, the subjects of his late-century successes remained entrenched in his imagination. He returned to the theme of Pan in the painting *Fantasy* c1916–17 (a painting that he reworked from his earlier *Pastorale* 1909), a non-nationally specific landscape with flattened form and colour, marking the extreme of Long's ventures into abstraction. Demonstrating the Arts and Crafts ideal of the exchange between painting and the decorative arts, Mildred Lovett developed the composition of Long's earlier *Pastorale* in a vase design, where the painting's flattened Art-Nouveau pattern is transposed by the rhythmic rise of the object's form. These works are perhaps the most successfully realised of the collaborative ventures between art and craft forms in Australia, both developing the common composition and language of decorative art within the distinctions of their chosen medium.

Long harnessed the qualities of Art-Nouveau expression to encapsulate mystery in the figurative form. In *Sadder than a single star that sets at twilight in a land of reeds* 1899, he draws on the cryptic female of Symbolist art, also demonstrated locally in Alice Muskett's work. Long knew Muskett from the Julian Ashton School, and the Society of Artists. In 1898, when Muskett exhibited *A lost halo*, Long was in sync with its Symbolist intentions, displaying *Spirit of the plains* at the same exhibition. When Long was shifting to Symbolist realms in his art, he would have noted Muskett's capacity to contain suggestive meaning in the figure.

Sydney Long *The valley* **1898**, oil on canvas
Art Gallery of South Australia, Adelaide. Elder Bequest Fund 1898

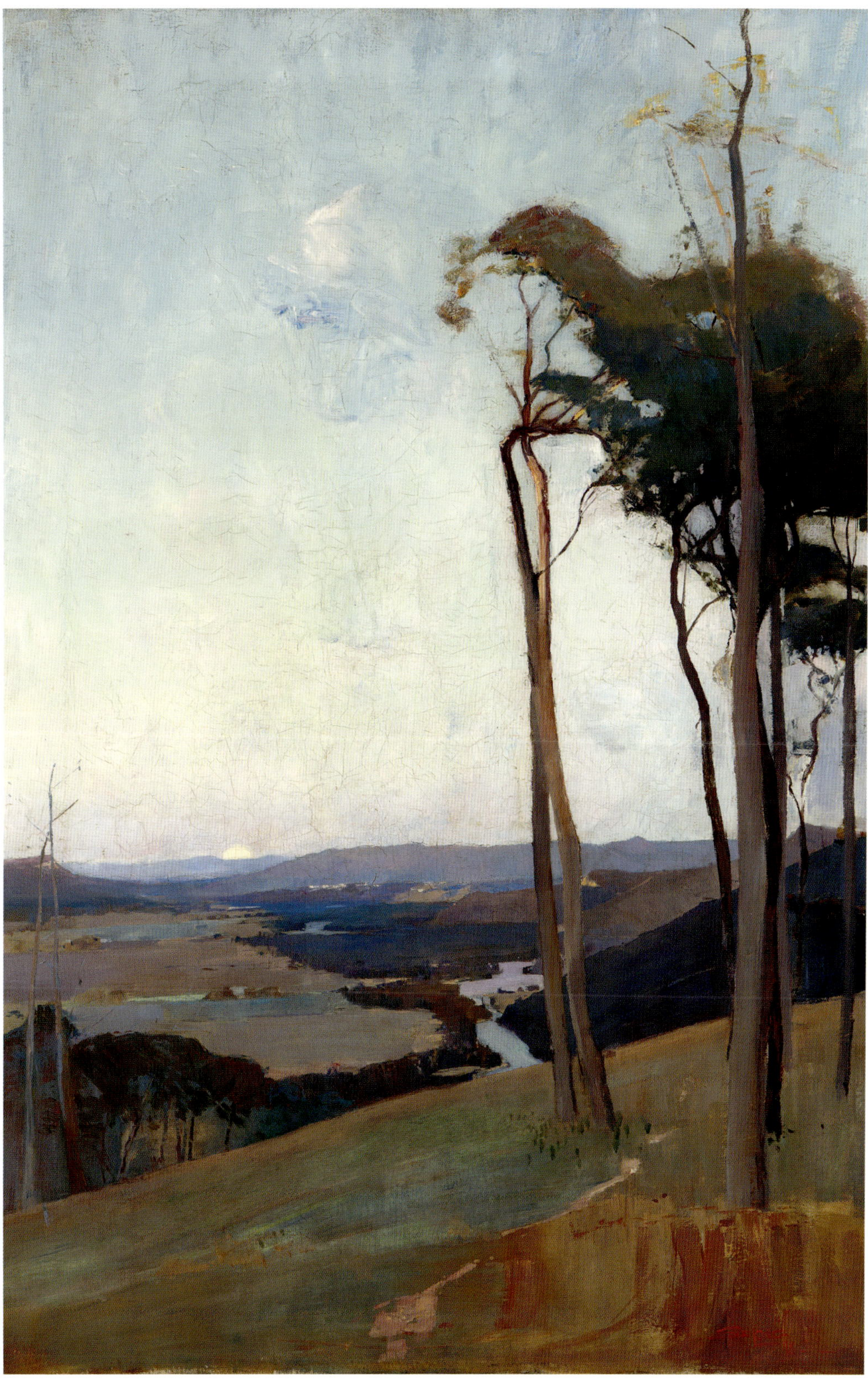

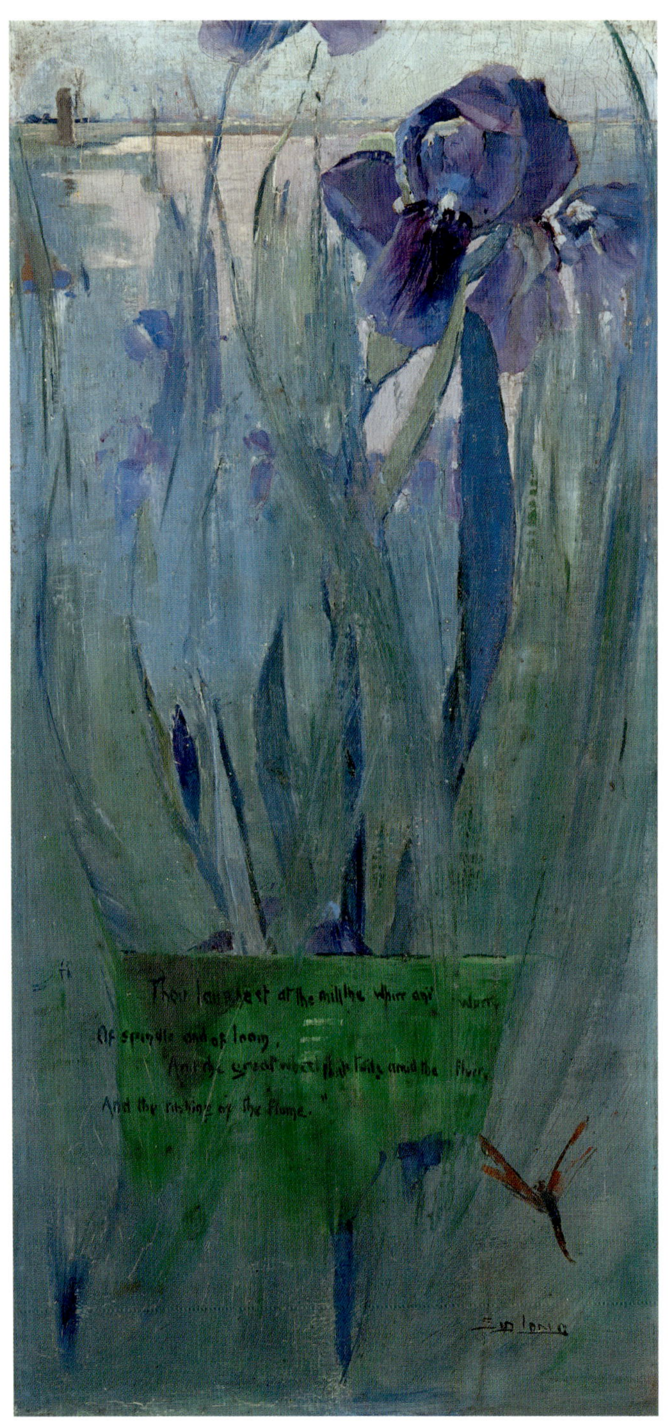

Sydney Long *(Landscape with irises)* c1898, oil on wood panel
Art Gallery of South Australia, Adelaide. On loan from the MJM Carter AO Collection 2006

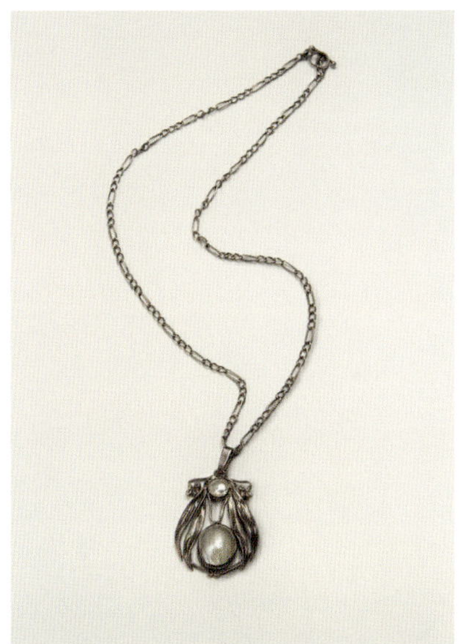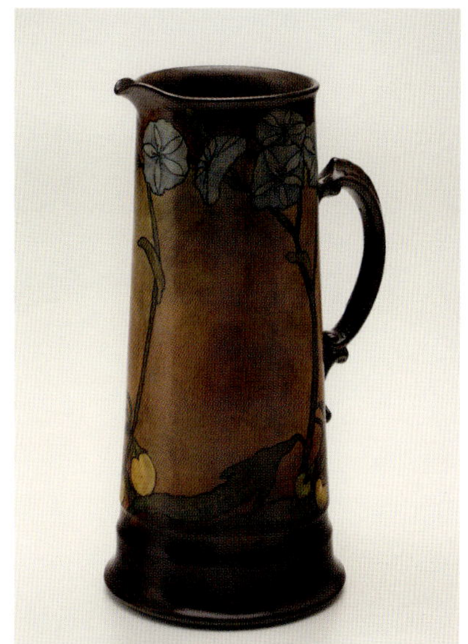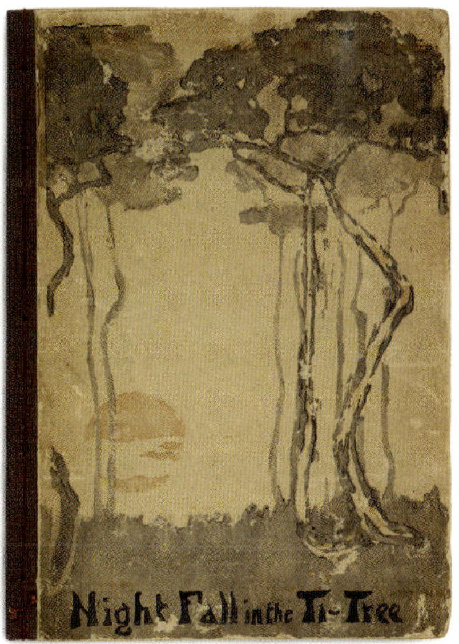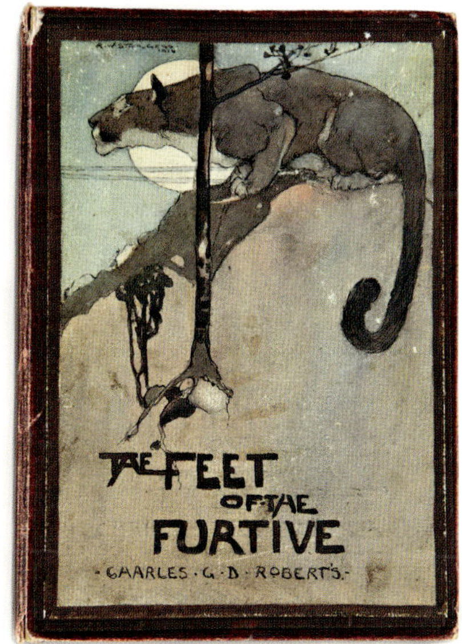

(clockwise from top left)

Mildred Creed *Gumleaf pendant and chain* c1914
Art Gallery of New South Wales. Purchased 1914

Ada Newman *Jug with solanum design* c1897, hand-painted porcelain
Art Gallery of New South Wales. Purchased 1910–12

RW Sturgess illustrations for Charles Roberts's *The feet of the furtive* 1916
Ballarat Art Gallery, Victoria. Gift of Beth Sinclair 1978

Violet Teague illustrations for Geraldine Rede's *Night fall in the ti-tree* 1905
Art Gallery of New South Wales. Purchased 1983

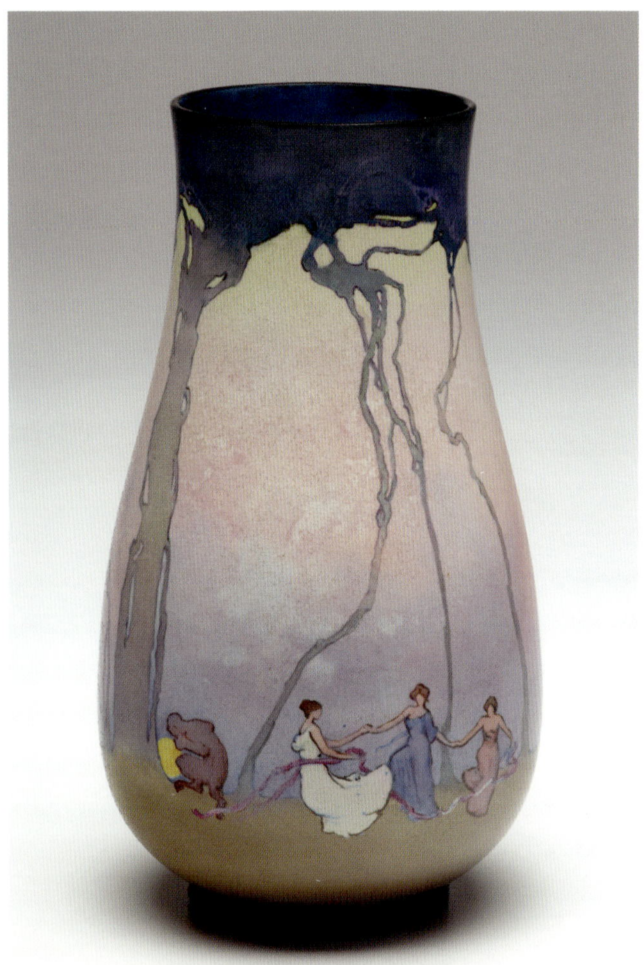

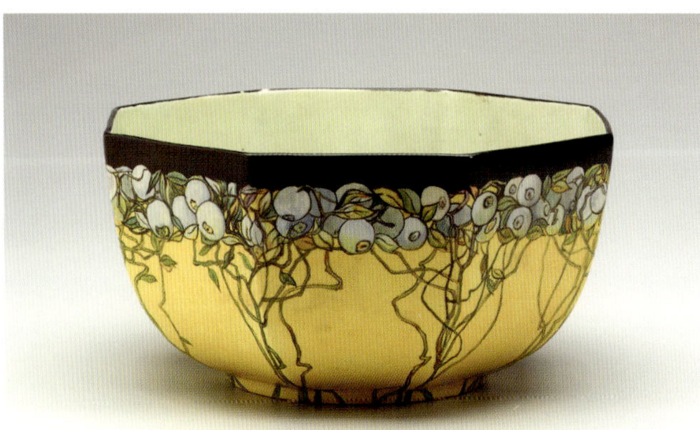

Mildred Lovett *Vase with pastoral design of dancing figures by Sydney Long* 1909, hand-painted porcelain
(see Long's *Fantasy* opposite)
Art Gallery of New South Wales. Purchased 1909
Amy Vale *Bowl with lillypilly design* c1897, hand-painted porcelain
Art Gallery of New South Wales. Purchased 1913

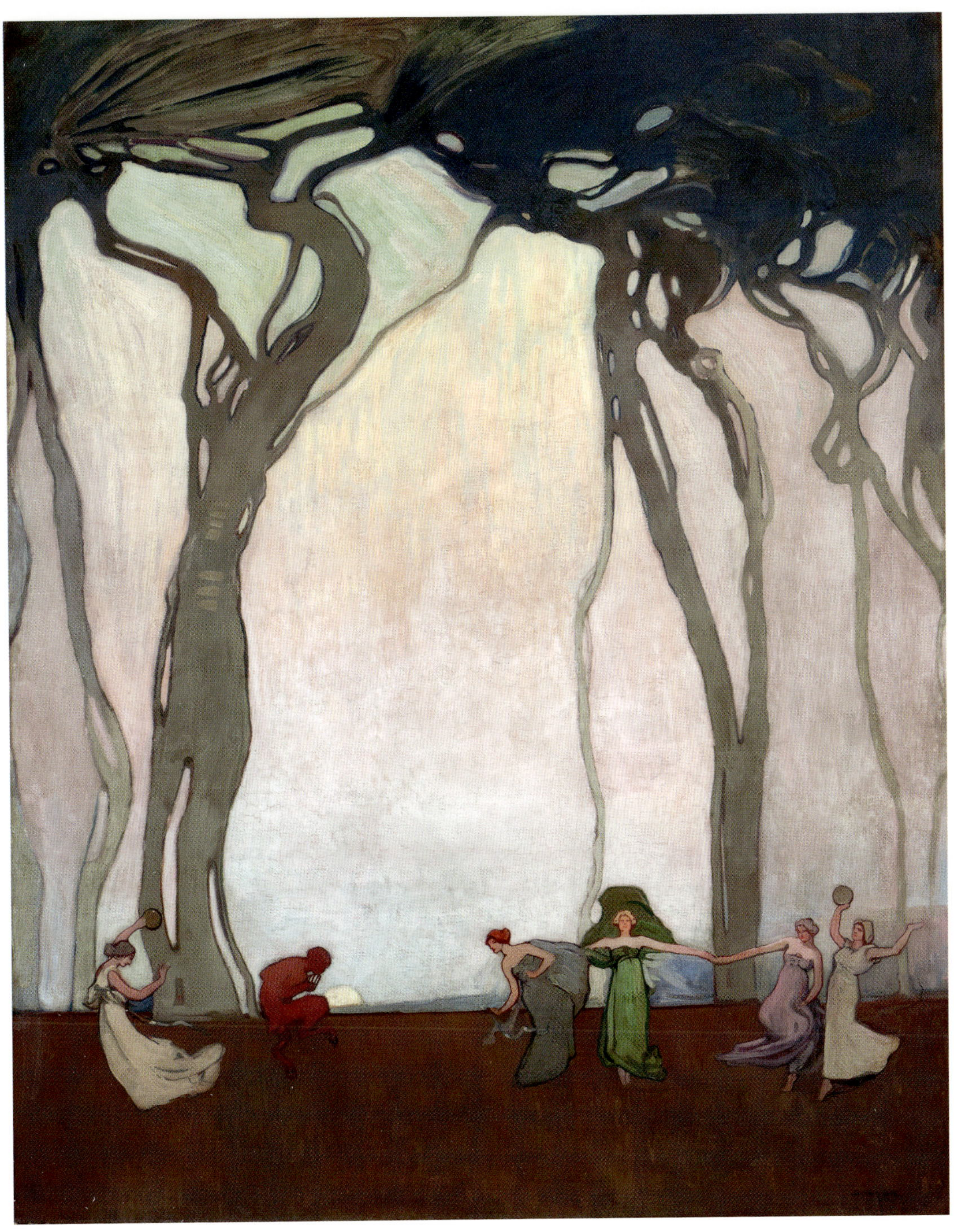

Sydney Long *Fantasy* c1916−17, oil on canvas (see detail pages 148−49)
Art Gallery of New South Wales. Purchased under the terms of the Florence Turner Blake Bequest 1971

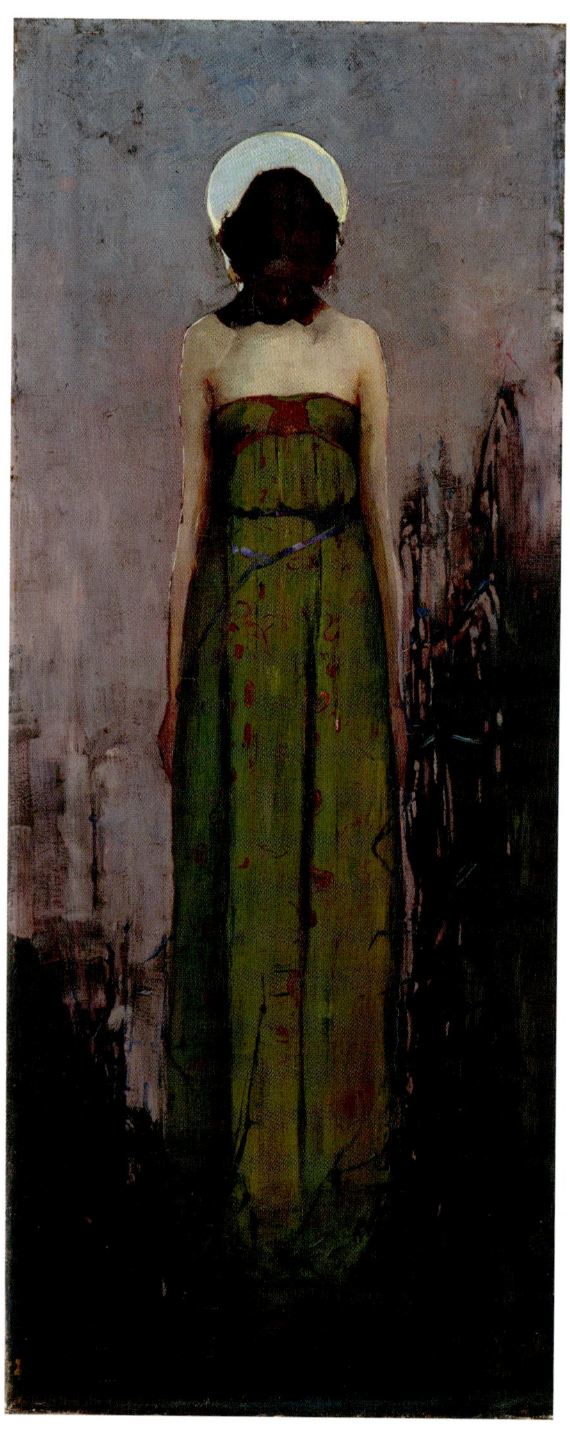

Sydney Long *Sadder than a single star that sets at twilight in a land of reeds* **1899,** oil on canvas (see detail page 157)
Art Gallery of New South Wales. Purchased 1899

Sadder than a single star is stripped of figurative detailing and presented as
a secret sprite of dusk. Rising like the reeds in her half-light environment, her
otherworldliness is accentuated by a vertical composition that propels her into
simplified and enigmatic form.

Artful atmospheres: Symbolism and photography

Decoratively shaped and poetically elucidated, Long's figure in *Sadder than a single
star* epitomises the fin-de-siècle spirit of Symbolist expression that was adopted
across a spectrum of art forms. The South Australian photographer Frederick
A Joyner's *A shaft of light* c1904, for example, echoed *Sadder than a single star*
by portraying a female figure rising from a bank of reeds with the bowed posture
of inward contemplation. The compositional similarities suggests how early century
Australian photographers followed an international pattern of exploring their
medium in terms of an aesthetic rather than functional practice. Symbolism
became one of the artistic languages drawn on by Pictorial photographers in their
move to redefine photography as an artistic practice that was differentiated from
the documentary, scientific and technical elements by which the medium was
largely recognised by the late nineteenth century. *A shaft of light* was part of a
series in which Joyner adopted rustic peasant figures that were reminiscent of
the subjects of Naturalism. Within this group of works, *A shaft of light* suggests
how the depiction of these figures was also amplified by a Symbolist emphasis on
female mystery. *Dawn* c1904 from this series features a woman from an unspecified
era who gazes intently forward as if peering toward an unknown destiny and the
work has been described as 'echoing the Pre-Raphaelites and their yearning for the
past pre-industrial age'.[42]

Australia's major Pictorialist Harold Cazneaux followed the work of the British
photographer Julia Margaret Cameron, particularly her pursuit of the psychological
enhancement of her portrait subjects. In *The orphan sisters* 1906 Cazneaux cropped
the conventional portrait composition for an intimate, close-up view of the two
figures. With softened tonal effects and dramatic shifts in light, their features are
paired by their dark mourning dress but their gazes are disparate and distanced,
shadowed by the inferences of their thoughts.

Both Joyner's and Cazneaux's development of Pictorial aesthetics was influenced
and encouraged by the South Australian photographer John Kauffmann. In
Kauffmann's pursuit of 'art photography' he produced a series of landscapes with
the quality of a dream state. *Nocturne* c1909 corresponds to the twilight ambience
of Whistler's paintings. The world is transcribed by chiaroscuro to become a place
where appearances are baffling and forms indeterminate. In an earlier photograph,

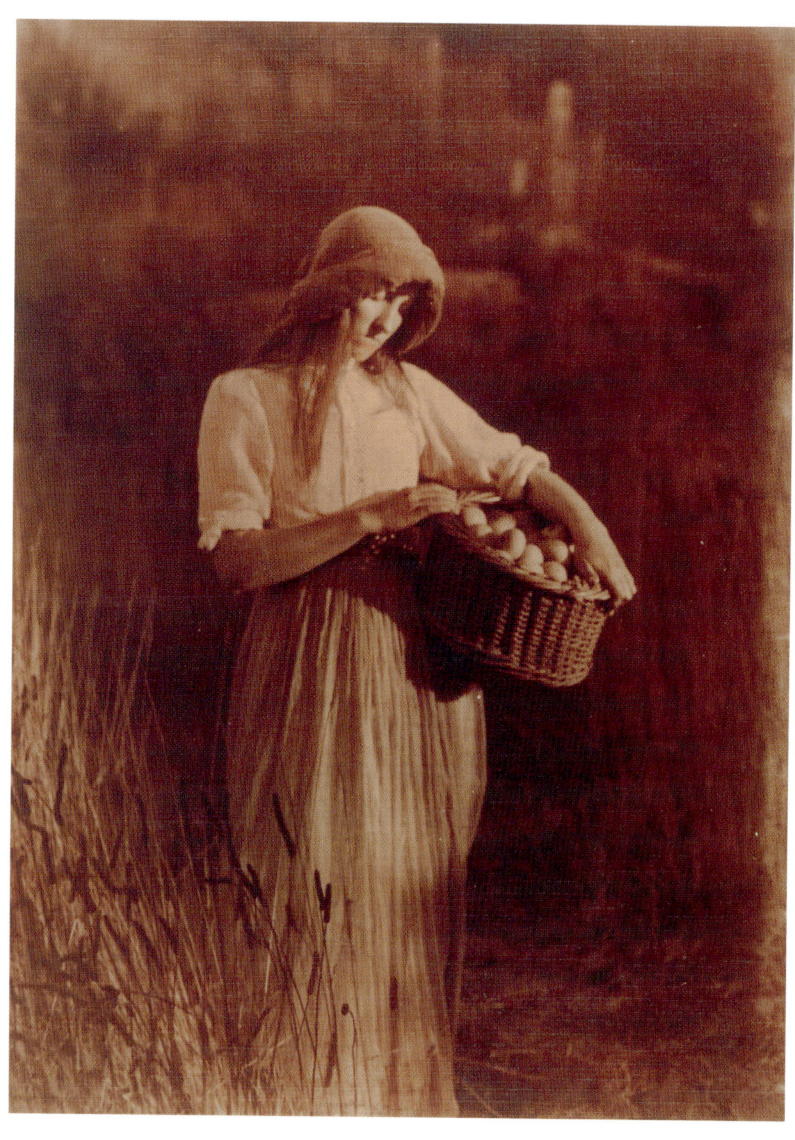

Frederick A Joyner *A shaft of light* c1904, gelatin silver photograph
Art Gallery of New South Wales. Gift of Mrs Max Joyner 1982

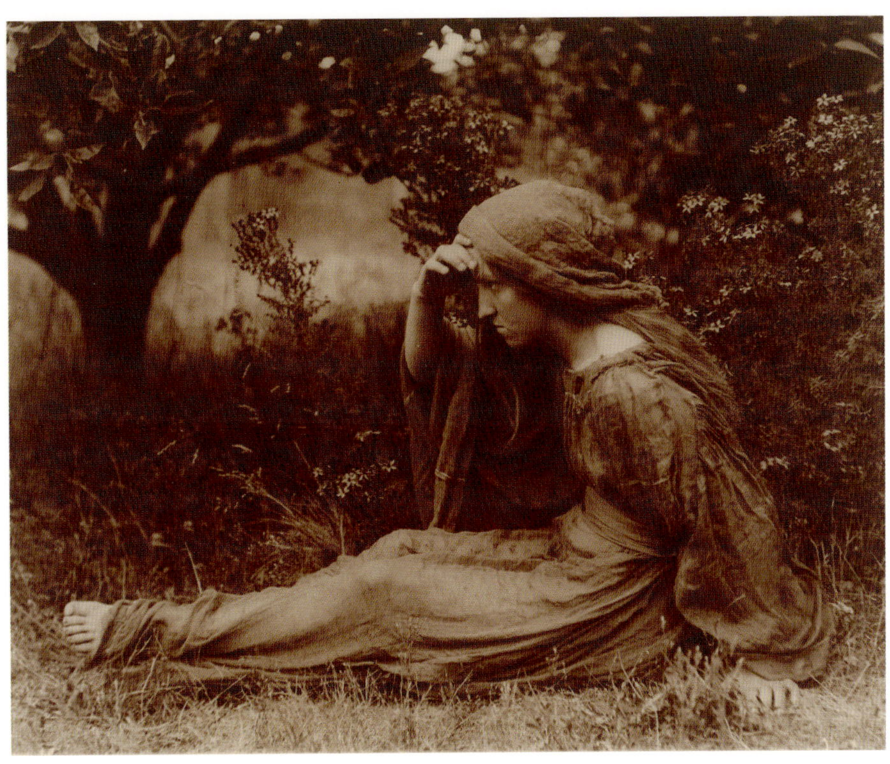

Frederick A Joyner *Dawn* c1904, gelatin silver photograph
Art Gallery of New South Wales. Gift of Mrs Max Joyner 1982

The Wetterhorn 1894, Kauffmann used sfumato effect to produce an image of sublime expanse, in which pinnacled mountain forms enigmatically rise beyond the picture frame as an unfolding force of light and shadow. Both works are carbon photographs, a process favoured by Kauffmann for its saturation of shadows with the potential for heightened emotional impact. Kauffmann's emotively driven view of nature was expanded in the lyrical *Fairy woods* c1920, where the twisting forms of nature interplay with light and shadow in Art-Nouveau movement. Like Long's stylised gum trees, Kauffmann depicts nature as a series of metaphysical rhythms.

George Lambert, Hugh Ramsay and the return to Europe

In a small, sketch-like composition George Lambert painted a scene that closely resembles the work of his studio partner Sydney Long. In *Syd Long bathing* c1896, Lambert uses his friend as a subject and also refers to Long's rendition of bathers in *By tranquil waters* where they feature as nymph-like beings that appear to radiate light from the glare of a backlit sun. Long's palette of vibrant blues and greens is referenced, and Lambert's condensed, intersecting, abstract landscape forms parallel Long's pursuit of decorative expression. The presence of a solitary figure strikes a somewhat uncanny note in this Arcadian setting. Lambert visually jots his impression of the style and substance of Long's art, probably pondering on how his friend's evolving aesthetic might inform his own.

Lambert departed Australia for Paris in 1900 after winning the NSW Society of Artists travelling scholarship with his 'large imaginative subject-picture', the dark pastoral fantasy *Youth and the river* 1899 (not located).[43] On leaving Australia, Lambert abandoned a Long-inspired vision and had his sights set on absorbing the art of Europe. En route to Paris he met the Melbourne artist Hugh Ramsay, who had graduated from the National Gallery School in 1897 and similarly yearned for the experience of France's artistic capital. Ramsay took with him from Melbourne a large incomplete canvas, *Consolation*, that he had begun in 1899 and which was based on John Keats's 1818–19 poem *Hyperion*. The work reinforces an element common to Symbolist practices in Australia: namely, the parallels that artists sought between poetry and visual form. In *Consolation*, Ramsay extracts from the poem an expression of yearning and grief, and gives physical charge to these sentiments through emphatic gesture. He revisited the canvas in Paris when his study of paintings at the Louvre propelled him to rework it with an almost baroque energy.

Like many Australian artists who travelled to Paris, Ramsay was immediately struck by the work of Puvis de Chavannes. *Venus and Adonis* c1901 is Ramsay's exercise in concentrating emotional expression into Puvis's aesthetic of simplified forms.

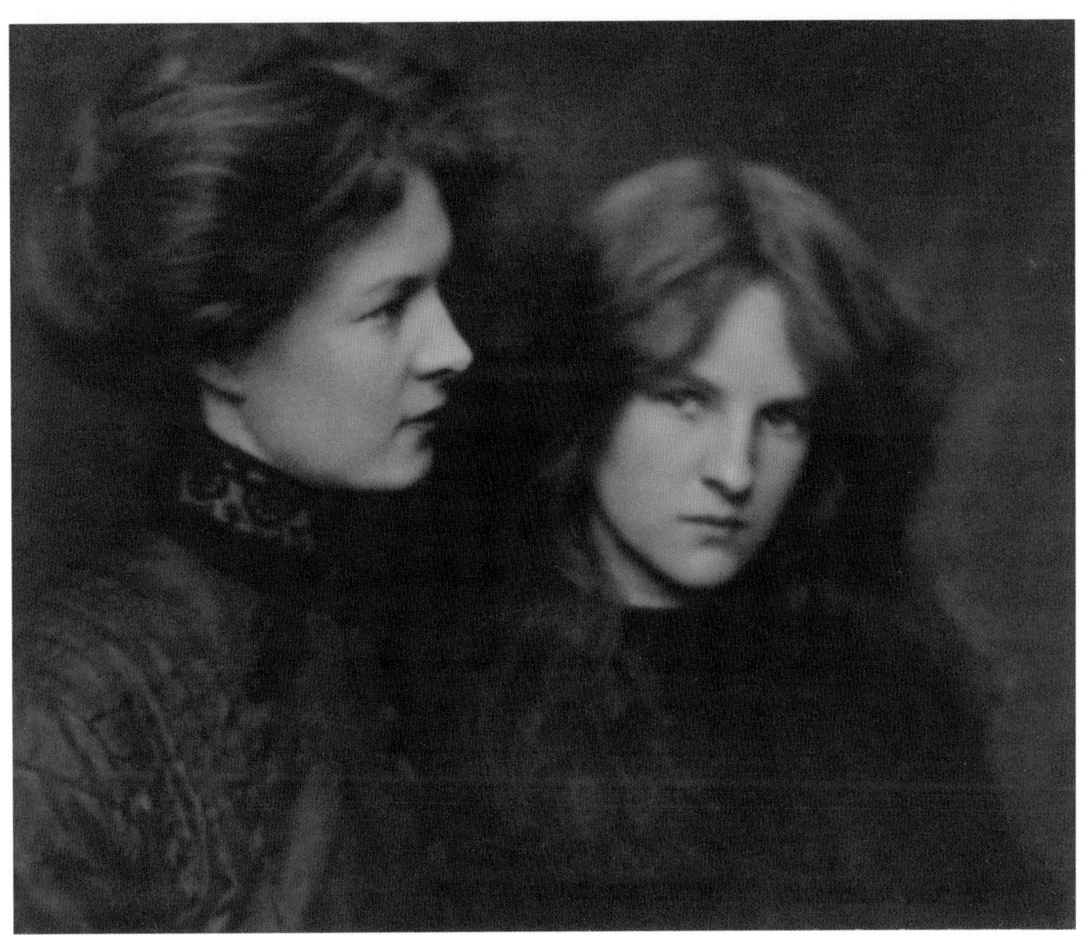

Harold Cazneaux *The orphan sisters* 1906, gelatin silver photograph
Art Gallery of New South Wales. Gift of the Cazneaux family 1975

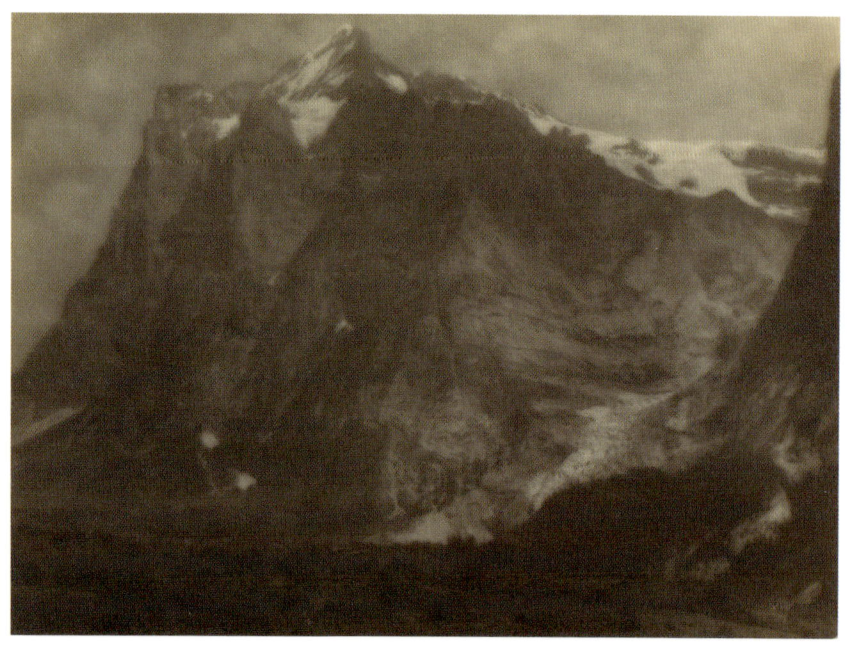

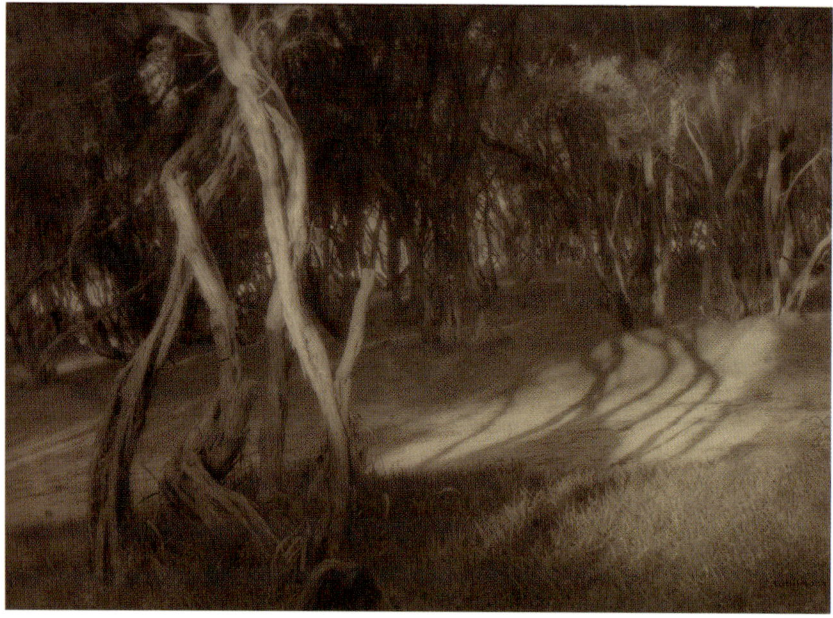

John Kauffmann *The Wetterhorn* 1894, carbon photograph
National Gallery of Australia, Canberra. Purchased 1980

John Kauffmann *Fairy woods* c1920, carbon photograph
Art Gallery of New South Wales. Gift of John Bilney 1979

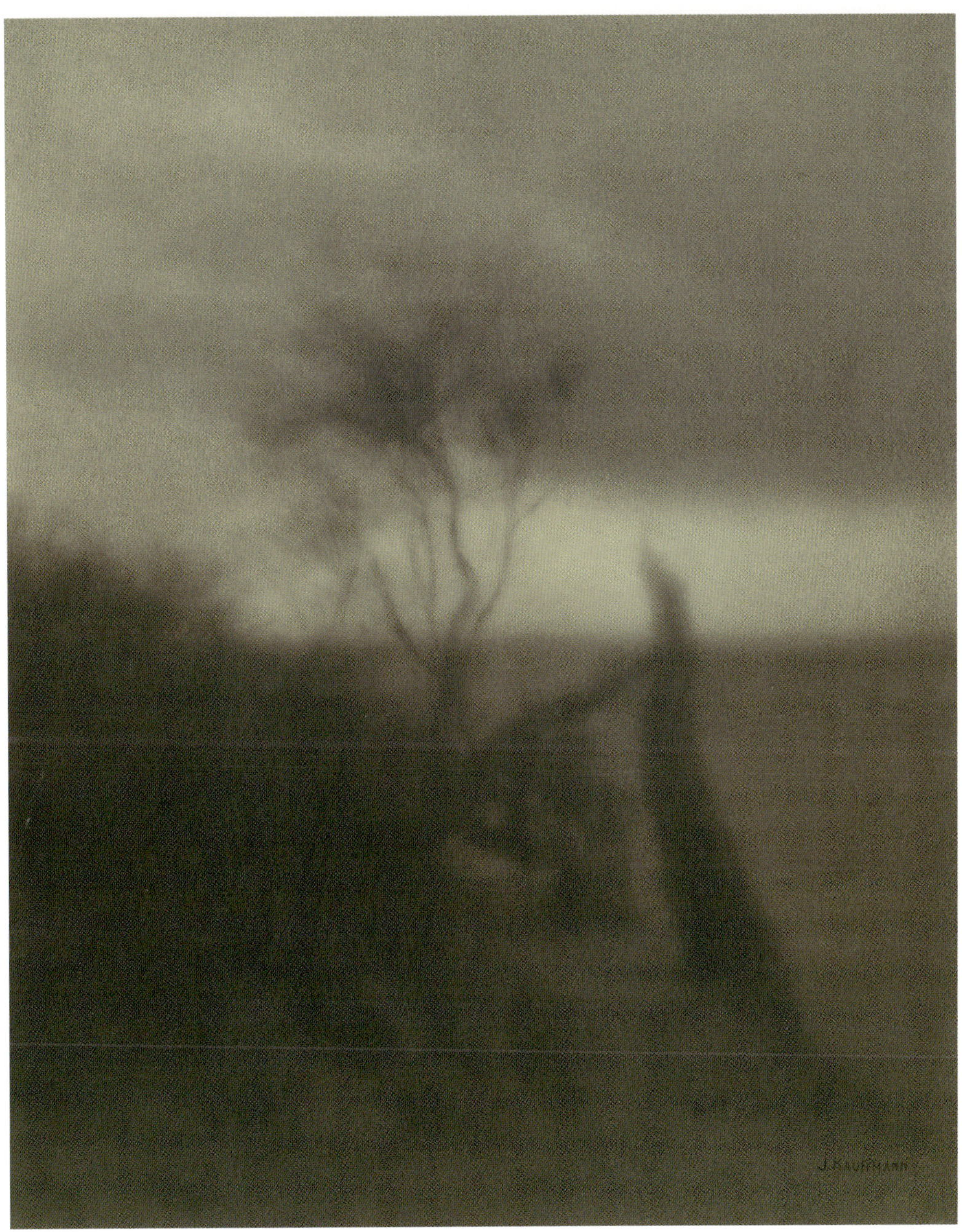

John Kauffmann *Nocturne* c1909, carbon photograph
National Gallery of Australia, Canberra. Purchased 1980

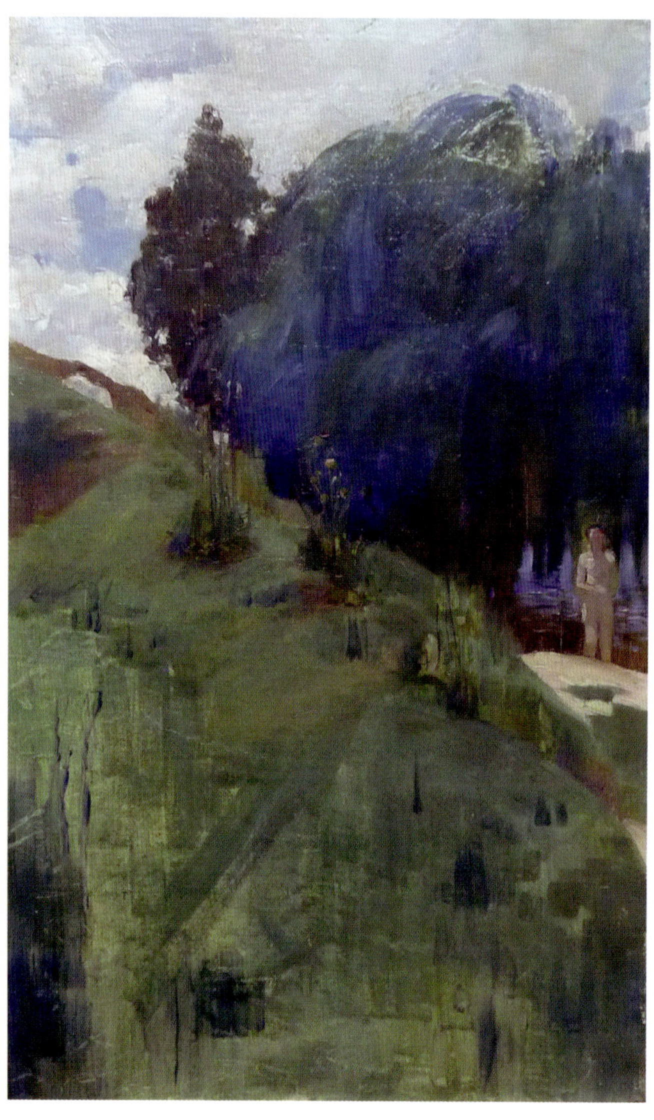

George Lambert *Syd Long bathing* c1896, oil on canvas
Devonport Gallery and Arts Centre, Tasmania. Purchased 1990

The work's backdrop rivals Ramsay's Australian peers in the degree of its abstraction. With a fluid, rhythmic composition emblematic of a grief-stricken state of mind, the tidal flow of the backdrop is reminiscent of that of Puvis's *The poor fisherman* 1881. Landscape here is formed through a psychological paradigm, yet the extent of such abstraction in *Venus and Adonis* is an anomaly in Ramsay's practice.

Puvis de Chavannes's work provided the artistic coda for Lambert's Symbolist practice. *Death of Adonis* c1901 was produced in response to Ramsay's homage. In a horizontal frieze with a subdued palette of close-range tones, Lambert presents death as poetic sleep. Adonis and wild boars appear as though under the influence of a soporific spell, in a mood lulled by compositional rhythms. Lambert would use this panel format in *Self portrait with Ambrose Patterson, Amy Lambert and Hugh Ramsay* c1901–03, a portrait tableau that self-consciously positions the artist and his immediate circle of Symbolist artists. Here, thinkers, pagan spirits (perhaps a nod to Long) and a mysterious woman are theatrically posed in the era's ubiquitous crepuscular landscape. Within this masquerade of fin-de-siècle personalities, meaning is imprecise and fraught with suggestion. While referring to a Symbolist mood of transience, the painting provides a glimpse of Lambert's practice in the new century, when the psychologically bound landscapes of Symbolism would be displaced by a broader shift in Australian art towards the elegant artifice of the Edwardian age.

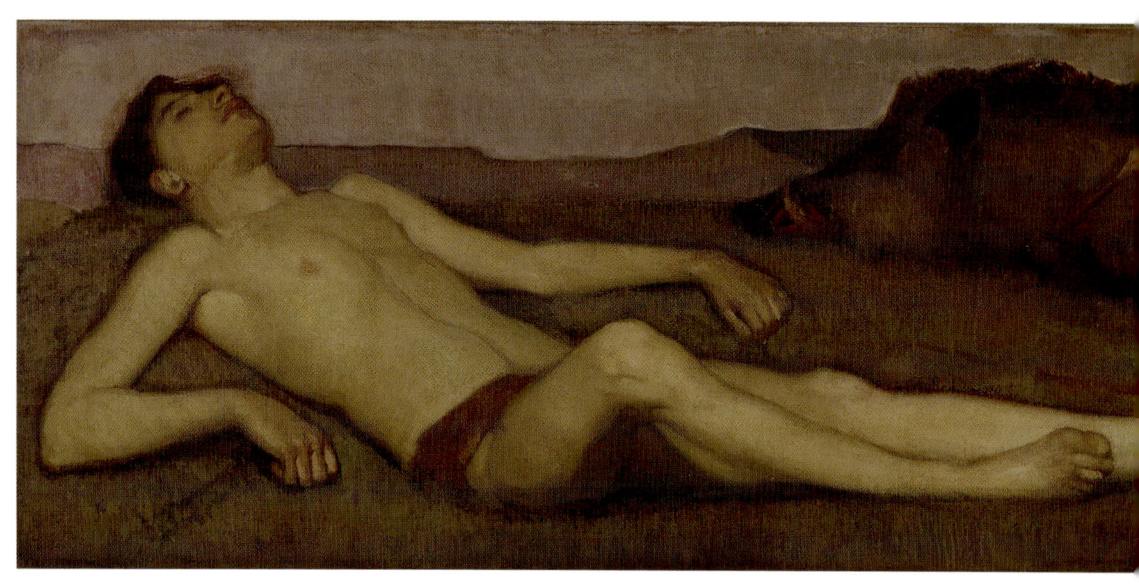

George Lambert *Death of Adonis* c1901, oil on canvas
 Manly Art Gallery and Museum, Sydney. Gift of PS Garling 1947

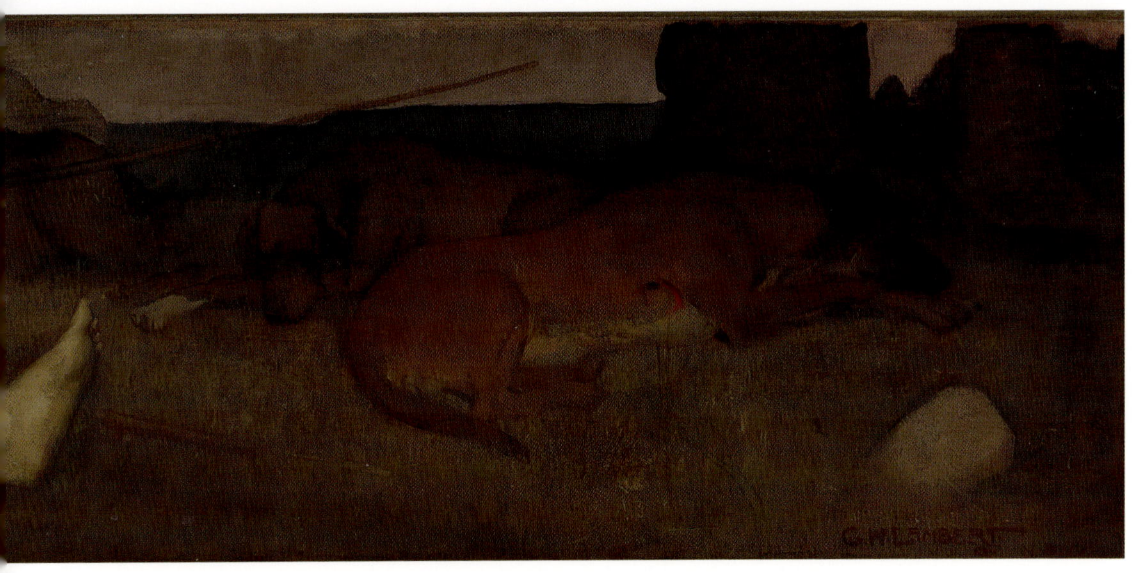

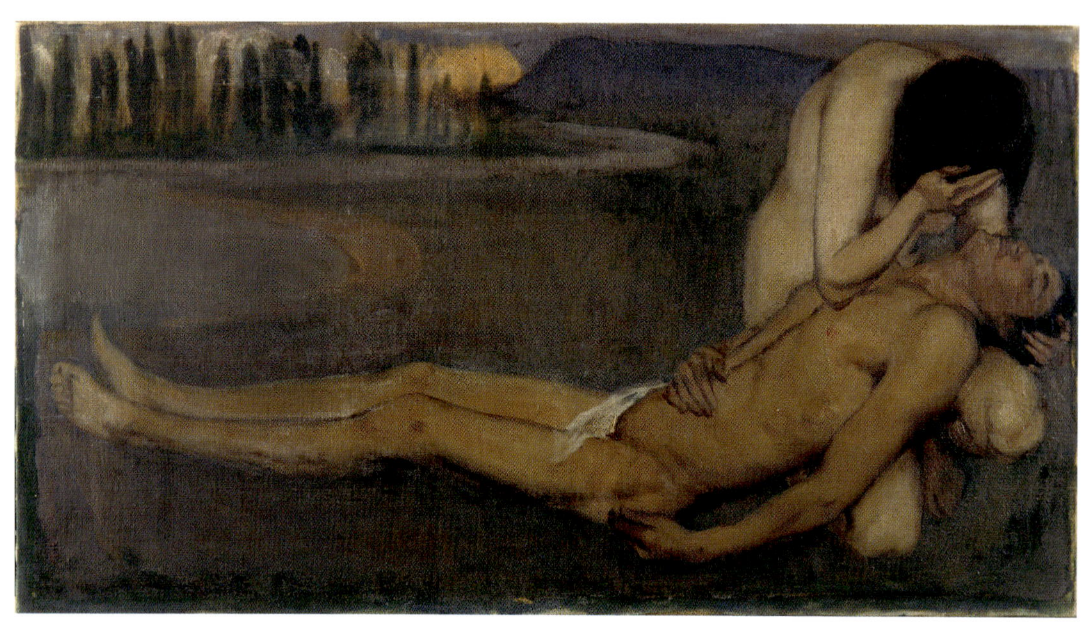

Hugh Ramsay *Venus and Adonis* c1901, oil on canvas
  Queen Victoria Museum and Art Gallery, Launceston. Gift of Lady Ramsay 1949

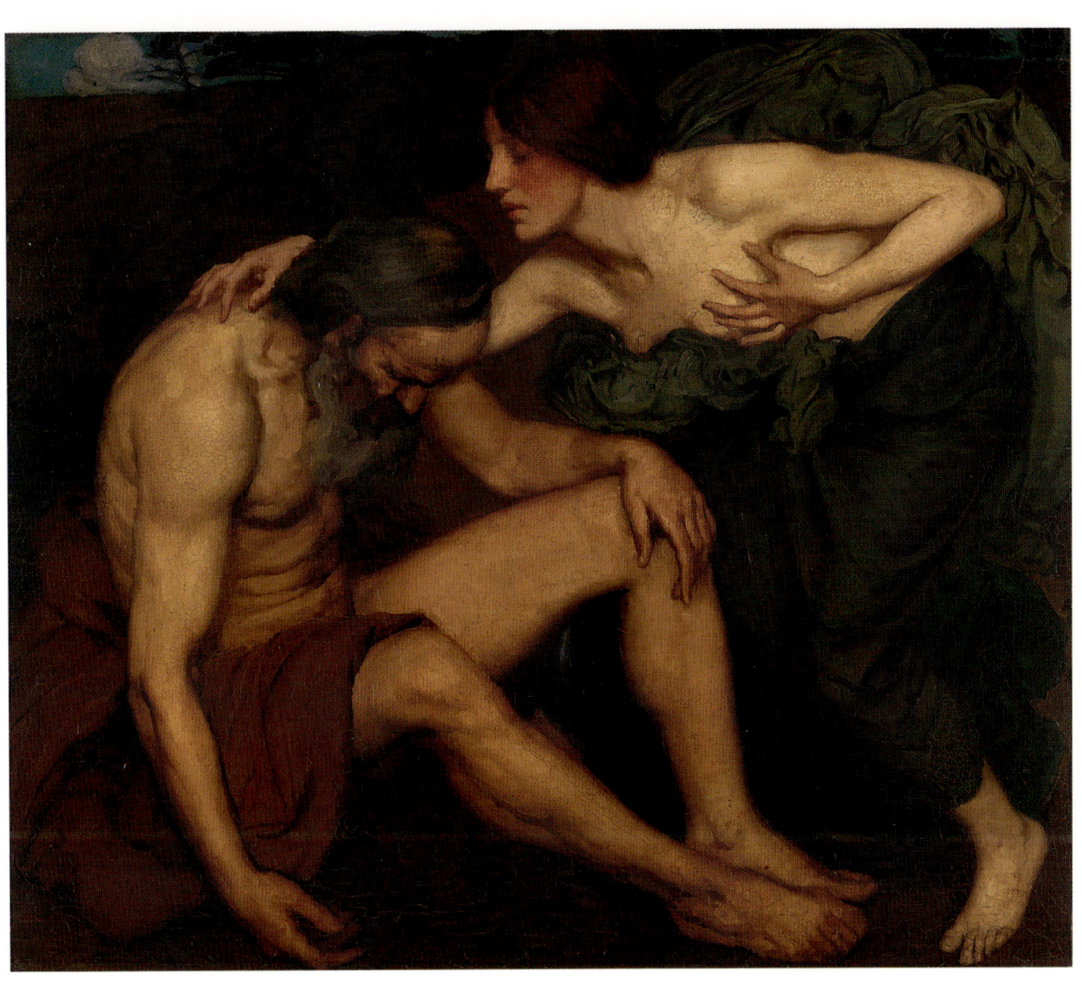

Hugh Ramsay *Consolation* 1899−1901, oil on canvas
National Gallery of Victoria, Melbourne. Gift of Royal Melbourne Hospital 1966

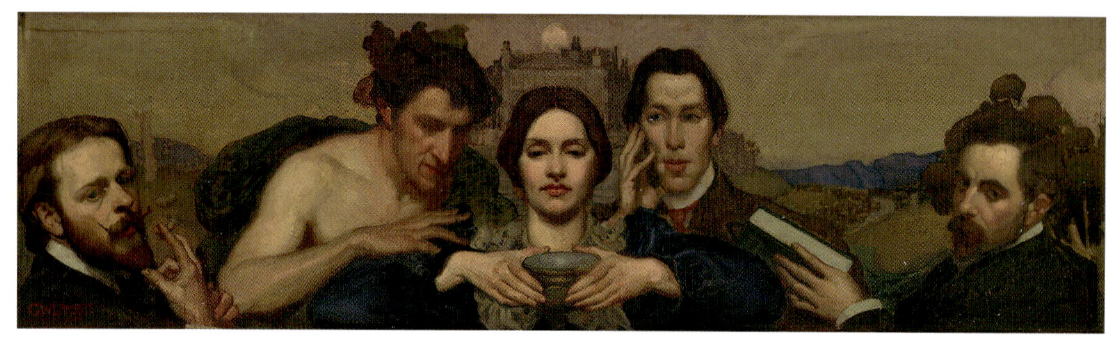

George Lambert *Self portrait with Ambrose Patterson, Amy Lambert and Hugh Ramsay* c1901–03, oil on canvas
(see detail pages 138–39)

 Queenland Art Gallery, Brisbane. Purchased with funds from Philip Bacon AM, through the Queensland Art Gallery Foundation

CONCLUSION

There are certain elements of Lambert's *Self portrait with Ambrose Patterson, Amy Lambert and Hugh Ramsay* that highlight the themes and undercurrents of Symbolism in Australia. As a group portrait it implies a series of connections – between painters, poets and muses; ancient ideals and modern formulation; and, with painter posed to the left of the group and writer on the right, of a crossover between visual and literary forms of artistic expression. In promoting these associations, Lambert's work alludes to the flow of ideas that was instrumental in fashioning Symbolist aesthetics in Australia. This exchange of ideas was crucial on both local and global levels in the dissemination of contemporary principles of art.

While Australians developed a Symbolist-inspired language to imply the distinctions of their local environment, such works also formed part of a broader set of responses to Symbolism across Europe in the late nineteenth century, where artists 'intended to maximise the emotional charge that their images would have on native audiences' in order to rouse national sentiment.[44] In a period that saw the rise of new nation states and the development and questioning of modern national identities, Symbolism also became key to figuring an artistic language that could allude to the idea of a national collective consciousness.[45] Fuelled by suggestions of dreams, poetry, legends and mythologies, Australian artists' use of Symbolist idioms in the years leading to Federation encouraged a spiritualised reading of the environment which could be seen to reinforce a nationalist sense of place.

Symbolist subjects and Art-Nouveau aesthetics continued to inform practices in Australia into the twentieth century, yet the onset of the First World War marked an endpoint to the momentum of art forms that had developed from the premise of Arcadian dreams. Art which explored the mind, its dreams and sensations, was revived in the new century in the guise of the Surrealist movement, and through practices that delved further in evoking irrational forces that determine the self. In Australia, as elsewhere, Surrealism developed as an art of a collective psyche that had been permanently marked by the experience of war and the Depression. Thus in the new century the expression of dreams shifted from the Symbolist domain of lyrical Arcadian landscapes populated by spirit beings towards urban terrains that were refigured as projections of the anxiety and angst of the modern age, and as an outcome of individual responses to the nightmares of the twentieth century.

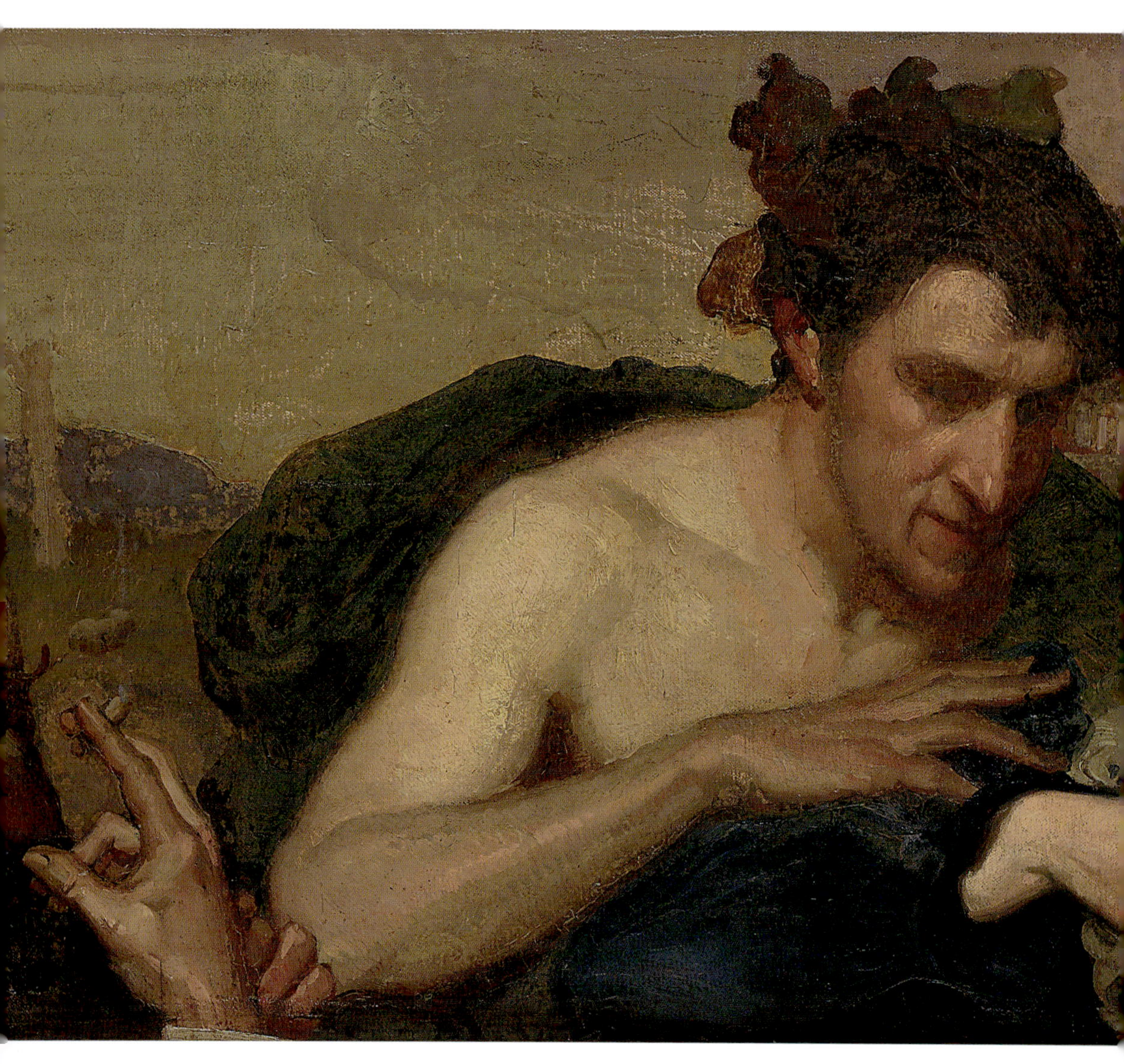

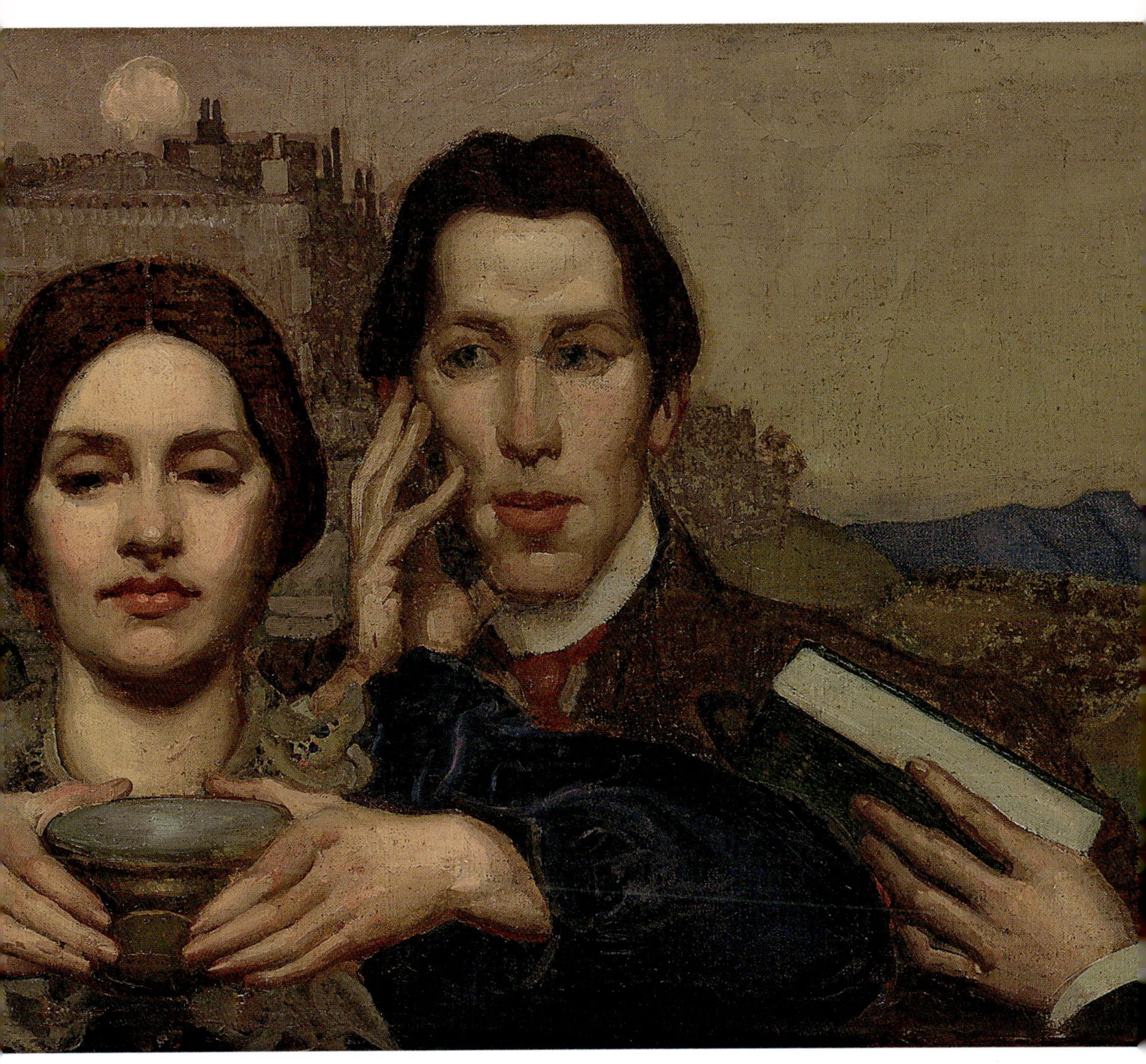

NOTES

Introduction

1. Charles Conder writing to GF Mann, 25 May 1889, GVF Mann correspondence, Archives, Art Gallery of South Australia, Adelaide.

2. Conder took the work to England in 1890 where it remained in a private collection after being rejected for selection by the Royal Academy of Arts in London in 1891. Its whereabouts were unknown until it was presented for auction at Sotheby's in Melbourne on 11 April 2006. *Hot wind* was referred to in histories of Conder's work by Frank Gibson (1914, when it was known to be in a private collection in London), John Rothenstein (1938), Ursula Hoff (1960), Mary Eagle (1997) and Ann Galbally (2002), and in Australian art histories by William Moore (1934) and Bernard Smith (1962).

3. Jean Moréas, 'Le Symbolisme', Supplement litteraire du *Figaro*, 18 September 1886, p 150; cited in Henri Dorra, *Symbolist art theories: a critical anthology*, University of California Press, Berkeley, Los Angeles 1995, p 151. There are various translations of Moreas's terms and the one referred to here was used in Jane Clarke, 'International classicists in the "Australian Impressionist" era: Arthur Loureiro and Bertram Mackennal', in Julie Ewington & Lynne Seer (eds), *Brought to light: Australian art 1850–1965 from the Queensland Art Gallery collection*, Queensland Art Gallery, Brisbane 1998, p 58.

4. Charles Harrison & Paul Wood (eds), *Art in theory 1900–1990: an anthology of changing ideas*, Blackwell, Oxford 1999, p 13.

Chapter 1

1. *Illustrated Australian News*, 22 December 1888, p 217, incorrectly reproduced as 'The crescent moon by G Loureiros'.

2. *Argus* (Melbourne), 16 November 1888, p 4.

3. Suggested as such by Jane Clarke in 'International classicists in the "Australian Impressionist" era: Arthur Loureiro and Bertram Mackennal', in Julie Ewington & Lynne Seer (eds), *Brought to light: Australian art 1850–1965 from the Queensland Art Gallery collection*, Queensland Art Gallery, Brisbane 1998, p 58. At the Victorian Artists' Society in May 1888 Frank Goldstraw exhibited two works, *Narcissa* (no 94 with drawn reproduction in the catalogue) and *The north wind* (no 95). The drawn reproduction of the former shows an allegorical maiden and the title of the latter also suggests allegorical form but it is difficult to determine to what degree – if any – the works embodied Symbolist qualities. Goldstraw became renowned as a portrait painter, yet the whereabouts of these allegorical paintings remains unknown.

4. Cited in Jane Clarke, 'Arthur Jose de Souza Loureiro 1853–1932', *Art & Australia*, vol 23, no 1, spring 1985, p 97.

5. Loureiro initially opened his School of Design in various city studio premises between 1884 and 1886, and from the following year operated a second studio from his residence in Kew. From 1890 he was head of the art department at the Presbyterian Ladies' College in East Melbourne and was also offered the influential position of Master of the National Gallery of Victoria Art School but was forced to decline due to ongoing ill-health.

6. *Argus* (Melbourne), 8 December 1885, p 8.

7. Loureiro had met Edith Huybers when she was studying with her sister at Cabanel's atelier (a further sister was the author Tasma).

The family remained close and when Edith returned to Australia she and her new husband, the sculptor Eugene Reverdy (Gustave Courbet's nephew), lived with the Loureiros in Melbourne from 1890. See *Table Talk*, 12 September 1890, p 6, and also Patricia Clarke, *Tasma: the life of Jessie Couvreur*, Allen & Unwin, Sydney 1994 on the Huybers siblings.

8. The oval works were commissioned by the former Melbourne mayor, Alderman James Cooper Stewart. See *Table Talk*, 19 October 1888, p 3. Stewart sold the works, along with other contents of his Kew residence (reported as Glenferrie), when he moved to Toorak in 1899. See the auction notice in the *Argus* (Melbourne), 30 August 1899, p 2, which lists Loureiro's paintings.

9. *Table Talk*, 19 October 1888, p 3, refers to the work's Portuguese subject. Jane Clarke identified the poem as Luís Vaz de Camões's *Os Lusíadas*. See Clarke 1998, p 302, fn 4.

10. *Os Lusíadas*, Book VI.

11. However, this was not a widespread trend. Richard Twopenny in *Town life in Australia* (1883) (reissued by Penguin, Melbourne in 1973) noted how the walls of Melbourne's middle-class homes were decorated with second-rate reproductions, pp 42–43.

12. *Table Talk*, 8 December 1893, p 3.

13. Jean Moréas, 'Le Symbolisme', *Supplement litteraire du Figaro*, 18 September 1886, p 150; cited in Henri Dorra, *Symbolist art theories: a critical anthology*, University of California Press, Berkeley, Los Angeles 1995, p 151.

14. See chapter 6, 'The arrival of the deviant: sexology', in Mike Jay & Michael Neve (eds), *1900: a fin de siècle reader*, Penguin, London 1999, pp 191–217.

15. Joris-Karl Huysmans, *Against nature (A rebours)*, Penguin Classics, London 2003, pp 53–54.

16. Edmund Gosse, 'The New Sculpture 1879–1894', *Art Journal* (London), 1894, p 200.

17. Bertram Mackennal to Theodore Fink, 1 July 1892, Theodore Fink papers, University of Melbourne; Bertram Mackennal to James Smith, 23 September 1892, James Smith papers, State Library of New South Wales, Sydney.

18. Mackennal to Smith, 23 September 1892.

19. 'Les Salon des 1893: la Peinture au Champ du Mars et al sculptures sans les deux salons', *Revue des deux Mondes*, vol 118, July 1893, np; cited in Deborah Edwards (ed), *Bertram Mackennal*, Art Gallery of New South Wales, Sydney 2007, p 31.

20. Oscar Wilde in a letter to Robert Ross, 7 July 1900, referred to Rodin's work at the 1900 Paris Exhibition: 'Rodin has a pavilion to himself and showed me anew all his great dreams in marble'; cited in Philippe Julian, *The triumph of Art Nouveau: Paris Exhibition 1900*, Phaidon, London 1974, p 138.

21. Mackennal quoted in *TP's and Cassell's Weekly*, 1925; cited in Edwards 2007, p 26.

22. Rodin in a 1911 interview with Paul Gsell; cited in Dorra 1995, p 79.

23. *London Morning Post*, 1913; cited in Edwards 2007, p 68.

24. Web Gilbert, who was working in London, had probably seen Mackennal's *The Earth and the elements*, which had been purchased for the Tate Gallery by the Chantrey Bequest in 1907.

25. William Moore, 'Notes on some younger Australian artists', *Studio* (London), vol 62, 1914, p 209.

26. This is also noted by Deborah Edwards in *Rupert Bunny: artist in Paris*, Art Gallery of New South Wales, Sydney 2009, p 35.

27. Zsigmond Justh, *Párizsi Napló (Half notes)*. This is the journal Justh kept with him from Hungary when he arrived in Paris in January 1888. The quote is from 21 February 1888 and taken from Eniko Hidas's translation from Hungarian, accessed June 2009 on http://mek.niif.hu/05600/05631/html/01.htm from The Hungarian Electronic Library.

28. Cited in Rodolphe Rapetti, *Symbolism*, Flammarion, Paris 2005, p 212.

29. Cited in Michelle Facos, *Symbolist art in context*, University of California Press, Berkeley, Los Angeles 2009, p 101. This position was similarly articulated by the playwright August Strindberg who closely documented his 'scientific work and metaphysical speculation' during the years of his mental breakdown, when his obsessive chemical experiments paralleled his anguished attempts at unlocking questions of the soul. See August Strindberg, *Inferno/ From an occult diary*, Penguin, London 1979, p 104.

30. Filiz Eda Burhan, *Vision and visionaries: nineteenth century psychological theory, the occult sciences, and the formation of the Symbolist aesthetic in France*, PhD dissertation, Department of Art and Archeology, Princeton University, New Jersey, June 1979, p 29.

31. Bunny is quoted as declaring himself a non-believer in Colette Reddin, *Rupert Bunny himself: his final years in Melbourne*, Colette Reddin, Melbourne 1987, p 225.

32. See Barbara Kane, *Sanctity and mystery: the Symbolist art of Rupert Bunny*, Ian Potter Museum of Art, University of Melbourne, Melbourne 2001. This is the catalogue of an exhibition based on the University of Melbourne's collection of Bunny's Symbolist-inspired work.

33. Monotypes are one-off prints. They are made by painting an image directly onto a glass or metal plate and then pressing damp paper onto the surface to create an imprint.

34. Wilde referred to Bernhardt in these terms. See Richard Ellmann, *Oscar Wilde*, Penguin, London 1987, p 350.

35. Justh 1888.

36. Justh 1888.

37. *Argus* (Melbourne), 11 July 1891, p 4.

38. Mackennal to James Smith, 19 August 1892.

39. The sonnet was first published in *The World* (London), 11 June 1879; cited in Ellmann 1987, p 113.

40. Ellmann 1987.

41. Rapetti 2005, p 13.

42. The dematerialisation of the image is seen as a defining trait of Symbolist abstraction as identified by Rapetti 2005, pp 147–74.

43. This term belongs to Gustave Moreau; cited in Jean Clair (ed), *Lost paradise: Symbolist Europe*, Montreal Museum of Fine Arts, Montreal 1995, p 236.

44. The work, which entered the collection of the French state in 1904, was particularly revered by the Nabis group of artists in Paris, as noted by Christine Dixon in *Masterpieces from Paris: Van Gogh, Gauguin, Cézanne & beyond: post-impressionism from the Musée d'Orsay*, National Gallery of Australia, Canberra 2010, p 238.

45. *Sydney Morning Herald*, 2 October 1897, p 7.

46. The original marble version of this work was placed in St John's Cathedral, Brisbane in 1933.

47. Robert Croll recalled that Web Gilbert had sourced the image of the Lotus leaf from its first blooming in the Royal Botanic Gardens in Melbourne around this time. See Robert Henderson Croll, *I recall: collections and recollections*, Robertson & Mullens Ltd, Melbourne, 1939, p 119.

48. Hysteria was medically defined in the nineteenth century by the French neurologist Jean-Martin Charcot who subjected his patients to public demonstrations of their condition and whose research was thoroughly documented through publications illustrated with photographs of his patients' traits. See Rapetti 2005, pp 256–57.

49. See Charles Darwin, 'The descent of man and selection in relation to sex', in Jay & Neve 1999, p 225.

50. William B Beattie, 'Hail – and farewell – Geo Washington Lambert', *Art in Australia*, no 33, August–September 1930, np. Much later, in around 1920, Lambert returned to Aestheticised design in his commission for decorative panels for his early patron Joseph Nield.

51. Beattie 1930.

52. The most recent comprehensive study of British Aestheticism was the exhibition *The cult of beauty: the Aesthetic movement 1860–1900*, Victoria and Albert Museum, London, 2 April –17 July 2011.

53. Andrew Wilton, *The age of Rossetti, Burne-Jones and Watts: Symbolism in Britain 1860–1910*, Tate Gallery, London 1997, p 19. Wilton identifies the image of the wistful, soul-gazing woman prevalent in the paintings of the Pre-Raphaelites 'as a paradigm of Symbolist iconography and … really where the story of Symbolism in Britain begins'.

54. Such principles were referred to in various articles published by Hall, but perhaps most significantly in 'The human basis of art' in the inaugural edition of *Art and Crafts*, vol 1, no 1, October 1895, pp 1–6.

55. As noted by Jillian Dwyer in 'The Lone Hand case: the critical response to Bernard Hall's Sleep in New Zealand', *Melbourne Art Journal*, no 2, 1998, p 23.

56. In a 1919 letter to an unnamed gentleman, Hall wrote that he had painted two large versions of *The quest* and was at work on a third. (Bernard Hall papers, sourced from copies held at the National Gallery of Australia, Canberra.) One version of *The quest* is in the collection of the National Gallery of Australia and is the version referred to in this catalogue. Another is in the collection of Queensland Art Gallery. The whereabouts of the third painting that Hall mentions is unknown. Hall also produced various smaller versions of the painting.

57. *The throne of Saturn* was illustrated in A Mary F Robinson, 'Elihu Vedder', in *Magazine of Art*, vol VII, 1884, p 124. Robinson referred to Vedder's work in these terms, p 122. *The throne of Saturn* has also been noted for influencing Watts's *Hope*.

58. The term 'seeker of souls' was used in relation to Symbolism by the French writer Jules Christopher in 1888; cited in John Christian (ed), *The last Romantics: the Romantic tradition in British art*, Lund Humphries, London 1993, p 33.

59. 'Australian artists today: C Douglas Richardson', *Age* (Melbourne), 4 May 1929, p 5.

60. The Nabis group in Paris, following Gauguin's example, developed religious imagery into a new abstract form with subjective colour and emotive design. At the Salon, in the context of the French revival of religious subjects, Bunny followed a pattern set by the

Pre-Raphaelites' modern interpretation of biblical imagery and exhibited a series of paintings on the lives of saints at the Salon in the 1890s. Loureiro, in his monumental *The vision of Saint Stanislaus* 1899 (National Gallery of Victoria), which was awarded a bronze medal at the Paris Exposition Universelle of 1900, also defines the crossover between academic form and the Symbolist quest for mysterious atmosphere through religious imagery.

61. There are references in the press, such as in the *Age* (Melbourne) 1929 (see fn 59), to Richardson's 'mystical values' and the fact that he, like others of Spiritualist faith, was a vegetarian and non-drinker.

62. *Argus* (Melbourne), 10 May 1895, p 6.

63. John Shirlow, 'CD Richardson', *Herald* (Melbourne), 25 September 1920.

64. Richardson, 'My recollections of Fred McCubbin as a fellow student', Victorian Artists' Society, 15 February 1918, p 7.

65. Richardson, 15 February 1918, p 7.

66. Ernest S Smellie, 'The art movement: an Australian artist, Mr CD Richardson', *Magazine of Art*, 1900, p 468.

67. George S Mann, 'Spiritualism – what is it?', Melbourne 1871; cited in FB Smith, 'Spiritualism in Victoria in the nineteenth century', *Journal of Religious History*, vol 3, issue 3, June 1965, p 247.

68. The work was one of two Richardson paintings that were later used to illustrate the Spiritualist poems of Annie MacDonald in her 1911 publication *Under the sign of the Southern Cross*.

69. Dillenger 1979, p 132. Richardson may have secured an introduction to Vedder through the expatriate Australian artist John Peter Russell as he had organised an introduction for Mackennal who visited Vedder in Rome in 1884.

70. *The cloud* was listed as 'model for a statue in metal' and priced at £800 in the Victorian Artists' Society annual exhibition catalogue, July 1901, no 229 (with the artist listed incorrectly as 'A Richardson').

71. Charles Douglas Richardson, 'The interior decoration of a house with sculpture', *Art and Crafts*, March 1898, pp 64–67.

72. The poem was also used by Loureiro as a reference for his painting *The spirit of the new moon*.

73. Altson contributed illustrations for magazines including *Pall Mall*, *Pearson's* and *Wentworth*.

74. Cited in Mary Eagle, 'Rupert Bunny', in Anne Gray (ed), *Australian art in the National Gallery of Australia*, National Gallery of Australia, Canberra 2002, p 92.

75. Referred to by Eagle 2002 in her discussion of this work.

76. Jennifer L Shaw documents how contemporary critics of Puvis's work repeatedly characterised his paintings as dreams. See Jennifer L Shaw, *Dream states: Puvis de Chavannes, modernism, and the fantasy of France*, Yale University Press, New Haven 2002, p 10.

77. This subject, as an academic exercise, had been similarly dealt with by the expatriate American artist Alexander Harrison in his painting *In Arcadia* c1885 that was purchased by the French state in 1886. Altson secured permission to paint his nude models on the island of Noirmoutier, and there are strange disjunctures in areas of the work between the attention to the qualities of the life models in the background and the expression of transcendental themes in the foreground.

78. Phillips Fox to Tom Roberts, 30 July 1887, State Library of New South Wales, Sydney, ML A2480.

79. See Eagle 2002, p 13. This is also noted by Bernard Smith in Len Fox, *E Phillips Fox and his family*, L Fox, Potts Point, NSW 1985, p 29.

80. G Albert Aurier, 'Le Symbolisme en peinture: Paul Gauguin', *Mecure de France 2*, March 1891; cited in Dorra 1995, pp 195–203. While Aurier's article on Gauguin remains the first significant visual manifesto on Symbolist painting, Reinhold Heller has noted that the Belgian poet Émile Verhaeren had earlier referred to the artist Fernand Khnopff as 'un peintre Symboliste' (a Symbolist painter) in 1887. 'Concerning Symbolism and the structure of surface', *Art Journal*, vol 45, no 2, summer 1985, p 146.

81. There is a carte de visite attached to this work with a signed note from Paul Gauguin to the collector Henri Rouart, the probable early owner of this work. Although the note does not mention Rae's name, its attachment to the work suggests an intriguing connection between Rae and the artists mentioned in it, including Gauguin.

82. Édouard Dujardin quoted in Dorra 1995, p 178.

Chapter 2

1. Virginia Spate, 'The sunny south: Australian impressionism', in Norma Broude (ed), *World impressionism: the international movement 1860–1920*, , Harry N Abrams, New York 1990, p 130.

2. Ada Cambridge, *Thirty years in Australia*, University of NSW Press, Sydney 1989, p 85; cited in Humphrey McQueen, *Tom Roberts*, Macmillan, Sydney 1996, p 85.

3. There are different versions of where the artists met in Sydney. William Moore, *The story of Australian art, vol 1*, Angus & Robertson, Sydney 1934, p 71, claims that it was at Roth's studio, as does Arthur Streeton in 'Eaglemont in the eighties', *Argus* (Melbourne), 16 October 1934, p 49 (although Moore's version of events may have been taken from Streeton's recollections).

4. *Table Talk*, 22 June 1888, p 9.

5. To the point of exhaustion, as one writer had already noted by 1885 (*Once a Month*, 15 May 1885, p 394). A description of Roberts's studio in 1889 referred to it as 'one of the best in Melbourne', matching that of countless other artists with 'Japanese screens, vases, stands, reeds and curtains … picturesquely arranged [along with] … draperies in rich soft tones'. *Table Talk*, 26 April 1889, p 5.

6. The *9 by 5 impression* exhibition works were priced at around £2 each, and Conder noted in an undated letter to his cousin Maggie that with works at this price, the exhibition 'ought to be' a success. State Library of New South Wales, Sydney, AC134.

7. Referred to as such in an undated letter from Streeton to Tom Roberts; cited in Ann Galbally & Anne Gray, *Letters from Smike: the letters of Arthur Streeton 1890–1943*, Oxford University Press, Melbourne 1989, p 52.

8. *Scottish Art Review*, June 1889, p 9, quoted in Ruth Zubans, 'Emanuel Phillips Fox: St Ives and the impact of British Art, 1890–1892', in Anthony Bradley & Terry Smith (eds), *Australian art and architecture*, Oxford University Press, Melbourne 1980, p 247.

9. Streeton's major panoramic work, *'Still glides the stream, and shall for ever glide'* 1890 (Art Gallery of New South Wales), for example, inscribes poetic sentiments on a moonlit landscape.

10. The phrase 'articulate surfaces' in reference to Whistler was coined by David Peters Corbett and is cited in Anna Gruetzner Robins, *A fragile modernism: Whistler and his impressionist followers*, Yale University Press, New Haven 2007, p 19. Robins notes the use of canvas textures on p 20.

11. Jane Clark & Bridget Whitelaw, *Golden summers: Heidelberg and beyond*, International Cultural Corporation of Australia for the National Gallery of Victoria, Melbourne 1985, p 193.

12. DH Souter, 'E Phillips Fox: Victorian painter', *Art and Architecture*, 1908, p 88; cited in Clark & Whitelaw 1985.

13. John Rothenstein, *The life and death of Conder*, Dent, London 1938, p 31.

14. Julian Ashton, 'Some recollections of Charles Conder', *Art in Australia*, no 2, 1917, np.

15. The significant influence of Browning was referred to in detail by Conder in a letter to his cousin Maggie Conder dated 11 February 1888 (State Library of New South Wales, Sydney, AC134). Browning's poetry was more generally influential on Australian artists of this period and in June 1889 Professor Henry S Laurie delivered a paper at the Victorian Artists' Society titled 'Robert Browning in relation to painting' which was reproduced in *Centennial Magazine*, vol 2, no 1, August 1889, pp 35–38.

16. Richard Twopenny, *Town life in Australia* (1883) (reissued by Penguin, Melbourne in 1973), p 3.

17. Rothenstein 1938, p 15.

18. Julian Ashton, 'Charles Conder's life', *Art in Australia*, 15 February 1939, p 61.

19. Toulouse-Lautrec was one of Conder's close associates in Montmartre, along with Louis Anquetin. Conder featured in a number of Toulouse-Lautrec's paintings, including as a distinct background figure in *Two waltzers at the Moulin Rouge* 1892.

20. Charles Conder to Maggie Conder, State Library of New South Wales, Sydney, AC134.

21. Arthur Streeton said of *Hot wind*: 'This design was a complete breakaway from conventional tradition and we were delighted with it.' Rothenstein 1938, p 32.

22. *Table Talk*, 2 August 1889, p 7.

23. Conder's portrait of Caffyn (not located) was reported in *Table Talk* on 23 August 1889 and was also mentioned by the artist in a letter to his cousin Maggie Conder on 11 February 1888 where he writes that Caffyn had directed his Spiritualist beliefs. Hugh McCrae noted Caffyn posing as a dryad in his book *My father, and my father's friends*, Angus & Robertson, Sydney 1935, p 24.

24. Mentioned in a letter from Charles Conder to Maggie Conder, 11 February 1888.

25. Tom Roberts, *Study for bookplate for Bernard Wise* c1890s, University of Queensland, Brisbane.

26. Streeton would later claim that the lines from Adam Lindsay Gordon, 'Where, with fire and fierce drought on her tresses, Insatiable Summer oppresses', possibly inspired Conder's depictions of this figure. Rothenstein 1938, p 32.

27. 'Mr Richardson is also exhibiting the decided novelty of sketches in wax', *Table Talk*, 16 August 1889, p 6.

28. *Table Talk*, 16 August 1889, p 6.

29. The term *Gesamtkunstwerk* was popularised in the late nineteenth century in relation to the Wagnerian notion of the synthesis of the arts, where musical expression merged with visual and literary practices to develop the 'total work of art'.

30. Marcus Clark referred to Verlaine's 'cult of faded things'; cited in Bernard Smith, *Australian painting 1788–1970*, Oxford University Press, Melbourne 1971, p 101. 'Your soul is an exquisite landscape', opens Verlaine's poem *Moonlight (Clair de Lune)*. Verlaine's 'Art of poetry' (1874) defined the conditions of his art; cited in Henri Dorra, *Symbolist art theories: a critical anthology*, University of California Press, Berkeley, Los Angeles 1995, pp 133–35.

31. WB Yeats, *Autobiographies*, Macmillan, London 1987, p 349.

32. David Rodgers, *Charles Conder 1868–1909*, Graves Art Gallery, Sheffield, UK 1967, p 3.

33. While Roberts worked as an assistant at a photographic studio, the practice of cropping the image in this way was not prevalent in Australia until well into the twentieth century.

34. At the cost, as one writer noted, of Long being the artist 'perhaps the least understood … and appreciated by the multitudes'. *AAA: All About Australians*, 2 March 1903, p 216.

35. *Studio* (London), vol 13, no 62, May 1898, pp 268–69.

36. DH Souter, 'Sid Long landscapist', *Art and Architecture*, March 1905, describing his decorative training (p 63) and *Circular Quay by moonlight* (p 64).

37. The Art Gallery of New South Wales purchased the work from that exhibition.

38. The Sydney-born Christopher Brennan (1870–1932) was influenced by the French Symbolist poet Stéphane Mallarmé after he encountered his work when on a travelling scholarship in Berlin from 1892. Long would later illustrate Brennan's poem *Secreta Silvarum* when it was published in the *Australian Magazine*, 29 April 1899.

39. As later claimed by Long in the *Sydney Morning Herald*, 23 July 1938.

40. Junios Junior, 'The personal element in design', *Australian Art Review*, 1 August 1899, pp 25–26.

41. See Debora L Silverman, *Art Nouveau in fin-de-siècle France: politics, psychology, and style*, University of California Press, Berkeley, Los Angeles 1989.

42. J Waterhouse, *Real visions: the life and work of FA Joyner, South Australian photographer 1863–1945*, Art Gallery of South Australia, Adelaide 1981, p 5.

43. The work was reproduced in the *Australasian* (Melbourne), 7 July 1900, p 26, and also described by Amy Lambert in *Thirty years of an artist's life: the career of GW Lambert, ARA*, Society of Artists, Sydney 1938, p 23.

44. Michelle Facos, *Symbolist art in context*, University of California Press, Berkeley, Los Angeles 2009, p 165.

45. See Michelle Facos and Sharon L Hirsh (eds), *Art, cultural and national identity in fin-de-siècle Europe*, Cambridge University Press, Cambridge 2003.

LIST OF WORKS

Measurements are given in centimetres (cm) as height by width by depth, unless noted otherwise.

Where a title is unknown, a descriptive title or the title it is known by is given in parentheses.

Abbreviations:

inscr	inscribed
cnr	corner
ll	lower left
lr	lower right
lc	lower centre
ul	upper left
ur	upper right
uc	upper centre

Abbey Altson (1866–1948)
born Yorkshire, England – died New York, USA
Melbourne 1883–91, France 1891–94, England 1894–24, India 1924–29, England 1927–39, USA 1939–48

The Golden Age 1893
painted in Paris
oil on canvas, 141.5 x 250.5 cm
inscr lr, oil: A. Altson./ 1893
National Gallery of Victoria, Melbourne.
Presented by the artist under the terms of the National Gallery of Victoria Travelling Scholarship, 1895

Fantasy – Angel drawing the cloth of the night 1897
painted in London
oil on academy board, 44 x 31 cm
inscr lr, oil: Abbey Altson/ 97
Kerry Stokes Collection, Perth

Rupert Bunny (1864–1947)
born and died Melbourne
England 1884–87, France 1887–1933, Melbourne 1933–47

Untitled (Witches' sabbath) 1887
probably the work orginally exhibited as
Une nuit de Valpurgis
painted in Paris
watercolour on paper, 25.5 x 19 cm (image)
inscr ll, ink: C.R.W. BUNNY/ PARIS
The University of Melbourne Art Collection.
Gift of the Bunny Estate 1948

(Burial of a saint) c1887–90
painted in Brittany or Paris
watercolour over pencil on paper, 42 x 54.5 cm
inscr ll, watercolour: Rupert C.W. Bunny
Philip Bacon Collection, Brisbane

Pastoral c1893
sketched in Brittany, painted in Paris
oil on canvas, 142 x 251 cm
inscr ll, oil: RUPERT. C.W. BUNNY
National Gallery of Australia, Canberra.
Purchased 1969

(Orpheus) c1898
printed in Paris
colour monotype, 24 x 33.6 cm (image),
24.4 x 34.8 cm (sheet)
inscr lc, monogram: RCWB, inscr ll, below platemark, pencil: Rupert C W Bunny
Art Gallery of New South Wales, Sydney.
Purchased 1969

Out of the sea c1898
printed in Paris
monotype, 23.8 x 33.6 cm (image),
32.1 x 44.6 cm (sheet)
inscr lc, pencil: To Miss Cary Elwes/ Souvenir of 59 [Avenue] de Sa[xe….illeg]/ Rupert Bunny./ Out of the sea
National Gallery of Victoria, Melbourne.
Gift of Mr CC Chisholm 1962

Harold Cazneaux (1878–1953)
born Wellington, New Zealand – died Sydney
Adelaide 1889, Sydney 1904–53

The orphan sisters 1906
photographed and printed in Sydney
gelatin silver photograph, 19.6 x 23.5 cm (image), 27 x 28.3 cm (card irreg)
inscr lr of card, pencil: H. Cazneaux,
inscr ll of card, sisters: The orphan sisters
Art Gallery of New South Wales, Sydney.
Gift of the Cazneaux family 1975

Charles Conder (1868–1909)
born Tottenham, England – died Virginia Water, England
Australia 1884–90, England and France 1890–1909

A dream of Handel's Largo 1889
painted in Melbourne
oil on wood panel, 26.5 x 16.1 cm
Art Gallery of South Australia, Adelaide.
MJM Carter AO Collection

Hot wind 1889
painted in Melbourne
oil on board, 29.4 x 75 cm
inscr ll, oil: CHARLES CONDER 89
National Gallery of Australia, Canberra.
Acquired with the assistance of the Yulgibar Foundation 2006

Moonlight 1889
painted in Melbourne
oil on canvas on board, 30.2 x 60.3 cm
inscr lr, oil and incised in paint: CHAS CONDER
Bastiaan Collection

Mirage c1889
painted in Melbourne
watercolour, 19.2 x 12.4 cm
inscr ll, watercolour: CHAS Conder; lc: Mirage
National Gallery of Victoria, Melbourne.
Purchased 1976

The hot sands, Mustapha, Algiers 1891
painted in Algiers
oil on canvas, 46 x 55.3 cm
inscr ll, oil: Charles Conder/ DEC. 1891; ll cnr: Charles Conder / 91
Art Gallery of New South Wales, Sydney.
Purchased with assistance from Katies 1982

'Mayday' 1892
painted in Chantemesle, France
oil on canvas, 81 x 45 cm
inscr lr, oil: CHARLES/CONDER/ CHANTE[SMESLE]
National Gallery of Australia, Canberra.
Purchased 1978

Moonlight at Mustapha 1892
painted in Algiers
oil on canvas, 38 x 46 cm
inscr ll, oil: CHARLES CONDER
MUSTAPHA.92
Philip Bacon Collection, Brisbane

Mildred Creed (1874–1943)
born Scone, New South Wales – died Sydney

Gumleaf pendant and chain c1914
silver and mother-of-pearl, 40.4 cm (chain),
4.4 x 2.5 cm (pendant)
Art Gallery of New South Wales, Sydney.
Purchased 1914

David Davies (1863–1939)
born Ballarat, Victoria – died Cornwall,
England
France and England 1890–93, Melbourne
1893–97, England and France 1897–1939

Moonrise 1893
painted in Melbourne
oil on canvas, 50 x 60 cm
inscr ll, oil: D. Davies
Art Gallery of South Australia, Adelaide.
Elder Bequest Fund 1947

E Phillips Fox (1865–1915)
born and died Melbourne
Europe/England 1887–92,
England/Europe 1901–13

Sunlight effect c1889
painted at Le Pouldu, Brittany, France
oil on canvas, 41 x 32.2 cm
National Gallery of Australia, Canberra.
Gift of the artist's nephew Len Fox in memory
of his mother Irene Fox 1984

Moonrise, Heidelberg 1900
painted in Melbourne and London
oil on canvas, 76.3 x 126.5 cm
inscr ll: E Phillips Fox 1900
National Gallery of Victoria, Melbourne.
Purchased 1948

Charles Web Gilbert (1867–1925)
born Cockatoo, Victoria – died Melbourne
London, England 1914–20

The dreamer 1915
modelled in London
bronze, 34.3 x 48.6 x 37.5 cm
inscr lc: Web Gilbert / 1915
National Gallery of Victoria, Melbourne.
Felton Bequest 1922

The Sun and the Earth 1918
modelled and carved in London
marble, 97.8 x 66 x 39.7 cm
inscr ul: C Web Gilbert 1918
National Gallery of Victoria, Melbourne.
Gift of Mrs Web Gilbert 1927

Bernard Hall (1859–1935)
born Liverpool, England – died London,
England
Melbourne 1892–1934

The quest c1905
painted in Melbourne
oil on canvas, 154 x 94.5 cm
inscr ll, oil: B.Hall
National Gallery of Australia, Canberra.
Purchased 1977

Sleep c1906
painted in Melbourne
oil on canvas, 64 x 141.1 cm
inscr lr, oil: B. Hall
National Gallery of Victoria, Melbourne.
Felton Bequest 1919

Alice Hambidge (1869–1947)
born and died Adelaide

By the light of the candle 1899
painted in Adelaide
watercolour on paper, 33.5 x 51.6 cm
inscr ur, watercolour: Alice Hambidge/ 1899
Art Gallery of South Australia, Adelaide.
Elder Bequest Fund 1899

Frederick A Joyner (1863–1945)
born and died Adelaide

A shaft of light c1904
photographed in Adelaide
gelatin silver photograph, red tone,
27.6 x 20.2 cm (image), 31.7 x 26.6 cm
(sheet)
inscr lr, pencil: F.A. Joyner
Art Gallery of New South Wales, Sydney.
Gift of Mrs Max Joyner 1982

Dawn c1904
photographed in Adelaide
gelatin silver photograph, brown tone,
22.5 x 27.6 cm (image), 26.6 x 31.6 cm
(sheet)
Art Gallery of New South Wales, Sydney.
Gift of Mrs Max Joyner 1982

John Kauffmann (1864–1942)
born Turo, South Australia – died Melbourne
London 1887, Zurich 1890–93, Vienna
1893–96, Adelaide 1897–1908, Melbourne
1909–42

The Wetterhorn 1894
photographed in Switzerland, printer later
carbon photograph, 21.6 x 29.7 cm
inscr lr: J KAUFFMANN
National Gallery of Australia, Canberra.
Purchased 1980

Nocturne c1909
photographed and printed in Victoria
carbon photograph, 28.5 x 23 cm
inscr lr, pencil: J KAUFFMANN, ll, on card:
"Nocturne"
National Gallery of Australia, Canberra.
Purchased 1980

Fairy woods c1920
photographed and printed in Victoria
carbon photograph, 21.2 x 29.6 cm (image),
25.3 x 32.2 cm (card)
inscr lr, ink: J Kauffmann
Art Gallery of New South Wales, Sydney.
Gift of John Bilney 1979

George Lambert (1873–1930)
born St Petersburg, Russia – died Cobbity,
New South Wales
Australia 1887–1900, England 1900–01,
France 1901–02, England 1902–21,
Australia 1921–1930

Syd Long bathing c1896
painted in Sydney
oil on canvas, 39.4 x 24.2 cm
Devonport Gallery and Arts Centre, Tasmania.
Purchased 1990

The serpent 1898
painted in Sydney
oil on canvas, 50.1 x 50 cm
inscr lr, oil: Geo Lambert/ 1898
Private collection

Death of Adonis c1901
painted in Paris
oil on canvas, 41.5 x 176.5 cm
inscr lr, oil: GW LAMBERT
Manly Art Gallery and Museum, Sydney.
Gift of PS Garling 1947

*Self portrait with Ambrose Patterson,
Amy Lambert and Hugh Ramsay*
c1901–03
painted in Paris
oil on canvas, 51.5 x 177 cm
inscr ll, oil: G.W. LAMBERT/ OF NSW. 1903
Queenland Art Gallery, Brisbane. Purchased
with funds from Philip Bacon AM, through the
Queensland Art Gallery Foundation

James Walter Robert Linton
(1869–1947)
born London, England – died Perth,
Western Australia

Australian landscape casket c1910
produced in Perth
copper, enamel on copper, 8.2 x 17 x 10 cm
Art Gallery of South Australia, Adelaide. South
Australia Government Grant 1985

Sydney Long (1871–1955)
born Goulburn, New South Wales – died
London, England
England/Europe 1910–21, Australia 1921–
22, England 1922–25, Australia 1925–52,
England 1952–55

Spirit of the plains 1897
painted in Sydney
oil on canvas on wood, 62 x 131.4 cm
inscr lr, oil: Sid Long
Queensland Art Gallery, Brisbane. Gift of
William Howard-Smith in memory of his
grandfather Ormond Charles Smith 1940

Pan 1898
painted in Sydney
oil on canvas, 107.5 x 178.8 cm
inscr lr cnr, oil: SID LONG
Art Gallery of New South Wales, Sydney.
Gift of JR McGregor 1943

The valley 1898
painted in Sydney
oil on canvas, 91.5 x 61.2 cm
inscr lr oil: SID LONG/ 98
Art Gallery of South Australia, Adelaide.
Elder Bequest Fund 1898

(Landscape with irises) c1898
painted in Sydney
oil on wood panel, 39.7 x 19.2 cm
inscr lr, oil: SID LONG
Art Gallery of South Australia, Adelaide.
On loan from MJM Carter AO Collection 2006

*Sadder than a single star that sets
at twilight in a land of reeds* 1899
also known as *Sadder than a single star* and
Decoration
painted in Sydney
oil on canvas, 92.7 x 38.7 cm
Art Gallery of New South Wales, Sydney.
Purchased 1899

Isabella 1904
painted in Sydney
oil on canvas, 150.5 x 107 cm
inscr ll. oil: SID LONG
Private collection

Fantasy c1916–17
painted in London
oil on canvas, 132.5 x 107 cm
inscr lr cnr, oil: SYDNEY LONG
Art Gallery of New South Wales, Sydney.
Purchased under the terms of the Florence
Turner Blake Bequest 1971

All works by Sydney Long © Estate
of Sydney Long. Courtesy Ophthalmic
Research Institute of Australia

Arthur Loureiro (1853–1932)
born Oporto, Portugal – died Braga, Portugal
Italy 1877–79, Paris 1879–81, Surrey,
England 1881, France 1882, Melbourne
1884–1904, Portugal 1901, and 1904–32

Study for 'The spirit of the new moon'
1888
painted in Melbourne
oil on canvas, 56 x 165 cm
Queensland Art Gallery, Brisbane. Purchased
1995. Queensland Art Gallery Foundation
Grant with the assistance of Philip Bacon
through the Queensland Art Gallery
Foundation. Celebrating Queensland Art
Gallery's Centenary 1895–1995

The spirit of the Southern Cross 1888
painted in Melbourne
oil on canvas, 168 x 136.5 cm (oval)
inscr lr, oil: ARTHUR LOUREIRO/ 1888
National Gallery of Victoria, Melbourne.
Purchased 2003

Mildred Lovett (1880–1955)
born and died Hobart, Tasmania
England, Belgium, France and Italy 1929

*Untitled (Vase with pastoral design
of nude figures with swans)* 1909
produced in Sydney
hand-painted porcelain with overglaze
decoration, 15 x 16.7 cm (diam)
inscr on case: M.L.
Art Gallery of New South Wales, Sydney.
Gift of Howard Hinton 1915

*Vase with pastoral design of dancing
figures by Sydney Long* 1909
produced in Sydney
hand-painted porcelain with overglaze
decoration, 26.4 (h) x 14 (diam) cm
Art Gallery of New South Wales, Sydney.
Purchased 1909

Bertram Mackennal (1863–1931)
born Melbourne – died Torquay, England
England, France, Italy 1882–88, Melbourne
1888–91, France 1891–94, England
1894–1931

La tête d'une sainte (Head of a saint)
1892
modelled in Paris
bronze relief, 53 x 39.5 x 11.2 cm
inscr ll: E/B MacKenn…[dissolves] PARIS;
inscr, lr: 1892
Private collection

Circe 1892–93
modelled in Paris
original lifesize plaster 1893, lifesize bronze
1901
240 x 79.4 x 93.4 cm
inscr lr, back of base: Bertram Mackennal/
1893
National Gallery of Victoria, Melbourne.
Felton Bequest 1910

Sarah Bernhardt c1892–93
modelled in Paris
bronze relief, 43.2 x 40.6 x 2.2 cm
inscr ll: Bertram Mackennal
Art Gallery of New South Wales, Sydney.
Bequest of Mrs JR McGregor 1944

Daphne 1897
modelled in London
bronze, 50 x 15 x 15 cm (with base)
inscr lr of base: B. MacKENNAL
Queensland Art Gallery, Brisbane.
Purchased 1974

The Earth and the elements 1907
modelled and carved in London
marble on onyx base, 71.5 x 65 x 65 cm
(with base)
inscr lr: B. MacKennal
Tate Gallery, London, presented by the
Trustees of the Chantrey Bequest 1907

Paul Montford (1868–1938)
born London, England – died Melbourne
Australia 1923–38

Memorial to youth 1895
modelled and cast in England
bronze, 85 x 56.4 x 14.5 cm
inscr lr: Paul R Montford/ Sc, stamped
(in reverse): 95
National Gallery of Australia, Canberra.
Purchased 1979

Alice Muskett (1869–1936)
born Melbourne – died Sydney
France 1895–98, Egypt 1911, England
c1914–18, Australia 1919–36

A lost halo 1897
drawn in Paris
pastel, 56.4 x 40.2 cm
inscr lr, pastel: Alice Muskett/ 1897
National Gallery of Australia, Canberra.
Purchased 1992

Ada Newman (1869–1949)
born Tumut, New South Wales – died Sydney

Jug with solanum design c1897
produced in Sydney
hand-painted porcelain,
31.5 (h) x 15.5 (diam) cm
Art Gallery of New South Wales, Sydney.
Purchased 1910–12

Harold Parker (1873–1962)
born Aylesbury, England – died Brisbane,
Queensland
Australia 1876–96, England 1896–1930
(visits to Australia 1911, 1921–22), Australia
1930–62

Ariadne 1919
modelled and carved in England
marble, 49.5 x 82 x 40.5 cm
inscr lc of base: Harold Parker/ 1919
National Gallery of Victoria, Melbourne.
Felton Bequest 1921

Iso Rae (1860–1940)
born Melbourne – died Brighton, England
France 1887–1932, England 1932–40

(Breton girl with goat) c1889
drawn in Brittany, France
pastel and black chalk on card, 47 x 17 cm
(image), 48.3 x 17.5 cm (sheet)
inscr lr, pastel: ISO RAE
National Gallery of Victoria, Melbourne.
Purchased with funds donated from the
estate of Quida Marston 2011

Hugh Ramsay (1877–1906)
born Glasgow, Scotland – died Melbourne
Melbourne 1878–1900, England and France
1900–02, Melbourne 1902–06

Consolation 1899–1901
commenced in Melbourne and completed
in Paris
oil on canvas, 126.2 x 145.7 cm
inscr ll, oil: Hugh Ramsay
National Gallery of Victoria, Melbourne.
Gift of Royal Melbourne Hospital 1966

Charles Douglas Richardson
(1853–1932)
born London, England – died Melbourne
arrived Australia 1858, Melbourne 1860–81,
London, Italy and France 1881–89,
Melbourne 1889–1932

The passing of Arthur 1885
painted in London
oil on canvas, 71 x 51.5 cm
inscr ll, oil: C. Douglas Richardson 1888 [sic]
Bayside City Council, Melbourne

Wind 1889
modelled in Melbourne
wax, 11.7 x 8.9 x 0.6 cm (work),
16.3 x 11.2 x 0.5 cm (mount)
inscr lr: CDR/ 1889
National Gallery of Australia, Canberra.
Rudy Komon Fund 1981

Memories 1895
modelled and cast in Melbourne
patinated plaster, 65 x 65 x 8 cm
inscr lc: C. Douglas Richardson 1895
Bayside City Council, Melbourne

Casting the spell 1896
painted in Melbourne
oil on canvas, 171.5 x 76.9 cm
inscr lr, oil: C. Douglas Richardson/ 1896
State Art Collection, Art Gallery of Western
Australia, Perth. Purchased with funds from
the Great Australian Paintings Appeal 1992

The hillside, Bacchus Marsh 1899
painted in Melbourne
oil on canvas, 61.2 x 92.2 cm
inscr ll, oil: C. Douglas Richardson / 1899
Geelong Gallery, Victoria. Purchased with the
generous assistance of the Friends of the
Gallery and the JB Ryan Perpetual Trust
2008

The cloud 1900
modelled and cast in Melbourne
patinated plaster, 190 x 40 x 44 cm
inscr back of base: C. Douglas Richarsdon
[sic] 1900
Bayside City Council, Melbourne

The undeveloped soul 1901
painted in Melbourne
oil on canvas, 170 x 105 cm
inscr ll, oil: C Douglas Richarson/ 1894 [sic]
Bayside City Council, Melbourne

Tom Roberts (1856–1931)
born Dorchester, England – died Kallista,
Victoria
Melbourne from 1869, England/Europe
1881–85, 1903–19

Adagio c1893
painted in Melbourne
oil on paperboard, 29 x 54.5 cm
Art Gallery of New South Wales, Sydney.
Purchased 1947

A study of Jephthah's daughter 1899
painted in Melbourne
oil on canvas, 76.5 x 50.7 cm
inscr lr, oil: Tom Roberts
Art Gallery of New South Wales, Sydney.
Purchased 1899

Arthur Streeton (1867–1943)
born Mt Duneed, Victoria – died Olinda,
Victoria
Melbourne from 1874, Melbourne – Sydney
1890–97, England 1897–1906, 1907–23

The flight of summer c1890
painted in Melbourne
oil on panel, 52.1 x 23cm
Private collection

Ariadne 1895
painted in Sydney
oil on wood panel
12.7 x 35.4 cm
inscr ll, oil: STREETON 95
The estate of the late Stuart Johnston,
Sydney

Scheherazade 1895
painted in Sydney
oil on cedar panel, 58.2 x 39.4 cm
inscr lr, oil: A STREETON/ 1895
National Gallery of Victoria, Melbourne. The
Joseph Brown Collection, presented through
the NGV Foundation by Dr Joseph Brown
AO OBE, Honorary Life Benefactor, 2004

A bush idyll 1896
painted in Sydney
oil on wood panel, 54.3 x 31.5 cm
inscr ll, oil: ARTHUR STREETON/ 1896
Art Gallery of New South Wales, Sydney.
Gift of Dr Joseph Brown 1991

The spirit of the drought 1896
painted in Sydney
triptych, watercolour, 25.2 x 11 cm (left),
12 x 31 cm (centre), 30 x 12.5 cm (right)
inscr lr of left panel: A STREETON 96.
Private collection

The spirit of the drought c1896
painted in Sydney
oil on wood panel, 34.7 x 37.2 cm
National Gallery of Australia, Canberra.
Joseph Brown Fund

Reginald Ward Sturgess
(1892–1932)
born Melbourne – died Williamstown, Victoria

The feet of the furtive 1916
(text by Charles Roberts)
hardbound book, watercolour and ink
illustrations, 15.3 x 21.4 cm
inscr on cover ul, ink: R.W. Sturgess/ 1916,
inscr ur, inside front cover, ink:
R.W. Sturgess 1916
Ballarat Art Gallery, Victoria. Gift of Beth
Sinclair 1978

Violet Teague (1872–1951)
born Melbourne – died Frankston, Victoria
Europe 1889–95, 1935–37

Night fall in the ti-tree 1905
(text by Geraldine Rede 1874–1943)
hand-bound book of colour woodblock prints
with letterpress text, 24.3 x 17.7 x 1 cm
(book)
Art Gallery of New South Wales, Sydney.
Purchased 1983

Amy Vale (1874–1951)

Bowl with lillypilly design c1897
hand-painted porcelain with overglaze
decoration, 12.5 (h) x 24.2 (diam) cm
inscr to come
Art Gallery of New South Wales, Sydney.
Purchased 1913

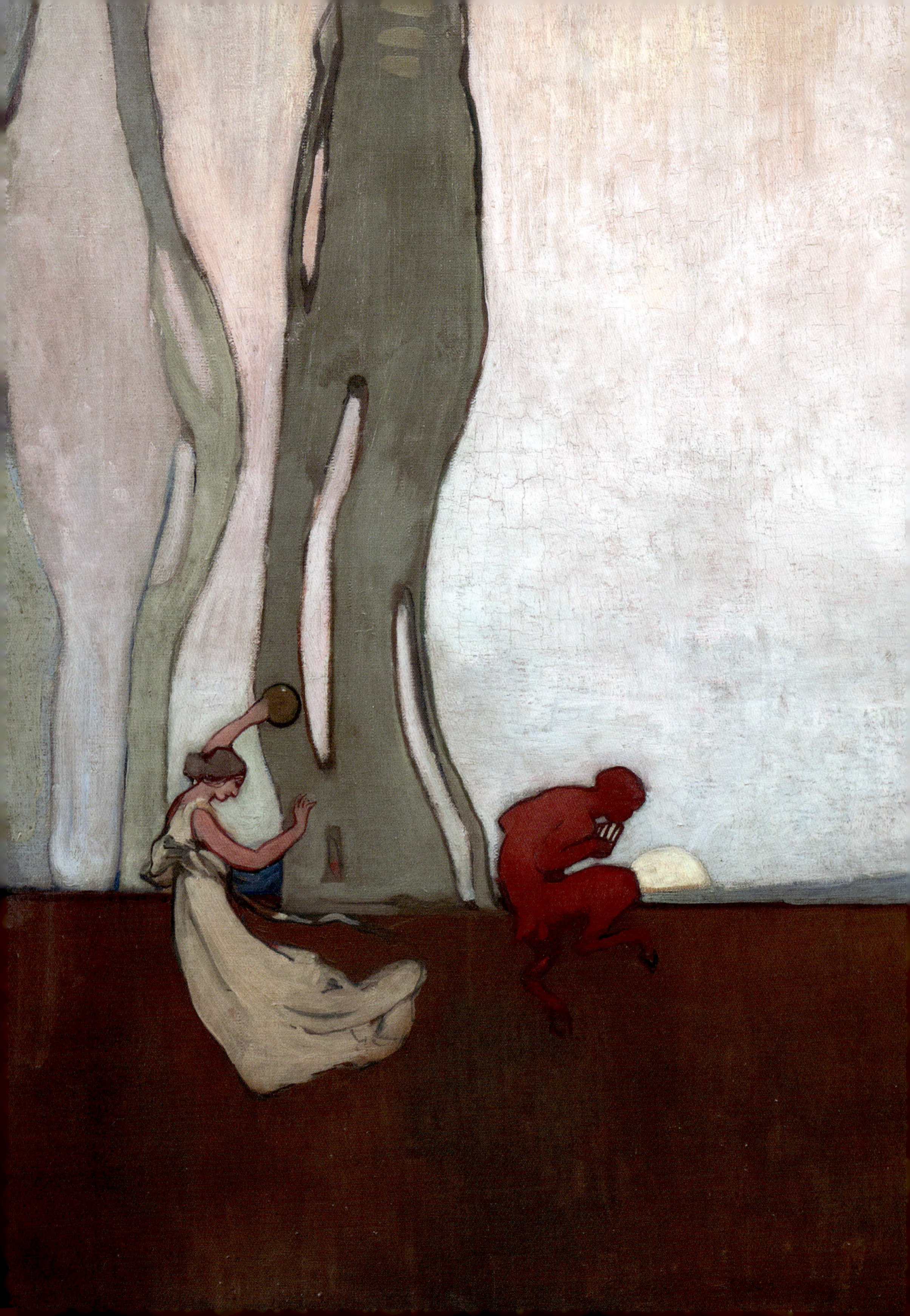

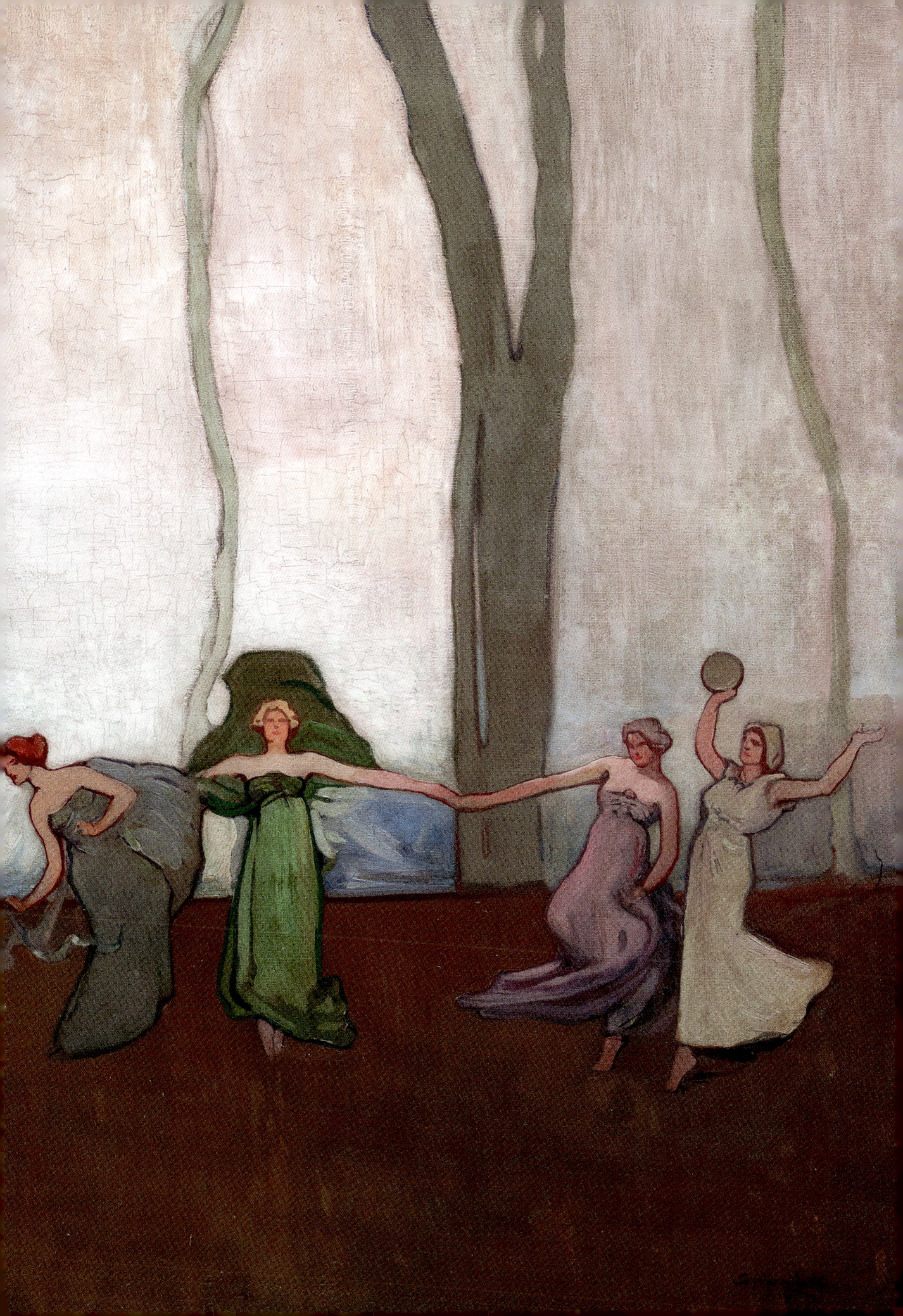

SELECT BIBLIOGRAPHY

Calloway, Stephen & Federle Orr, Lynn. *The cult of beauty: the Aesthetic movement 1869–1900*, Victoria and Albert Museum, London 2011

Clair, Jean (ed). *Lost paradise: Symbolist Europe*, Montreal Museum of Fine Arts, Montreal 1995

Clark, Jane & Whitelaw, Bridget. *Golden summers: Heidelberg and beyond*, International Cultural Corporation of Australia Ltd, Sydney 1985

Clark, Jane. 'International classicists in the "Australian Impressionist" era: Arthur Loureiro and Bertram Mackennal', in Julie Ewington & Lynne Seer (eds), *Brought to light: Australian art 1850–1965 from the Queensland Art Gallery collection*, Queensland Art Gallery, Brisbane 1998

Dorra, Henri. *Symbolist art theories: a critical anthology*, University of California Press, Berkeley, Los Angeles 1995

Edwards, Deborah. *Rupert Bunny: artist in Paris*, Art Gallery of New South Wales, Sydney 2009

Edwards, Deborah. *Bertram Mackennal*, Art Gallery of New South Wales, Sydney 2007

Facos, Michelle. *Symbolist art in context*, University of California Press, Berkeley, Los Angeles 2009

Galbally, Ann. 'Aestheticism in Australia', in Anthony Bradley & Terry Smith (eds), *Australian art and architecture: essays presented to Bernard Smith*, Oxford University Press, Melbourne 1980

Gott, Ted. '"Gently I wave the visible world away": Charles Conder, Arthur Streeton and the "problem children" of Australian Impressionism', in Terence Lane (ed), *Australian Impressionism*, National Gallery of Victoria, Melbourne 2007

Mendelssohn, Joanna. *The life and work of Sydney Long*, McGraw Hill, Sydney 1979

Peers, Juliette. 'Religious images of the Heidelberg School', *Art and Australia*, vol 23, no 3, autumn 1989

Radford, Ron. *Art Nouveau in Australia*, Art Gallery Director's Council, Sydney 1980

Rapetti, Radolphe. *Symbolism*, Flammarion, Paris 2005

Rothenstein, John. *The life and death of Conder*, Dent, London 1938

Silverman, Deborah L. *Art Nouveau in fin-de-siècle France: politics, psychology, and style*, University of California Press, Berkeley, Los Angeles 1989

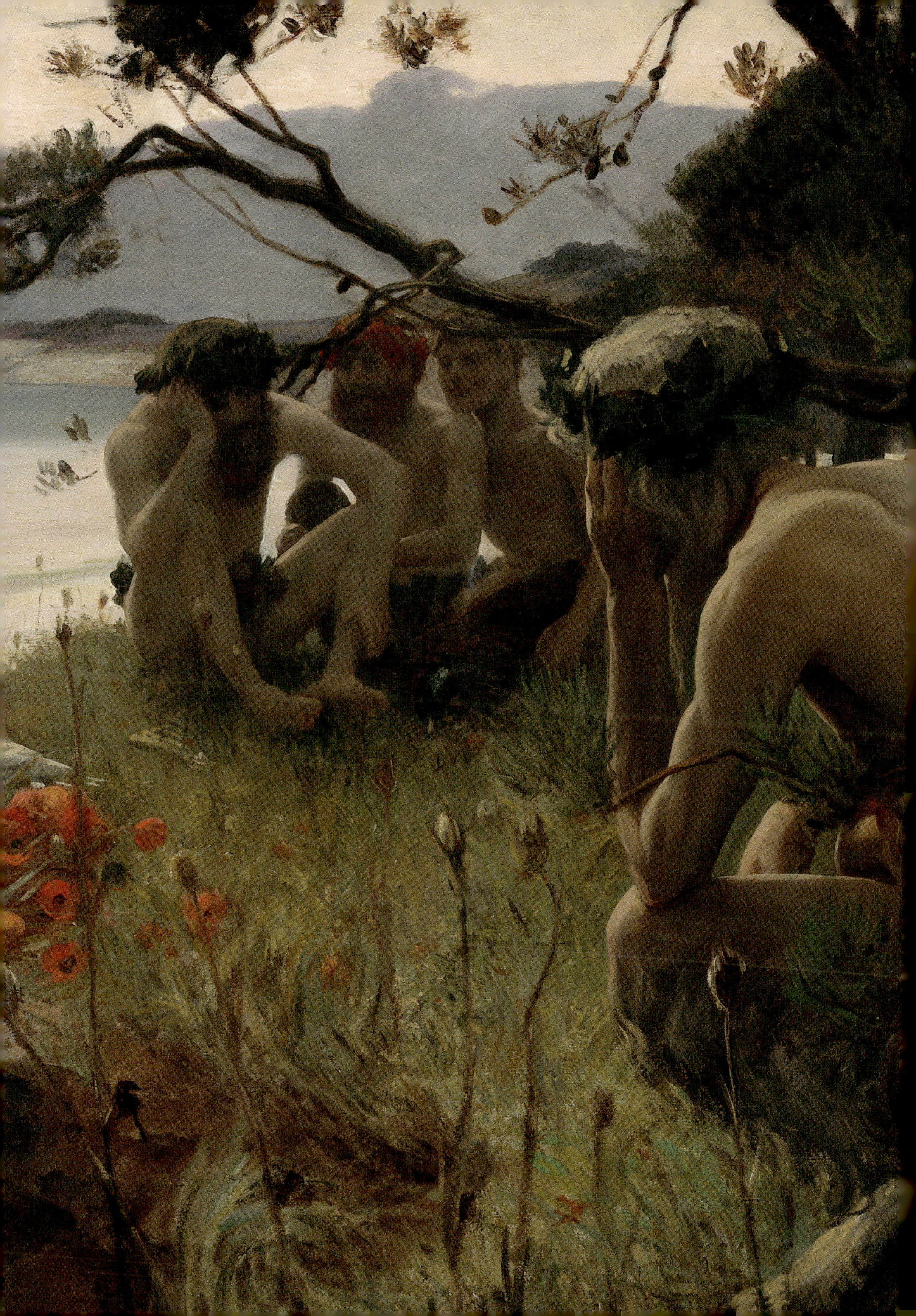

ACKNOWLEDGMENTS

While *Australian Symbolism:the art of dreams* is the first exhibition and publication on Symbolist art in Australia, various curators and scholars have contributed to this area of study and have influenced my formulation of the show. I would like to acknowledge Jane Clark's seminal research on nineteenth-century Australian artists, especially Arthur Loureiro; her usual generosity in sharing her expertise, as well her role in repatriating Charles Conder's *Hot wind* – a work central to my conception of this exhibition. Dr Juliette Peers's exceptional scholarship has been critical in establishing the significance of lesser-known histories of Australian art, and in particular her work on Charles Douglas Richardson and Australian New Sculpture has informed aspects of this project. Mary Eagle's pivotal research on artists from this period has also proved invaluable.

An exhibition such as this is only made possible by the generosity of its lenders, and my sincere thanks go to all the public institutions and private collectors who have taken part in this show. Several museums have lent a significant number of works, and I would like to acknowledge the invaluable support of the National Gallery of Australia, director Ron Radford and curatorial staff Anna Gray, Miriam Kelly, Sarina Noordhuis-Fairfax, Gael Newton and Anne O'Hehir; the National Gallery of Victoria, director Gerard Vaughan, and curators Alisa Bunbury, Humphrey Clegg, Kirsty Grant, David Hurlston and Elena Taylor; Queensland Art Gallery, director Tony Ellwood and curators Julie Ewington and Angela Goddard; Art Gallery of South Australia, director Nick Mitzevich, curator Rebecca Capes-Baldwin and Max Carter AO; and Bayside City Council, mayor Louise Cooper-Shaw, and Helen Kaptein and Grainne Murphy.

At the Art Gallery of New South Wales thanks go to Anne Flanagan, acting director and Wayne Tunnicliffe, head of Australian art for supporting this project. I am particularly grateful to Deborah Edwards, senior curator of Australian Art, whose work on Bertram Mackennal and Rupert Bunny contributed to my interpretation of Australian Symbolist practices. I am also indebted to Deborah for her insightful advice on my essay and encouragement throughout this project. I am equally fortunate to have had the input of Terence Maloon, former curator of special exhibitions, and his constructive suggestions on the book's text. For invaluable assistance during the research process, my gratitude goes to intern Suzie Fraser and Steven Miller and the library staff, particularly Enikő Hidas.

For the publication, thanks to: Jenni Carter, senior photographer, for her image coordination and exceptional photography; Karen Wong for her inspired catalogue design; Claire Armstrong for her painstaking editing; Julie Donaldson, managing editor; Cara Hickman production and studio manager; Graham Maslen (Spitting Image); and Analiese Cairis and Karen Hancock for their design input. I would also like to acknowledge the lessons learnt from working with Mark Boxshall.

For the exhibition, thanks to: the Gallery's conservation team, particularly, Kerry Head, Donna Hinton, Simon Ives, Carolyn Murphy, Analiese Treacy and Kate Wilson; Erica Drew, senior exhibitions manager; Charlotte Cox, exhibition registrar; Tanguy Le Moing, exhibition designer; Claire Martin, media relations manager; Emma Smith and the Gallery's collection registrars; Stephanie Tarvey and the installation crew. Thanks for assistance in varied forms to Judy Annear, Craig Brush, Matt Cox, Vigen Galstyan, Anne Gerard-Austin, Peter Raissis, Josephine Touma and Andrew Yip. And to former colleague Ursula Prunster whose eager response to my initial idea for a Symbolist exhibition remains much appreciated.

The tireless efforts of Emma Hicks in London have been vital to securing particular works for the exhibition. I am also thankful to Oliver Streeton who has very graciously offered his time and knowledge of his grandfather's work; and to Philip Bacon, as both a generous lender and for his role in securing several key Symbolist works for public collections.

I would like to also acknowledge the assistance of: Geoffrey Smith and Fiona Hayward (Sotheby's Australia); Andrew Crawford and Tim Abdallah (Menzies); Geoffrey Edwards, Lisa Sullivan and Veronica Filmer (Geelong Gallery); Nick Nicholson (National Gallery of Australia); Jennie Maloney (National Gallery of Victoria); Tracey Dall (Art Gallery of South Australia); Kylie Challenor and Kirsty Burow (Queensland Art Gallery); Anne Rowland and Julie Collett (Art Gallery of Ballarat); Sarah Yukich and Erica Persak (Stokes Collection); Jay Miller (The University of Melbourne Art Collection); Jackie Dunn and Katherine Roberts (Manly Art Gallery of Museum); Ellie Ray (Devonport Art Gallery); Melissa Harpley (Art Gallery of Western Australia); David Thomas; and Col and Daniella Fullagar.

Denise Mimmocchi

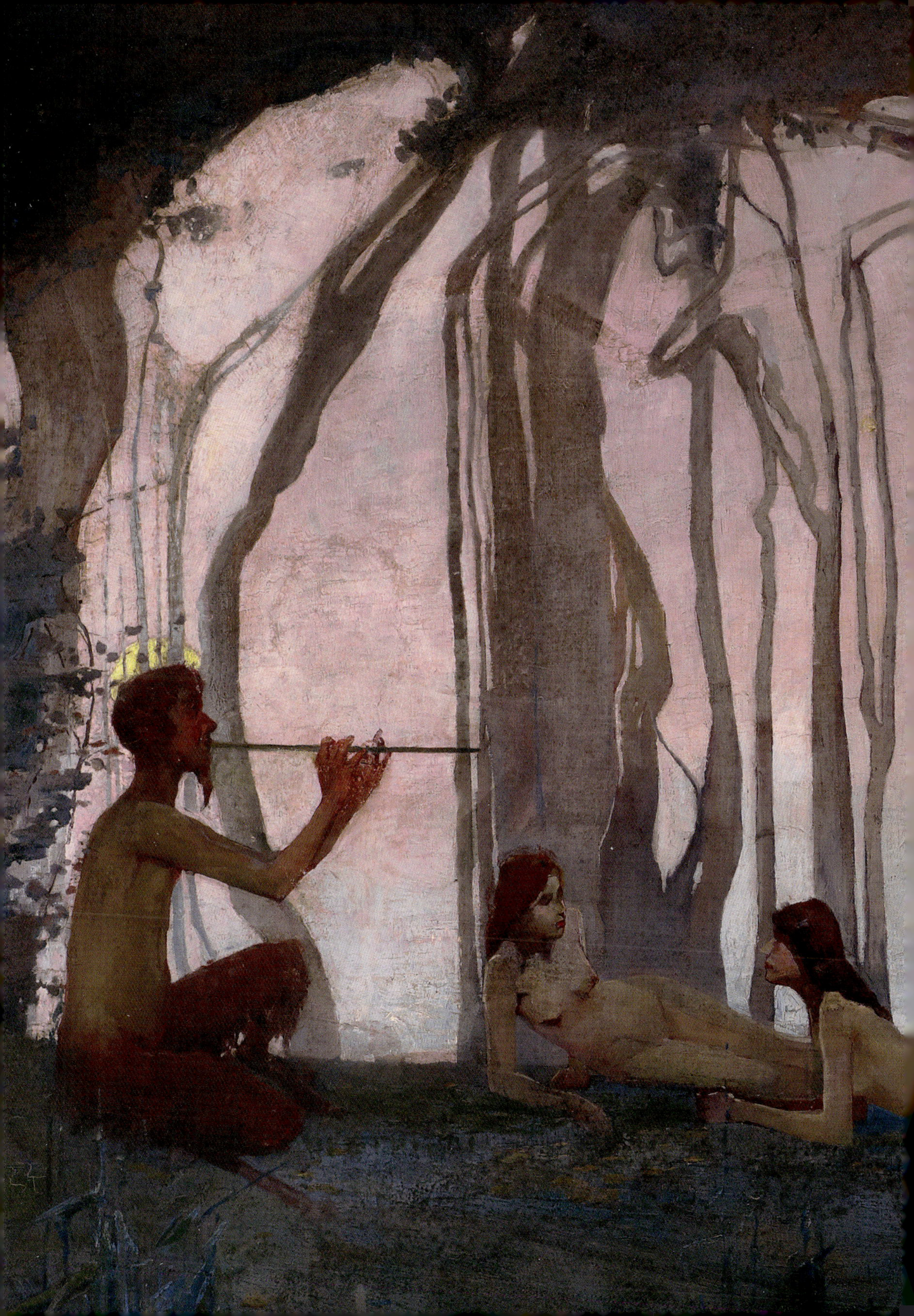

INDEX

Illustrations are indicated by italic page numbers; principal entries for artists are indicated by bold page numbers.

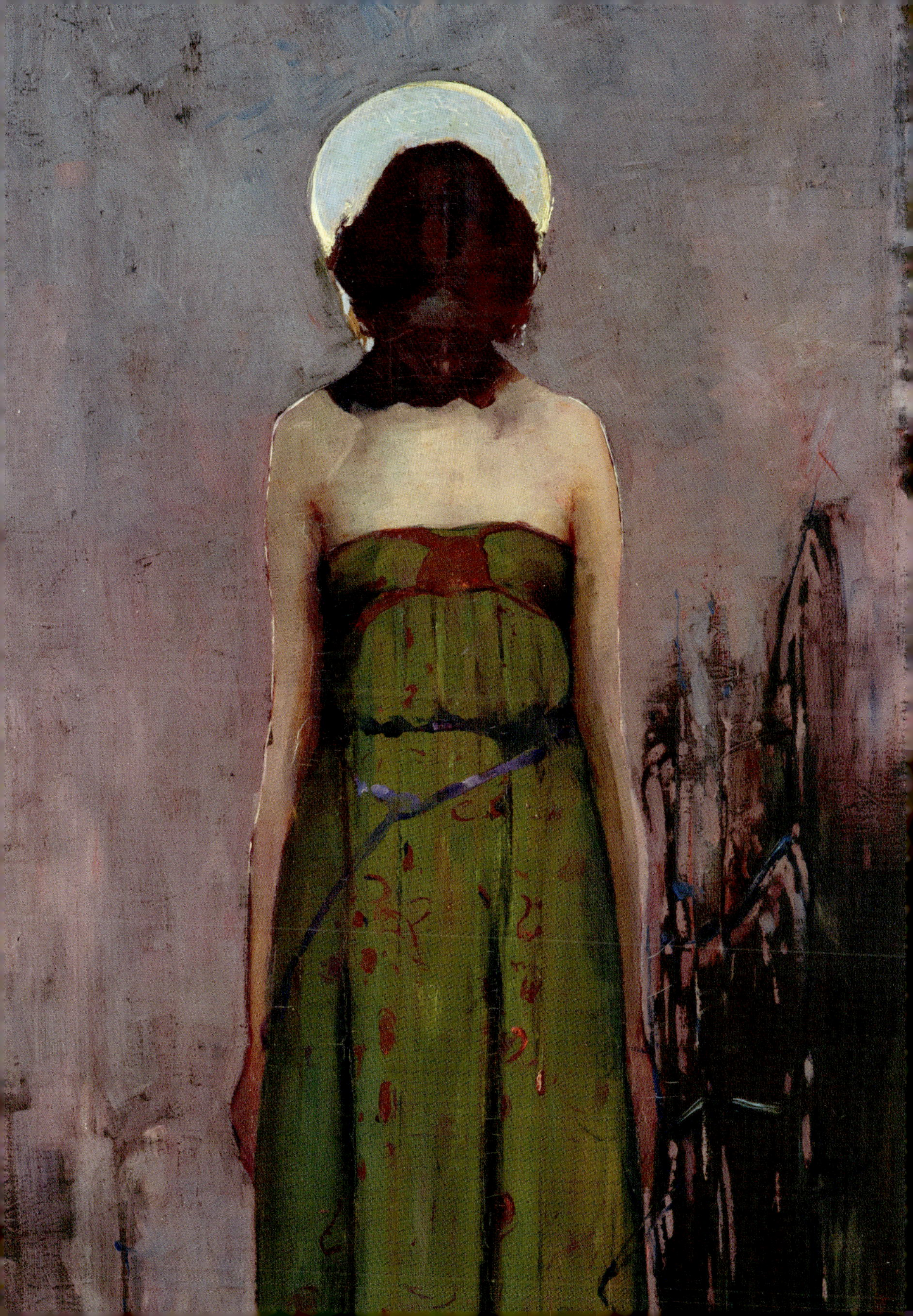

FROM THE PRESIDENT'S COUNCIL

The President's Council of the Art Gallery of New South Wales is delighted
to sponsor *Australian Symbolism: the art of dreams*, the first exhibition to focus
on this movement in Australian art. The exhibition provides a fresh context to
appreciate the work of some of Australia's most well-known artists of the late
nineteenth and early twentieth centuries including Rupert Bunny, Charles Conder,
Bernard Hall, George Lambert, Sydney Long, Bertram Mackennal, Tom Roberts
and Arthur Streeton.

The President's Council, whose members are Australian business leaders, provides
important counsel and financial support to the Gallery. Since its inception in 1995,
the Council has established a strong partnership between the corporate community
and the Gallery and has grown to become the major sponsor of the Gallery's
extensive and stimulating exhibition program.

Steven Lowy AM, President

PRESIDENT'S COUNCIL MEMBERS

Michael Fraser, AGL Energy Limited

Nigel Williams, ANZ Banking Group

John Symond AM, Aussie Home Loans

Giam Swiegers, Deloitte

Greg Everett, Delta Electricity

Sandra Chipchase, Destination NSW

Damian Hackett, Deutscher and Hackett

Rob McLeod, Ernst & Young

Peter Fray, Fairfax Media Limited

Kathryn Everett, Freehills

Emmanuel Pohl, Hyperion Asset Management

Scott MacDonald, Investa Property Group

David Clarke, Investec Bank (Australia) Limited

Stephen O'Connor, JCDecaux Australia

Rob Priestley, J.P. Morgan

Chris Jordan AO, KPMG

Robin Bishop, Macquarie Capital

John Clayton, Marsh

David Hornery, National Australia Bank

Kim Williams, News Limited

Paul O'Sullivan, Optus

Kerr Neilson, Platinum Asset Management

Alan Joyce, Qantas Airways

Alfred Moufarrige OAM, Servcorp

Ryan Stokes, Seven Group Holdings

Virginia Mansell, Stephenson Mansell Group

Luca Belgiorno-Nettis AM, Transfield Holdings

Philip Coleman, UBS AG Australia

Jeff Mitchell, Westpac Banking Corporation

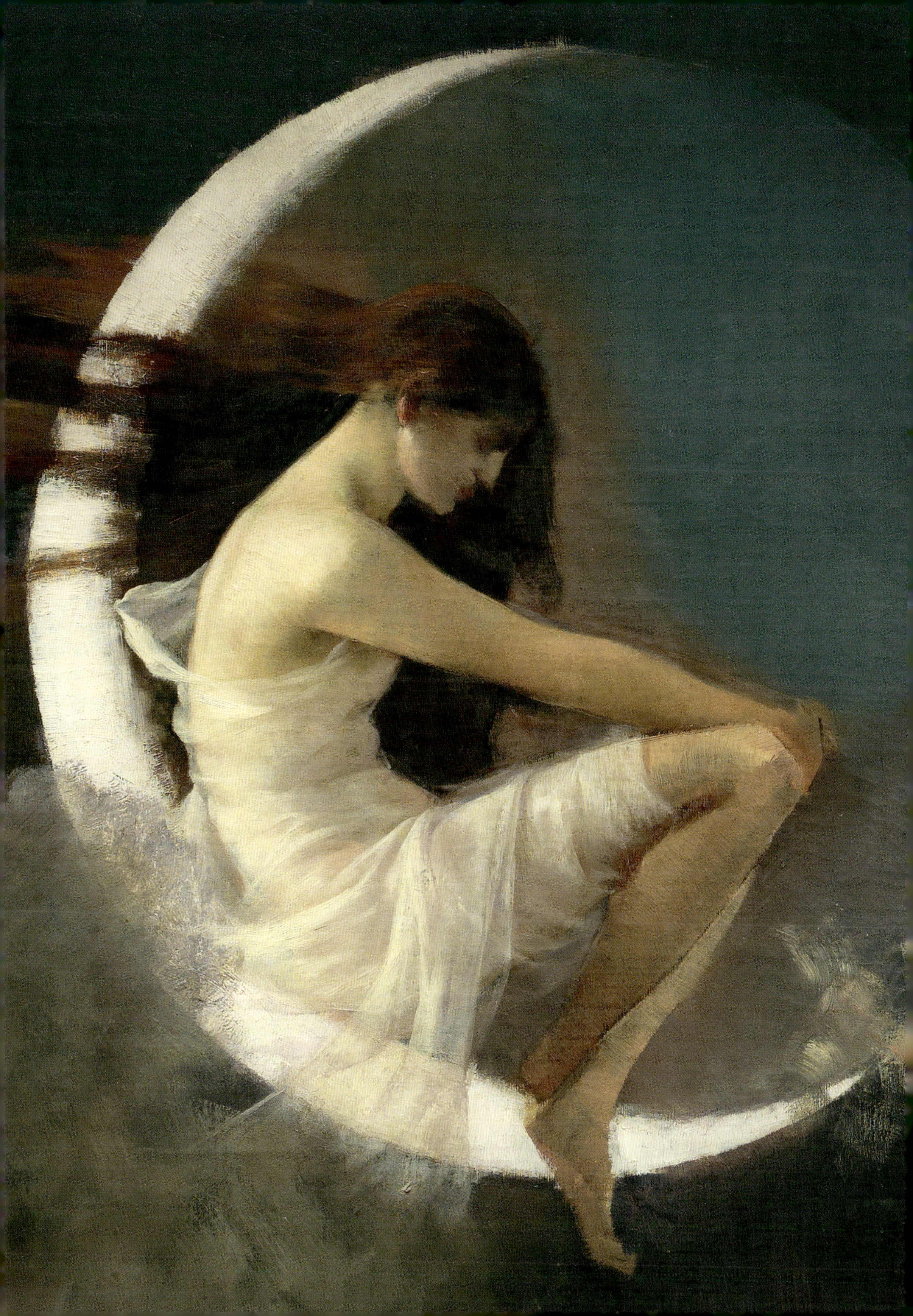

Published in conjunction with the exhibition
Australian Symbolism: the art of dreams
11 May – 29 July 2012
Art Gallery of New South Wales

First published 2012
Art Gallery of New South Wales
Art Gallery Rd, The Domain, Sydney NSW 2000, Australia
artgallery.nsw.gov.au

Managing editor: Julie Donaldson
Text editor: Claire Armstrong
Rights and permissions: Michelle Andringa
Design: Karen Wong
Photography: Jenni Carter
Index: Sherrey Quinn
Production: Cara Hickman
Pre-press: Spitting Image Pty Ltd
Printing: KHL Printing Co, Singapore

Art Gallery of New South Wales Cataloguing-in-publication
Mimmocchi, Denise.
Australian Symbolism: the art of dreams / Denise Mimmocchi

9781741740769

Includes bibliography and index.
1. Symbolism (Art movement) – Australia – Exhibitions. 2. Art, Australian – 20th century –
Exhibitions. 3. Art, Australian – 19th century – Exhibitions. I. Art Gallery of New South Wales. II. Title

Cover: Charles Conder *Hot wind* 1889 (detail), see pages 12–13

ABOUT THE AUTHOR

Denise Mimmocchi is a curator of Australian art at the Art Gallery of NSW. She is author
of *Sydney Long: Pan* (2009) and has contributed to numerous publications including
Rupert Bunny (2009) *Bertram Mackennal* (2007) and *Margaret Preston* (2005).